True, ... the media, misused
by pol... derstood by most
Americans. That's why everyone will benefit from reading this book — whether
you are a skeptic, a seeker, a new believer, or a longtime follower of Christ. The
combination of Chuck Colson's thoughtful brilliance and Harold Fickett's engaging prose gives us a clear, concise, and compelling summary of what followers of
Jesus actually believe.

DR. RICK WARREN, *The Purpose Driven Life*, Saddleback Church

This book reads like a novel and packs the wallop of a sledgehammer. It
is quite possibly the most important book Chuck has ever written.

BILL HYBELS, Senior Pastor, Willow Creek Community Church

The Faith will no doubt become a classic like *Loving God*. This book
will be used, and should be used, by every evangelical church and believer
in America. It succinctly speaks the truth about the basics of the faith so
that faith can be described, believed, and shared with a world that needs hope.
As a masterful storyteller who interweaves powerful, hard-hitting stories,
Colson has truly done a wonderful job. I commend it without reservation and will
be asking all those within my sphere of influence to read this book.

FRANK S. PAGE, President, Southern Baptist Convention

In an age of muddled thinking about what Christianity is about, Chuck's new
book clears the air, sets straight the facts, and invigorates the mind and soul,
reminding us all of the historical and timeless truths of our faith!

JONI EARECKSON TADA

This is vintage Charles Colson — carefully reasoned and passionately argued.
His chapter on how the gospel comes to prisoners is, by itself, enough to make
your mind stretch and your heart sing.

JOHN ORTBERG, pastor and author, Menlo Park Presbyterian Church

Chuck Colson is the most compelling witness for the Christian faith I know, and
the strength of his convictions is matched by the credibility of his life. He has
given us a contemporary statement of the apostolic faith — articulate, persuasive,
and winsome. A book of wisdom for believers and seekers alike.

TIMOTHY GEORGE, founding Dean of Beeson Divinity School of Samford
University, senior editor at *Christianity Today*

Colson and Fickett are in cracking form as they hit the high spots of Christian
belief, behavior, and blessedness against the black background of our runaway
decadence. Thank God for such men and for such a book.

J. I. PACKER, Regent College

Here Chuck Colson asks and answers the hardest questions of the Christian faith, knowing that those who need most to hear will not listen if he will not dare to enter the darkness of their doubts, fears, and challenges.

BRYAN CHAPELL, President, Covenant Theological Seminary

This book helps equip us to believe more strongly, to love more deeply, to serve more obediently, and to rejoice more exuberantly. Read it yourself, and then buy two more copies: one for a believer you're discipling and one for a skeptic you're evangelizing.

RUSSELL D. MOORE, The Southern Baptist Theological Seminary

Vintage Colson.... Indeed, the gospel is right at the center of these doctrinal studies making the book anything but the dry, lifeless outlay of loci that one finds too often.

WILLIAM EDGAR, Westminster Seminary

His best book yet. It is just the right length and strikes a great balance of being engaging and accessible yet thoughtful and informative.

J. P. MORELAND, Talbot School of Theology

A moving and inspiring guide to the Christian faith shared by believers of all times and places. It sings in unison with the great cloud of witnesses: prophets, martyrs, and saints, many of whose stories come to life in the telling.

DR. THOMAS C. ODEN, author and former Professor of Theology at Drew University

Concise, insightful, and helpful, Chuck's book nails down "the Faith" that must be grasped, kept, guarded, and passed on.

GREG WAYBRIGHT, Senior Pastor, Lake Avenue Church

Chuck Colson asserts that *God is* and then marshals the arguments of centuries of evidence to make an airtight, winsome case.

ERIC B. DENT, University of North Carolina, Pembroke

Chuck Colson has helped us again with clarity about our faith and what and why we believe. Thanks, Chuck, we've needed this!

JOE STOWELL, Teaching Pastor, Harvest Bible Chapel, former President, Moody Bible Institute

An indispensable, powerful, and highly readable guide to the world from the perspective of eternity.

JOHN C. MAXWELL, Founder of INJOY Stewardship Services and EQUIP

Overall, the strength of *The Faith* is that it shows the vital connection between justice, reality, and truth.

DR. SARAH SUMNER, Haggard School of Theology at Azusa Pacific University

THE
FAITH

GIVEN ONCE, FOR ALL —*Jude 3*

———— ◆◆◆ ————

What Christians Believe,
Why They Believe It, and
Why It Matters

———— ◆◆◆ ————

CHARLES
COLSON
AND HAROLD FICKETT

ZONDERVAN®

ZONDERVAN.com/
AUTHORTRACKER
follow your favorite authors

The Faith
Copyright © 2008 by Charles W. Colson

This title is also available as a Zondervan audio product.
Visit www.zondervan.com/audiopages for more information.

Requests for information should be addressed to:

Zondervan, *Grand Rapids, Michigan 49530*

ISBN-13: 978-0-310-27604-3
ISBN-10: 0-310-27604-7

International Trade Paper Edition

Interior design by Beth Shagene

Printed in the United States of America

08 09 10 11 12 13 • 24 23 22 21 20 19 18 17 16 15 14 13 12 11 10 9 8 7 6 5 4 3 2 1

This book draws upon the work
of the saints who over 2,000 years
have courageously defended —
and in many cases given their lives for —
Christian orthodoxy.

And it is dedicated to two of those saints,
my colleagues Timothy George and Richard John Neuhaus,
whom God has raised up for this time
to defend the faith given once for all time.

Also by Charles Colson

Born Again

Loving God

Kingdoms in Conflict

Against the Night

Why America Doesn't Work
(with Jack Eckerd)

The Body
(with Ellen Santilli Vaughn)

Gideon's Torch
(with Ellen Vaughn)

How Now Shall We Live?
(with Nancy Pearcey)

Being the Body
(with Ellen Santilli Vaughn)

God and Government

The Good Life
(with Harold Fickett)

CONTENTS

or·tho·doxy: \ ör-thə-**däk**·sē \ *noun* **1 :** that which adheres to the accepted or traditional and established faith, especially in religion; proper, correct or conventional; **2 :** that which adheres or conforms to the Christian faith as expressed in the early Christian ecumenical creeds and confessions.

PREFACE

[I] urge you to contend for the truth that was once for all entrusted
to the saints.   —Jude 3

Would you give your life for a cause you didn't fully understand?
Would you try to convince someone else to join you? No, neither
would I. Which is why I decided to write this book and invited Harold Fickett to join me.

Most professing Christians don't know what they believe, and so
can neither understand nor defend the Christian faith — much less
live it. Many of the things we tell nonbelievers do not represent real
Christianity. And most nonbelievers draw their impressions of the
Christian faith from the stereotypes and caricatures that popular culture produces.

When I told friends that I wanted to write an accessible book that
would summarize in about 240 pages the basic truths of Christianity,
several thought it would be impossible — too big a subject, they said,
not to mention the theological minefields. And still others thought
no one would be interested in dusty doctrine and history. But the
past not only shapes the present; it can also show us the future. We
can see much more and further ahead by standing on the shoulders
of those who have gone before us.

So this book is about the faith that was "once for all entrusted
to the saints" — those essentials that all true Christians have always
believed, what C. S. Lewis called "mere Christianity." In one sense,
there is nothing new here; nothing that is not found in Scripture and
in our creeds, which reflect the apostolic teaching — or cannot be

reasoned out from the Scripture as we try to understand today's world. And yet, what is here is new — ever new — because it is eternal.

We have written this book with the deep conviction that this is what people need to defend and live the Christian faith in the midst of the extraordinary challenges of our time.

This book reflects the most profound influences on my life, starting with C. S. Lewis's *Mere Christianity*, which was hugely influential in my own conversion. We also draw upon Dorothy Sayers' classic *Creed or Chaos*, and the signature book of the great Christian statesman and abolitionist William Wilberforce, *Real Christianity*.

Other authors whose work has profoundly influenced me: the various and highly accessible writings of John Stott, like *Basic Christianity*; the work of J. Gresham Machen who, seventy-five years ago, courageously defended the faith in a great book entitled *Christianity and Liberalism*. Many arguments you will see come as well from G. K. Chesterton, particularly his book *Orthodoxy*; and the works of Abraham Kuyper and Francis Schaeffer, whose writings shaped my theology and worldview.

I have drawn from Berkhof's *Systematic Theology*, which has been a handbook for me for years, and now, in more recent years, the *Systematic Theology* of Thomas Oden, an extraordinarily helpful understanding of the patristic era, when the teaching of the apostles was freshest in mind. From more modern times you will see the influence of Rodney Stark, a great sociologist who began as a skeptic and ended up as a believer, and Timothy George, Jim Packer, Neal Plantinga, and Richard Neuhaus.

The cover has proven provocative to early readers. There is a door by which all humans pass from darkness into the light. The way through it is narrow, the Doorkeeper tells us, but He promises to open the door and welcome us into His light. For He is the light by which everything else is enlightened, which is why the Christian faith is attractive and inviting; far from an imposition, the faith is the world's great hope.

You will note that the door is still open, but just ajar. Western culture is doing everything in its power to shut that door. But the Doorkeeper (who is the Door) will never allow it to be fully shut.

He invites you to pass through it.

When Jesus spoke again to the people, he said, "I am the light of the world. Whoever follows me will never walk in darkness, but will have the light of life." —*John 8:12*

PROLOGUE

In Nickel Mines, Pennsylvania, love would have to prove stronger than death.

On the morning of October 5, 2006, twenty-five children were studying in the local one-room schoolhouse, a barnlike structure with a simple bell tower and a front porch supported by steel rods. The building, as plain as notebook paper, reflected the values of the Amish community that educated its children there. The Amish trace their lineage back to pacifist Swiss Christian communities, who, during the sixteenth and seventeenth centuries, renounced the trappings of worldliness.

On that morning, in the midst of the Amish, the worst of the world's madness appeared. At 9:51 a.m., Charles Carl Roberts IV, a thirty-two-year-old milkman, burst into the West Nickel Mines Amish schoolhouse and shattered the community's serenity. He had thought about the violence he was about to perpetrate long in advance, and he came prepared. He carried a 12-gauge shotgun, a 9 mm handgun, a .30–06 bolt-action rifle, about six hundred rounds of ammunition, a stun gun, and two knives. He also had tools and building supplies with him.

He ordered the young girls to line up quickly in front of the chalkboard. Then he demanded that the teacher, Emma Mae Zook, take her fifteen male students, a pregnant woman, and three mothers with infants outside. Once they were gone, Charles Roberts used the tools and the 2 x 6 and 2 x 4 foot boards he was carrying to barricade himself inside. Next, he used flex ties to bind the hands and legs of the young girls, who ranged in age from six to thirteen.

Evidently, he meant to take his time. He called his wife on a cell phone to confess, in partial explanation of the suicide notes he had left at home, that he had molested two young relatives twenty years before. This tale seems to have been a delusion. He also spoke of his grief at the death of an infant daughter. When the Amish girls asked Roberts why he meant to hurt them, he said he was angry at God.

The community responded more quickly than Roberts may have anticipated, and the schoolgirls themselves would alter his plans. Roberts's plan to molest the girls seems apparent from the lubricant he was carrying, but their teacher, Emma Mae Zook, ran to a neighboring farmhouse and called the police at 10:36 a.m. The police arrived in force nine minutes later. From the loudspeakers on their cruisers they spoke to Roberts. He responded that if the grounds weren't cleared in two seconds he'd kill everyone.

The oldest of the girls, Marian Fisher, spoke up. The Amish speak Swiss German as their mother tongue, but she used the best English she could muster. She pleaded, "Shoot me and leave the others one loose." Marian's eleven-year-old sister, Barbie, asked to be next. They demonstrated the greatest love a human possibly could.

Unnerved by the girls' courage and the police, Roberts tried to execute all ten girls, pouring bullets into them as fast as he could.

At the sound of gunfire the police rushed the building. With one final blast, Roberts committed suicide before they could reach him.

Although Roberts shot all ten children at point-blank range, and several of them repeatedly, he did not fully exact the revenge against God he had planned. Five children survived. Marian's sister, Barbie, was one of them, which is why we know some of the details of what happened inside the schoolhouse that horrible day.

Charles Roberts's death seemed sad only in that he was no longer available to prosecute.

But that's where this story turns in an unexpected direction. The entire Amish community followed young Marian Fisher's lead of sacrifice and love of one's neighbor. While Charles Roberts chose to unleash his anger on the innocent, the Amish chose to bestow forgiveness on the guilty. Newsreel footage showed the Amish horse-and-buggy cortege rolling along the main road in Nickel Mines on their way to the funerals of the slain children. It was a poignant and picturesque scene. But the images that stayed in the imagination were of Amish men and women attending Charles Roberts's funeral in the graveyard of his wife's Methodist church. They insisted it was not their place to judge him. Amish leaders even asked their community to refrain from thinking of Roberts as evil.

The Amish also reached out to Marie Roberts and her children. They invited the family to attend the girls' funerals — for the Bible says to mourn with those who mourn, and the Roberts family was mourning their own loss. As money poured in to address the medical bills of the wounded girls, Amish community leaders stipulated that a fund be set up from these resources to take care of the killer's widow and three children.

——

Christians practiced the same inexplicable sacrifice and love in Roman times. Catastrophic events were far more common in the ancient world than in our own. The ancient city of Antioch, for example, suffered forty-one natural and social catastrophes during Roman rule — an average of one every fifteen years.[1] Riots, floods, earthquakes, fires, military sieges, and plagues constantly threatened to wipe the centers of Roman civilization off the map.

In size, most Roman cities were little more than urban postage stamps. Most people lived in multistory tenements, divided like rabbit warrens into one-room apartments. Every household had an open fire for cooking, and whole city blocks often went up in flames like so much kindling. The filth of chamber pots often rained down on the public thoroughfares, as the records of public citation attest.

With sewage in the streets, the air smoke filled, and the incredible crowding — at a time when soap was not yet used — the cities of ancient Rome were perfect cultures for communicable diseases. Plagues in Roman times sealed the fates of 30 to 40 percent of a city's inhabitants. At the onset of plague, the wealthy fled to their country estates. Paganism didn't teach that human life was sacred.

The growing number of people who called themselves Christian, however, believed that each human being was made in the image of a loving God. The Christians' God expected that His followers would acknowledge His love by sacrificing themselves for others. They were to extend God's love not merely to their families and friends but to their enemies as well. "Love one another" became their standard.

Imagine a young Christian—we'll call him Fortunus—living in one of Rome's deathtrap cities in AD 166, at the time of the first great plague, which was probably smallpox.

In the street, Fortunus meets a fellow believer, Crispus, and together they pull a hand-drawn cart toward the fountain at the city's center. The place is usually alive at this early hour, neighbors calling out to one another from tenement windows, shops opening up, and the streets rumbling with heavy carts bearing wares. But now it remains quiet except for Fortunus's own cart's creak and clatter and the intermittent wails of plague victims in the apartments overhead, which make the chill of the morning that much colder and each step harder.

The fountain is the last place the diseased and dying can go for water, once their neighbors and families notice their illness and abandon them, as was the common practice. There Fortunus and Crispus find another twenty plague victims, many lying on the ground, their clothes bloodied by the hemorrhaging pustules brought on by the disease's first phase. Others are already dead. The two Christians load those who cannot walk into their cart and encourage those who can to come along. Later that morning Fortunus and Crispus will come back for those who have already died and see that they are properly buried.

Their city's Roman garrison probably had a hospital, complete with an isolation ward for cases of communicable diseases like smallpox, but this was only for Roman soldiers and would have been unavailable to Christians. Fortunus and Crispus take the plague victims to the house of a wealthier member of their community. Smallpox causes high fever, headache, back and stomach pain, along with vomiting. After these flulike symptoms comes the pox, white-jellied, running sores that spread in a polka-dot pattern over the face, down the throat, into the eyes, and over the hands and feet. There would have been little for the ancient Christians to do but give the victims water, keep them as clean as possible, and encourage them with kindness and prayer.

Fortunus, who had left his wife and children at home that morning so he could to spend the day carting victims to makeshift hospitals and trying to ease their pain, knew that his care for the ill would probably end his own life. Every time he looked into the pocked face of a victim, he was looking into the face of death.

The care Christians showed often did result in their succumbing to the plague themselves. But paradoxically, their compassion did not deplete Christian ranks in the long term—quite the reverse. Tending to the sick increased the disease survival rate by as much as two-thirds,[2] and this witness attracted many new converts. By acting on the teachings of Christ, without regard to their own welfare, these Christians, against all expectations, progressed from being a small sect to the dominant cultural group.

The unprecedented teachings of Christianity gave people a reason to care for the sick and destitute. Only Jesus taught that His followers could find Him in their neighbor. "For I was hungry and you gave me something to eat, and I was thirsty and you gave me something to drink.... I tell you the truth, whatever you did for one of the least of these brothers of mine, you did for me" (Matthew 25:35, 40). People who saw Christians behave this way were amazed.

Just as we are amazed at the forgiving example of the Amish. "Love your enemies and pray for those who persecute you" (Matthew 5:44). In the tragic case of their slaughtered children, the Amish were practicing the love *every* Christian ought to practice.

In one way, we should wonder why the forgiveness of the Amish surprises anyone. It's nothing but the Gospel, although admittedly an all-too-rare instance of its full practice. But why don't Christianity's bitter critics understand that the practice of love and forgiveness are hallmarks of Christianity, *real* Christianity? Because we Christians do not truly understand the tenets of our faith and therefore cannot live the faith.

When we do, as we shall see, we are called to the most exciting adventure imaginable. God wants to make us new creations in Christ. That means joining Christ in His work in the world. So the skeptics will understand—that *real* Christianity is no threat but a glorious proposal.

PART I

GOD AND THE FAITH

CHAPTER 1

EVERYWHERE, ALWAYS, BY ALL

What we witnessed at Nickel Mines and in the times of the Roman plagues is true Christianity—sacrificial love, concern for all people, forgiveness and reconciliation, evil overcome by good. These two examples, drawn from thousands I might have selected, represent signs of the Kingdom of God announced by Jesus and lived by His followers to this day.

Admittedly, Christianity has not always been practiced this way. Christians are fallen, flawed, and broken people who often profess one thing and do another. But contrary to the public misconceptions about Christianity today, the Christian Church and the truth it defends are the most powerful life- and culture-changing forces in human history. This enduring truth has been tested and proven true over two thousand years.

Christianity—The Enduring Truth

My wife, Patty, and I were visiting London on a ministry trip some years ago. We found a few free hours one day for sightseeing and visited Christopher Wren's architectural masterpiece, St. Paul's Cathedral, in the heart of the old city. Hundreds of visitors were milling around, looking at the art treasures and sculptures, admiring the grand rotunda above. One look at the narrow walkway curling upward into the dome cured us of any desire to climb the steps.

To our surprise, an Anglican Mass was being celebrated at the high altar and, interestingly, broadcast over the loudspeakers. Most of the sightseers regarded it as little more than Muzak. But we made our way to a back pew and sat among perhaps a hundred other worshipers.

Although I am from a low-church tradition, I found myself caught up in the beauty of the liturgy, riveted by its scriptural basis. We decided to take a few minutes to sit quietly and enjoy the power of the Word in such a glorious setting.

We were caught up in the church's history. I remembered Winston Churchill's funeral had been conducted here in 1965, and we had visited the memorial chapel that commemorates the American contribution to winning World War II. The history of St. Paul's extends back through the centuries. Queen Elizabeth I (1533–1603) contributed to repairs after a lightning strike. A side chapel is dedicated to St. Dunstan, who almost single-handedly revived British Christianity in the tenth century after the Danish invasions, and no doubt he had a hand in the St. Paul's of his day.

When the service reached the acclamation — "Christ has died! Christ is risen! Christ will come again!" — I was struck by the realization that the congregation and casual sightseers alike were listening to the heart of the Gospel, which was being proclaimed with force and power as it had been on this very spot for at least 1,400 years, when the first St. Paul's was built, and likely earlier, back to Roman times.[1] The same Gospel — every doctrine — was rooted in Scripture, given by the apostles, and expressed in the creeds of the early Church. Jesus Christ, the same yesterday, today, and forever.

I whispered my thoughts to Patty, who nodded in agreement. The realization sent shivers up our spines. "The faith that was once for all entrusted to the saints" (Jude v. 3) was being boldly proclaimed from this altar, and hundreds of unsuspecting tourists, if inadvertently, were soaking it in. It has always been this way and always will be!

Then I had a second moment of inspiration as I realized that our ancient faith provided answers to the deepest questions in the hearts of all those visiting St. Paul's that day and to secularized Britain as a whole. This witness was being given in the heart of a cosmopolitan city and in a nation that has largely turned against God in increasingly desperate times. The Christian West is under assault by the twin challenges of secularism and radical Islam — whose roots have some unsuspected likenesses. Only through Christianity, I believe, can Western Europe and America meet these desperate challenges.

Even as we sat there, radical Islam was transforming Britain's capital into "Londonistan." The city's underground and buses were soon to be bombed by these radicals, confronting secular society with a religiously motivated challenge it could not comprehend. Only the God of love celebrated that day at St. Paul's could provide the renewal needed.

Skipping a Stone across Ages and Cultures — A Time-traveler Visits Christian Communities

The core beliefs that have united Christians for two thousand years certainly built Western civilization, but it is a mistake to think that Christianity belongs to Western culture. Christianity did not originate in the West and has never been confined to it. The core elements of the faith have brought about a tremendous unity in a diversity of cultures, as the renowned writer on Christian missions Andrew Walls demonstrates, imagining what a time-traveler would see if he dropped in on five Christian communities living in different cultures over the centuries.

First, the time-traveler visits the founding church in Jerusalem in AD 37. He notes that these new Christians are hard to distinguish from a branch of Judaism. They simply identify the Jewish teaching about the Messiah, the Son of Man, with Jesus of Nazareth. These Christians are mostly drawn from the ranks of tradesmen and laborers. They have large families, and their faith is marked by celebrations and by helping one another to face life's material challenges.

Next, our time-traveler visits Christians about the time of the Council of Nicea in AD 325. These Christians are no longer Jewish but drawn from all over the Mediterranean world. Many of the leaders now practice celibacy. They are familiar with the ancient Jewish Scriptures but give equal value to writings that have been generated by their own community — the "New Testament." The subject of their discussion centers, as did the first community's, on the death and resurrection of Jesus of Nazareth. Culturally, these two Christian communities are already worlds apart.

Our time-traveler then visits Irish monks of the seventh century. They practice such spiritual disciplines as fasting and praying for long hours with their arms outstretched in the form of a cross. They are otherworldly in a way the first two communities were not, but they have the same evangelical zeal; they want those near and far to understand Jesus' significance as the Messiah. Some of their members are about to depart for the Scottish coast in tubby leather and wood boats, where they will call the Scottish clans to exchange their nature worship and bloody practices for the joys of heaven.

The time-traveler drops in on one of the great English missionary societies of the 1840s. Unlike the Irish monks, these Christians seek a spirituality marked by social activism instead of severe spiritual disciplines. While the monks lived on virtually nothing, these people are almost too well fed. But they feel exactly the same burden to spread the message. They are funding missions to the Far East, Oceania, and Africa. They are also working to improve conditions within their own society brought on by the Industrial Revolution.

Finally, the time-traveler comes to Lagos, Nigeria, in the 1980s. He sees white-robed Christians dancing and chanting their way through the streets. They call themselves Cherubim and Seraphim, and they invite their neighbors to experience the power of God. They are not social activists like the English. They fast like the Irish monks but more for fixed purposes. They talk more about the Holy Spirit and its power to inspire preaching, bring healing, and provide personal guidance.

The time-traveler notes that, culturally, these five Christian groups could hardly be more different. Yet they think of themselves as connected, and indeed, their thinking is remarkably similar. They believe that in Christ the world has been rescued from the power of evil and death; they believe in God's sovereignty over history; they make the same use of the Scriptures and of bread and wine and water.

Surprising historical connections among these groups come to mind as well — those activist English missionaries first brought the faith to the dancing Nigerians, for example. (Today, in a fitting reversal, these Nigerians and other peoples of the Global South are bringing the faith back to the West.) The Jews evangelized the Mediterranean Gentiles, from whom both Ireland and England received the faith. All five groups, despite cultural appearances, are part of the same legacy: the one Lord, one faith, one baptism they profess holds true for all.

Right Belief and Today's Confusion

We call the core beliefs that have united Christians through the ages *orthodoxy*, or "right belief." Understanding this faith, once entrusted for all, is critically important today, for we live in a time, as I realized in St. Paul's, when Christians and the civilization they helped to build are under assault.

Surveying the press coverage over the last couple of years makes it clear that Christianity is reeling from a bruising and perhaps unprecedented attack by aggressive atheism—or what one critic ominously calls "anti-theism." In 2006, Richard Dawkins, a clever and articulate Oxford evolutionary biologist, published *The God Delusion*, which took up near-permanent residence on the *New York Times* bestseller list. Dawkins considers religious instruction a form of child abuse and suggests that governments should put a stop to it. Tufts professor Daniel Dennett argues that religion is a dangerous toxin that may be poisoning believers. Similar books have appeared from Sam Harris (*Letter to a Christian Nation*) and the brilliant if caustic Christopher Hitchens (*God Is Not Great*). The title of Chris Hedges' *American Fascists: The Christian Right and the War on America* could hardly be more direct. Regularly, critics liken politically active Christians to the Taliban.[2]

This is not a fringe phenomenon. According to the *Wall Street Journal*, these authors sold close to a million books in one twelve-month period alone.[3] Richard Dawkins, responsible for half of those sales, can attest to how lucrative attacking God has become. These critics say we are trying to "impose" our views on American life—that we want to create a "theocracy," or a government run by the Church. But this is absurd; theocracy is contrary to the most basic Christian teaching about free will and human freedom. Christianity gave the very idea of separation of Church and state to the West. And Christianity advances not by power or by conquest, but by love.[4]

Postmodernism and the Death of Truth

What's really at issue here is a dramatic shift in the prevailing belief of Western cultural elites; we have come into a postmodern era that rejects the idea of truth itself. If there is no such thing as truth, then Christianity's claims are inherently offensive and even bigoted against others. Tolerance, falsely defined as putting all propositions on an equal footing—as opposed to giving ideas an equal hearing—has replaced truth.

Millions acquiesce to the all-beliefs-are-equal doctrine for the sake of bettering their social position in our values-free, offend-no-one culture. But to succumb to this indifference is not to accept a tolerant or liberal view of Christianity; it is to embrace another religion, a belief in some supreme value—perhaps tolerance—but not in the God who is and who has spoken.

President Eisenhower, a great father figure of the post–World War II era, perfectly captured this spirit of the postwar age: "Our government makes no sense unless it is founded on a deeply felt religious faith—and I don't care what it is."[5] In 2007, an Episcopal priest carried this view so far she became a Muslim and remained a priest, while publicly denying there was any inconsistency.[6]

All the while, those making their truth claims are publicly demeaned with impunity. Christians are called "wing nuts" and "flat-earthers," or as one major national paper famously put it: "Poor, uneducated, and easily led."[7]

Clash of Civilizations

Even as we provide a reasoned defense against postmodernist disbelief, we must renew our culture—the only true remedy to radical Islam's aggression.

The West has been slowly, almost reluctantly, becoming aware of its clash with radical Islamists. Millions of fascist-influenced jihadists, feeding on revivalist teachings as a counter to Western decadence, seek death for infidels and global rule for Islam. Many Westerners would like all of this simply to disappear somehow. As the polls show, secular Europeans, for whom religion has become inconsequential, cannot fathom a religiously motivated challenge to their way of life. They and others like them throughout Europe and America are eager to deputize competent authorities to handle the problem, so they can get back to their pleasurable lives.

Others ask, "What can be done? Can anyone come up with a new plan or vision of things?" But neither complacency nor fear serves us well. We don't need a new vision of things; rather, we need an eternal vision—to raise our eyes once again to the light that has always guided Christians during times of great distress. One of the greatest virtues of the Christian faith is that it is life affirming and culture building. No other worldview or religion protects the sanctity of life and human dignity as Christianity does; no other worldview has ever created as humane and progressive a culture as Christianity has. Our faith and our experience teach us that the power that created the universe can provide answers to today's dilemmas.

Challenge for the Church

The challenges of anti-theism and radical Islam could not come at a worse time for the Church, because most Christians do not understand what they believe, why they believe it, and why it matters. How can a Christianity that is not understood be practiced? And how can it be presented in its true character as peace, freedom, and joy? How are skeptics to understand Christianity's positive aspects?

Tragically, postmodern culture has infected and weakened the Church, particularly in the West. Spain, once the most Catholic country in Europe, has become, within a generation, among the most secularized. A recent report among Spain's bishops lays the blame squarely on heretical teaching as to the nature of Christ and His atoning work. Likewise, when I asked a priest friend why church membership was declining so rapidly in once rigidly Catholic Ireland, he answered, "Because the priests don't preach the Gospel."

Even evangelicals, known for their fidelity to Scripture, have not been exempt from postmodernist influence. Both George Gallup and George Barna, eminent pollsters and close Church observers, have in recent years decried the declining biblical literacy in the Church. The majority of evangelicals—whom Barna calls "born-again Christians"—do not believe in absolute truth. Sixty percent of Americans can't name five of the Ten Commandments; 50 percent of high school seniors think Sodom and Gomorrah were married.[8]

I viewed these findings with some suspicion until I did my own survey in preparing for this book. Over the past two years, whenever I had occasion, I asked mature believers to name the fundamental doctrines of the Christian faith. Many of them looked surprised, even perplexed. Of the twelve critical doctrines that I have identified in this book, most of my friends, admittedly unprepared, could name only four, at best five. One or two actually told me they thought that doctrine only confused, that we should simply focus on Jesus. Pastors were not much better informed than the laity; Barna found that 49 percent of Protestant pastors reject core biblical beliefs.[9]

On a number of occasions I have stopped in the middle of giving talks and asked, "What is Christianity anyway?" At one dinner in the Bible Belt, the group of mature believers hesitated for what seemed like a full minute of painful silence. No one volunteered.

Finally one man said, "To love the Lord your God with all your heart, mind, and soul." I replied that was good, but only part of the whole. There followed three or four other answers, all based on what could be called broad scriptural truths, like the Ten Commandments and the Sermon on the Mount.

These, I explained, are true but only parts of the whole. Christians must see that the faith is more than a religion or even a relationship with Jesus; *the faith is a complete view of the world and humankind's place in it.* Christianity is a worldview that speaks to every area of life, and its foundational doctrines define its content. If we don't know what we believe—even what Christianity is—how can we live it and defend it? Our ignorance is crippling us.

From the Beginning:
Mere Christianity

If the Church has any hope of answering today's challenges, it must pursue what we call radical Christianity or orthodoxy. *Radical* is a good term; it means going back to the "root." This is why throughout this book we will be sending you back to the writings of the apostles themselves and of Church leaders and theologians of the first five centuries of the Christian era.

If we are to face today's grave threats to the Christian Church and to Western civilization, we must look across the sweep of Christian communions, Protestant, Catholic, and Orthodox, to find the original consensus of the early Church; that is, those essential elements of our faith that, from the beginning, all true Christians have believed—what Oxford scholar C. S. Lewis meant by the title of his classic book *Mere Christianity*.

Centuries of Christian reflection and public debate have produced classic and lesser creeds that all say much the same. From the Apostles' Creed and the Nicene Creed forward, the words differ little when addressing the great articles of faith. The Lutheran Augsburg Confession begins by explicitly citing the ancient Nicene Creed.[10]

This unanimity didn't happen by chance or as a result of secret cabals. Theology has always been a public activity. The nature of Christ was the subject of shoptalk throughout the later Roman Empire. People did not take sides lightly. Many, like Athanasius, risked their lives for the sake of the "faith that was once for all entrusted to the saints" (Jude v. 3).

It may seem odd to rely on the ancient roots of Christianity at a time when progress is so exalted. But progress does not always mean discovering something new. Sometimes it means rediscovering wisdom that is ancient and eternal. We all find our identity in our roots. Visit nearly any family and you'll see pictures of grandparents and earlier generations. People go to great lengths to trace their ancestry. Adopted children seek their birth parents.

Where we come from tells us who we are, and so it is in the Church. A fifth-century French monk, St. Vincent of Lerins, famously counseled: "Hold fast that faith which has been believed everywhere, always and by all."

———

We pray that the Kingdom of God will rule in our hearts and once again transform the places in which we live. That will happen only by knowing and living the faith. To the best of our ability, then, here is *what Christians believe, why we believe it,* and *why it matters.* As you read on, carefully examine each of the propositions set forth with these three questions in mind and note how each proposition leads to the next, showing the internal coherence and logic of the Christian view, as compared to other belief systems. For whether you are a seeker or a believer, if you understand why each proposition matters and see their coherence, I'm confident you'll be as convinced as I am that this is the truth you can stake your life on.

We begin, as does the faith, with this proposition: *God is.*

CHAPTER 2

GOD IS

One of the faith's most persuasive contemporary critics is Sam Harris, who articulates the powerful doubts that we all know in our moments of soul searching. In *Letter to a Christian Nation*, he speaks of the losses the citizens of New Orleans suffered as a result of Hurricane Katrina:

> But what was God doing while Katrina laid waste to their city? Surely he heard the prayers of those elderly men and women who fled the rising waters for the safety of their attics, only to be slowly drowned there. These were people of faith. These were good men and women who had prayed throughout their lives. Do you have the courage to admit the obvious? These poor people died talking to an imaginary friend.[1]

My thoughts have been as dark at times. In January 2005 I got the shocking news that my oldest son, Wendell, was diagnosed with cancer of the spine. The day of the surgery was the longest day of my life. Our family kept a vigil in the sterile hospital waiting room, jammed with other anxious families. We'd been warned that taking a tumor out of the spine is a delicate and lengthy operation. One hour passed, two, three. A friendly receptionist kept advising us that Wendell was still in surgery.

As the hours dragged by, we watched all the highs and lows of life played out on the stage before us—doctors in white coats and masks arriving to consult with other families in a small conference room, from which most emerged beaming and jubilant, but others sorely downcast. Although I did my best to cheer others in our family, after six hours I thought my nerves could stand it no longer. *How can any operation take this long?*

Eleven hours later we were the last family left when the doctor finally arrived to give us a report. The tumor was excised, bone grafts and steel plates attached to the spine. The good news was that Wendell would not be mentally or physically impaired, as we had feared. But later we learned that cancer cells had remained in the spine. A yearlong debilitating regimen of chemotherapy and radiation — massive doses of each — was to follow.

While Wendell was recuperating in the spring, my daughter Emily discovered a black mole on her leg that turned out to be melanoma, moderately advanced, potentially deadly. So I was soon back in the same hospital for Emily's surgery. Wendell was there at the time, receiving his chemotherapy, so I spent several hours shuttling between my two sick children — any parent's ultimate nightmare.

In still other ways, 2005 was a tough year, including a major surgery for my wife, Patty, and extra struggles with my ministry. At night I would pace the floor and question God. How and why could all of this be happening? Hadn't I served Him faithfully for thirty years? Wasn't I responsible for a ministry reaching hundreds of thousands around the world? Didn't He hear my prayers? I was spiritually drained and exhausted — as if I'd wrestled with demons in the darkness. Where was God when I needed Him?

In late August, Patty and I took a weeklong break at a friend's home in western North Carolina. One morning I got up early and walked out on the deck. I was greeted by the magnificent sight of the Blue Ridge Mountains rising out of the mist, the sun throwing the shadows of the lower peaks against the higher summits, the foliage glistening with dew. The scene took my breath away. I was seeing God's magnificent creation as if it were newborn. There was no explanation for what I was seeing — the intricate details of nature, genuine beauty — apart from a creator God. This could not be an illusion, an accident, or the result of some random process. While the other planets are sterile and lifeless, this one throbs with life and beauty. *God is.* I knew God exists at a deeper level than I had ever known anything in my life before. His existence didn't depend on my feelings, either. I might feel desperate, weary of praying, ready to throw in the towel, but God still is. There is no other explanation for reality. What I saw, I realized, was the answer to what I had thought were unanswered prayers.

Anyone looking at the majesty of the mountains or the vastness of the churning seas or the quiet beauty of a sunset has to wonder about the origins of what they see, and question, as we all do, where we humans came from.

Three Ideas of Origin

Theory #1: A Godless Material Universe

Today, three major ideas compete about the universe's origin. The first is that the material universe is the sum and substance of all that exists and that it has either always existed or it came into existence without a cause. Therefore, natural explanations suffice to answer all questions about the nature and origin of the universe and of life.

The idea that the universe has always existed goes back to the Greek philosophers and was dominant for much of Western history. When the idea of a static eternal universe was shown to be false by Einstein's general theory of relativity,* the material theory took refuge in a universe that expands and collapses in a cycle with no beginning or end. But recent discoveries have virtually invalidated this idea. (There is not enough mass-energy in the universe for gravity to halt its expansion, for example.)

Materialists who accept that the universe — or "multiverse,"† as some theories frame it — has an absolute beginning, as in the Big Bang, are stuck with pulling the rabbit of creation out of a nonexistent hat, that is, out of absolute nothingness. In this view, galaxies, supernovas, and black holes are merely the result of chance combinations taking place over immense stretches of time. Likewise, the structure of matter itself, with its basis in atomic and subatomic

---

*As well as by Hubble's observation of the universe's expansion, and Penzias's and Wilson's discovery of the cosmic microwave echo from the Big Bang.
†According to chaotic inflationary cosmology.

particles, springs from forces that must be considered purely random. In the same way, while all of life is based on highly complex arrangements of information, called DNA, life must be considered simply the product of blind, unintelligible chance, when a single cell popped into existence in the primordial sea.

The material theory leaps from nonexistence to intelligible existence to information-based life on the basis—literally—of *nothing*.

Theory #2: God Is an Intelligent Presence in All Things, a Universal Mind

Our universe has an intelligible character for which the material theory cannot account. It can be investigated, reasoned about, and its phenomena translated into elegant mathematical expressions, like Einstein's $E = MC^2$. How can the intelligible, the predictable, and the uniform emerge out of pure chance?

Some try to cope with this dilemma by contending that life's origin is based in reason or a Universal Mind. That's why Greek philosophy embraced the concept of the *logos*, an ultimate creative reason as the source of all things. It's also why many of the greatest scientists have concluded that an ultimate intelligence must be present in all things, if not behind them. Einstein called for a "cosmic religiosity ... enraptured wonder at the harmony of the laws of nature ... a deep faith in the rationality of the structure of the world."[2]

This is one of today's prominent ideas, not only among scientists but among those interested in Eastern religions. The faiths of the East often see the material world as expressing an underlying spiritual unity. Books discussing the convergence of modern physics and Eastern religion line the shelves.

Believers in a Universal Mind usually see their god and the universe as synonymous and assume an attitude of reverence toward creation; they join environmental groups and even flock to mountain tops to experience the "harmonic convergence" of natural forces. Often they see the world's evolution as the way in which this universal intelligence comes to consciousness.

This view leaves the human mind without any real purpose. Scientists who believe in a Universal Mind, as Einstein did, are strict determinists—they don't believe people make their own decisions. Einstein rejected any conception of a personal God as "anthropomorphic" and detested the "religion of fear" and "religion of morality" a personal God inspires. He thought human beings were no more responsible for their own actions than a chicken laying an egg.

Theory #3: A Personal God

Christians believe that the most likely explanation for a reasonable universe and one in which we experience ourselves as free can be found in a reasonable, personal God. As I said, Greek philosophy embraced the concept of *logos*, an ultimate creative reason as the source of all things. The Gospel of John applies this concept to Christ, as the *Logos* or Word of God through whom all things came to be (John 1:1 – 3).

Christians see the creation as an indicator of God's character. When we look at nature, we are immediately impressed by its creativity and beauty. Think for a moment of chameleons with their independently bobbling eyes, or deep-sea creatures that glow to light their own way. Apple blossoms and honey bees cooperate to assure that fruit develops and the bees are sustained. Nature is incredibly varied and astoundingly beautiful.

The beauty of the world gives us a primary clue about the character of this *Logos*, often defined as the plan of creation. The scientist may look at the white clouds of apple blossoms as nothing more than an adaptive response, but if only an adaptive response were required, then why this dazzling display? And why should the ingenious cooperation of the blossoms and bees be called for?[3]

I certainly had to ask myself why this world should reveal such glory when the earth sprang up anew before my eyes that morning in the Blue Ridge Mountains of North Carolina. Could I deny that "the heavens declare the glory of God; the skies proclaim the work of his hands" (Psalm 19:1)? Christians wonder why beauty should exist in such abundance if the creative reason did not mean to communicate love.[4]

Only a creative reason, or *Logos*, does justice to our experience of the world. Further, only a *Logos* that is both unimaginably creative and loving accounts for our delight in the world. When we see the *Logos* as the source of creation and yet independent of it, when we reflect on the world's beauty and our own freedom, the *Logos* quickly assumes the character of the personal God described in the Scriptures. We have reason to confess, "In the beginning, God ..." (Genesis 1:1).

—

The choice we make among these three options as to the universe's origin is the most important choice in life. Everything else follows from it. It's the place where the search for the truth begins.

Considering the Three Choices

Few people actually think through these choices; rather, most are influenced by cultural prejudice, as I discovered a few years back when I attended an exclusive dinner the night before a governor's prayer breakfast.

The gentleman seated next to me greeted me with a blunt warning that he was an atheist. I looked at him for a moment — graying temples, a wise expression, handsomely attired — the very image of a community leader. I told him I was glad to sit next to him because "I've never really met an atheist."

As his eyebrows arched, I explained, "An atheist believes the existence of God can be disproved. So please, tell me how you've done that."

He looked momentarily uncomfortable. "Well, perhaps I should say I'm an agnostic."

"When did you give up studying about God?" I asked.

Now his neck began to redden. He admitted he'd really never tried.

"But an agnostic is one who says he doesn't think God can be known, and you can only be an agnostic if you've tried to know Him and exhausted the search." I'm not sure even now what made me so bold, but I added, "So I would say that while you appear to be a very well-educated person, you've made an unsupportable statement."

Not surprisingly, he was offended and rather quiet for the rest of the evening.

Some weeks later I received a copy of the editorial page of the state's largest newspaper. It turned out my dinner companion was the publisher. His lead editorial was an explanation of how my visit had affected his view of life, how religion was indeed an important element of all of our lives and something we needed to pursue. What struck the publisher was that his own point of view proved unsupportable.

Okay, that was simply a clever debating ploy, the reader may say. But it doesn't answer modern science, which has rendered belief in a personal God irrational. As Freud said, it is simply "wish fulfillment," or as Richard Dawkins describes it in his bestseller, "a delusion." A recent character on television captured the conventional wisdom: "I'd like to believe in God, but I'd have to leave my mind at the door."

The Proposition That "God Is"

One of the great philosophers of our day, Alvin Plantinga, has engaged his secular contemporaries in frequent debates over the rationality of asserting the first presupposition that *God is*. Most secular philosophers, who are scientific materialists — they believe only in physical phenomena and a material universe — challenge him and say there is no support for what he says.

Plantinga's response is to ask the philosophers whether they believe that other people have minds. Is this rational? The philosophers say yes. But Plantinga points out that individuals who call themselves solipsists each believe that they alone have a mind. (One has to wonder how solipsists communicate with others who have no minds.)

Plantinga argues that saying God exists is as rational as saying other people have minds. Both philosophical conclusions are logical in the same way. Since all basic presuppositions begin with faith, *God is* is as rational as any other first premise.

Evidence that points toward the intelligent design of the universe increases the probability that *God is*. The more that is learned of the structure of the billions of human cells that make up our body, the clearer it is that cells function based on intelligent information, DNA, that is more complicated, as Bill Gates has said, than any software ever written. And there is now abundant cosmological evidence that this planet is uniquely hospitable to human life—the unique orbit of the earth, the distance from the sun, and the like. It is as if, one scientist wrote, "the universe in some sense must have known that we were coming."[5]

The presupposition *God is* is today not without abundant supporting empirical evidence. It requires no flight from reason to believe it.

Is *God Is* Irrational?

But what about the frequently heard charge that belief in God is irrational? All of the current books of the anti-theists stress this. Is choosing God an irrational selection when its effects are considered?

Roman citizens could see that Christianity offered real tangible benefits that pagan religions did not. In the midst of the widespread plagues, urban squalor, and general hopelessness of Rome, Christians lived a profoundly different and more hopeful life. When people witnessed their flourishing families and healthy lifestyles, contrasted with pagan decadence, they rationally decided that Christianity was a better choice as to how they would live their lives.[6]

In modern times we see the same phenomenon at work.[7] In the early 1990s people in South America chose the evangelical, largely Pentecostal, faith for a very good reason: it resulted in changed behavior in a way that benefited the family. Women, for example, who were accustomed to their husbands going to the tavern at night and leaving them alone, suddenly discovered that when those husbands were converted they stayed home with the family. The word spread. They joined the churches that promoted personal conversions and transformed lives. The choice was informed by the evident results the choice produced. This exactly meets the criteria of secular social scientists as to what constitutes a rational choice.[8]

But even if we believe we are making rational choices, aren't we coloring our judgment by desiring a God we can turn to in time of need? Aren't we just engaging in an irrational wish fulfillment, as Sam Harris, viewing the tragic consequences of Hurricane Katrina, would have it? Wasn't that my situation when I stood on that porch, distraught over my children, engaging in an emotional and subjective wish fulfillment?

But the knowledge of God is innate within human beings — it's born into us (Genesis 1:26–27; Romans 1:18 and following). Today, even secular biologists and scientists studying the human mind have found strong evidence of this intuitive knowledge — what some have even called the God gene. This need to connect to God and to one another was documented in a recent scholarly study entitled, "Wired to Connect."[9] We are made to seek meaning beyond ourselves in ways a purposeless, random process could not explain.

That this is wired into us doesn't mean we all experience the same delusion or engage in wish fulfillment. It more likely means we are made this way because what we long for is real. As C. S. Lewis, the great Oxford scholar and apologist, argued, all humans are by nature hungry because food has been made to satisfy our hunger. We don't make up hunger and food to satisfy our fancies; we are made for it.

But Dawkins will have none of this. We are beguiled by the God delusion, he says, calling the biblical Yahweh "psychotic" and Aquinas's proofs of God's existence "fatuous" and religion "nonsense."

This is how Dawkins explains that belief in God is not rational: "Any God capable of designing a universe, carefully tuned to lead to our evolution, must be a supremely complex and improbable entity that needs an even bigger explanation than the one He is supposed to provide." "Thus," Dawkins says, "He's ruled out by the laws of probability." Dawkins is saying God can't be God because He is beyond our comprehension. But this is precisely the nature of God by definition — the classic ontological argument advanced by St. Anselm that God is that which is beyond what the human mind can comprehend. Isaiah 55 tells us, "'For my thoughts are not your thoughts, neither are your ways my ways,' declares the LORD (v. 8).

Dawkins says that he chooses to live as if God does not exist. But at the same time, he concedes that on a scale of 1 to 7, 1 being certainty that God exists, and 7 certainty He doesn't, Dawkins rates himself a 6, at least acknowledging that he cannot prove his position.[10]

But even a one-in-seven chance that life has meaning is better than a zero-in-seven chance. Blaise Pascal, one of the great philosophers of modern history, argues that if there is no God, and you bet your life there is, you've lost nothing. But if there is a God, and you bet your life there isn't, you've made the greatest mistake imaginable. I'm sure if Dr. Dawkins had been on the *Titanic* and was offered two lifeboats, one certain to sink as opposed to one with a one-in-seven chance of staying afloat, he would have instantly chosen the latter. To choose the boat with no hope would be clearly irrational.

If the choice *God is* is rational, why do people refuse it? Mortimer Adler, editor of the Great Books series and surely an intellectual giant in his time, accepted the rational conclusion that Christianity was true. But when asked why he hadn't converted, he said he wasn't "prepared to give up all [the] vices and the weaknesses of the flesh."[11] Soon after making that statement, Adler saw the irrationality of his position, recognized that his own will was the problem, and surrendered his life to Christ. He was baptized, and in his later years joined the Catholic Church.

———

What we choose really does matter. If we live in an exclusively material world, human life—including mine and yours—is absolutely meaningless. No matter how intense our passions, how great our accomplishments, or what side of history we choose, all of this will turn to dust in a universe doomed to extinction. Nothing apart from God counts, as Solomon so eloquently wrote four thousand years ago in Ecclesiastes—words that ring true today.

But if there is a personal Creator, if *God is*, then His creation can reflect His character; it can reveal God's purposes for us. Our lives instantly gain meaning. The world becomes a means of knowing God as well as our dwelling place. We can truly be the reasoning, imaginative, creative persons we believe ourselves to be.

How we understand ourselves and the world around us determines the kind of life we make. The early Christians showed us this as they swabbed the foreheads of plague victims; so have the Amish. Whether we believe that *God is* affects not only our families and our culture, but world history. But how do we know how we are to live in this world God has given us?

CHAPTER 3

HE HAS SPOKEN

When we say that God is "personal," we mean, at the very least, that He is rational, purposeful, self-conscious, and, above all, that He communicates. The loving God of Christianity reveals not only His own character but how He wants humankind to live in creation. Whether and how God has spoken may seem at first an abstract question, but it's a matter of life and death, as the following stories show.

Scillium, North Africa, AD 180

The runner brought the message that soldiers were on their way. Speratus, a silversmith, had to decide whether to take the church's sacred scrolls with him to jail. He went to the cedar chest where they were kept and began loading them into a satchel. The noise in the street grew louder until the rumble accompanying the legion to Speratus's door sounded like a stampede. Would the scrolls be safer with him or in hiding? Lately, the Roman authorities had been searching out, seizing, and burning the writings the Christian community considered authoritative — the letters of Paul and the four Gospels. To not guard these writings was in the eyes of the Church an act of betrayal — a renunciation of the faith and the hope of heaven.

Speratus was a Roman citizen with rights. Above all, the pagans would want him to recant his beliefs and would probably let him keep the letters with him as an inducement. He decided to take them along. The best hiding place is often right out in the open.

The emperor, Marcus Aurelius, had been scapegoating the Christian community, blaming them for the famine afflicting the empire, which resulted in persecutions as far as Gaul, where Christians were put on racks and dragged down onto beds of spikes, among many other grisly tortures. But Marcus Aurelius had died the previous month in March. His successor, Commodus, was said to be much more favorably disposed to the Christians because he had a concubine in his household who had converted. Word might come through any day that the persecutions were to cease. If Speratus could keep the letters of Paul safe for only a short time, they might remain in the church's possession. Speratus himself might even walk out of prison unharmed.

The announcement of his arrest was being called out to the town before his door. Speratus gave his wife, Lucy, and his children a quick embrace, then hurried out to the guard before they harmed his family.

—

Only in prison would Speratus fully understand why he had been led to take the letters of Paul with him into captivity. The Romans rounded up twelve members of the Scillium church: seven men, Speratus, Nartzalus, Cittinus, Veturius, Felix, Aquilinus, Laetantius; and five women, Januaria, Generosa, Vestia, Donata, and Secunda. They were kept in a cavelike dungeon underneath the Roman garrison. They sang songs and prayed together against the fear that felt weightier than their chains. They fed on the words Paul wrote before his own martyrdom.

Speratus's attention was particularly drawn to the concluding passages of Paul's first letter to Timothy: "Fight the good fight of the faith. Take hold of the eternal life to which you were called when you made your good confession in the presence of many witnesses. In the sight of God, who gives life to everything, and of Christ Jesus, who while testifying before Pontius Pilate made the good confession, I charge you to keep this command without spot or blame until the appearing of our Lord Jesus Christ" (1 Timothy 6:12–14).

Speratus's name meant "hope." Now, in the darkness, he tried to look past his fear to a hope that could survive the grave.

In July, the Christians of Scillium were brought to the African province's capital, Carthage.* Six of the twelve were examined in the judgment hall on July 17 by Proconsul Vigellius Saturninus. Images of the emperor and incense were brought into the hall so that the accused Christians could offer sacrifice to pagan Rome.

Saturninus told Speratus that he still might regain his freedom. "Swear by the genius of our Lord the Emperor."

Speratus thought of Paul's admonition to Timothy and paraphrased it in reply. "I cannot worship the empire of this world," he said, "but rather I serve that God, whom no man has seen, nor with these eyes can see. I know my Lord, the King of Kings and Emperor of all nations."[1]

"Do you truly believe this?" Saturninus asked the others. "Don't you understand it means your deaths?"

Cittinus said, "We fear nothing and no one, except our Lord God, who is in heaven."

Saturninus became curious and asked what Speratus had in the satchel he carried.

"Books and epistles of Paul, a just man."

The Proconsul took Speratus's belief in Paul's writings as a capitol offense against Rome's justice. "These men and women," Saturninus declared, "having confessed that they live according to the Christian rite, and having obstinately refused the opportunity to return to the traditions of Rome, are to be put to the sword."

The Christians of Scillium responded, "Thanks be to God."

The fame of the Scillitan martyrs, as they came to be known, spread throughout the empire. No doubt the letters of Paul that Speratus was carrying were burned, but the Scillitan martyrs are remembered for their absolute trust in the Word of God. A basilica was eventually built in their honor at Carthage (present day Tunis).

---

*In the present day, Tunis, Tunisia.

Henan Province, China, 1974

During Mao's Cultural Revolution in China another Christian community faced a hostile empire. Red Guards, mostly university and high school students, flooded into cities, towns, and villages and systematically persecuted anyone they believed in violation of Mao Tse-tung's Thought. As many as 100 million people were victimized through torture and imprisonment in forced-labor camps; 1 million were executed. To be caught in possession of a Bible meant torture and imprisonment at the very least.

A visitor to Henan Province in those days would have seen scrupulously quiet villages with women outside of ramshackle homes doing the washing or sweeping away the dust. A few of these women were actually lookouts, as groups of Christians risked death by studying the Scriptures together. The house church of a village in Henan Province was blessed if it had one copy of the Bible. The texts used for Bible study were hand-copied sheets. The community's Bible was often protected by being broken into several portions and distributed among different houses. If one house was raided and its Scriptures confiscated, the community would not lose the entire Bible. To secure more copies, the entire Bible was frequently hand copied, sometimes by teams of people who worked around the clock. When confiscating raids seized their Scriptures, the people of Henan would in desperation dig up the graves of Christians who had been buried with their Bibles before 1949. These copies would be mostly illegible from damp and decay, but the Christians of Henan longed even for fragments.

During the years of Mao's rule the patriarchs, or "uncles," of the Chinese house church movement were imprisoned. Perhaps the greatest among these Chinese patriarchs, Wang Mingdao, was arrested for a second time on April 29, 1958. He spent the next twenty-two years in prison. During the Cultural Revolution his treatment became especially brutal. He wore handcuffs for four months straight and was beaten daily.[2] When asked how in old age he had endured, he said, "The Word." The same could be said of the entire Chinese Church.

In 1949 when Mao came to power, there were about 4 million Christians in China. Today, there are reportedly over 100 million.

Henan Province, once considered an "atheistic zone," was said by the authorities to have caught "Christianity fever." Other provinces, including Anhui and Hebei, came to be known as "Jesus nests." There are probably as many evangelical Christians today in China as there are in the United States. In the last thirty years China's Christians have triumphed through suffering much in the way the first Christians did in Rome. No better example of an "emerging church" could be found!

And why? Could there be a better explanation than to imagine one of Henan's young women holding a hand-copied chapter of John's Gospel in her shaking but grateful hands?

Arrayed against the faithful in their evangelical house churches and the underground Catholics were state-church collaborationists.[3] What did they preach? A theological liberalism "infused" with Marxist-Leninist-Mao Tse-tung Thought. These collaborators decried the "fundamentalists" and mocked their love of the Scriptures.

I asked a China expert why Christianity took its genuine great leap forward during the darkest days of the Cultural Revolution.[4] He said, "Light shines in darkness."

The Recurring Battle

Why have I related these stories? Separated by eighteen centuries, the stories of the Scillitan martyrs and of the Chinese house church movement during the Cultural Revolution involve the same dynamics—Christians defending the Word of God, enemies doing their best to destroy it and persecuting Christians for cherishing it. These identical dynamics have come into play whenever in its two thousand-year history the Church has faced a hostile culture. Think of these stories as bookends, if you will, of Christian history. They illuminate the struggle that began with the early Church and continues to this day, always with the same battle lines over God's Word.

Just as in ancient North Africa, Christians today in North Korea, much of the Muslim world, and elsewhere risk violent punishment for even possessing the Scriptures. Pakistani Christians must hide their Bibles or endure severe attacks by imams and roving gangs.

In America and elsewhere in the West, the Bible continues to be attacked, if more subtly. Every Christmas and Easter the media run programs with titles like "Who was Jesus?" Their advertising suggests that new scholarly discoveries transcend the narrow confines of faith and provide a greater truth devoid of the supernatural. Conspiracy theory books like *The Da Vinci Code* and articles related to the publication of ancient Gnostic texts like the Gospel of Thomas and the Gospel of Judas abound. (The Gospel of Judas, touted as a great discovery, was actually rejected as heretical by Church Father Irenaeus in approximately AD 180.) Skeptics claim that the New Testament was cobbled together by religious leaders for their own benefit.[5] The Bible, they say, was simply one version among many of Jesus' life and teachings and therefore cannot be trusted.

Postmodernists, in fact, trust no writings, believing that history is nothing but a record of cultural prejudice, having been written by history's victors, particularly white Anglo-Saxon males. What's more, any truth claim, particularly one about ultimate reality, is offensive in this relativistic era. This has resulted in a cultural atmosphere in which to say one believes in the Bible is to invite derision. Even a Supreme Court justice like Antonin Scalia—one of the brightest intellects in the country—cannot acknowledge believing in Jesus' resurrection without being vilified and called too gullible to serve on the Court.

So what is it about this book, the Bible, that causes people to give their lives for it, causes oppressors to try to destroy it, and so infuriates the cultural elite today?

Clearly, the Bible is unique. Over the centuries many great books have been written, including those by Aristotle, Plato, Shakespeare, Cervantes, and on and on; they have had an influence, of course. But no book, not even Karl Marx's *Das Capital*, has ever caused the controversy aroused by the Bible or invited such severe resistance or inspired its followers to such extraordinary actions.

The reason is what the Bible claims for itself. Although it is in many respects a book like many others, a collection of ancient writings that includes a variety of genres from historical narrative to introspective philosophy, it is much more; it purports to be the Word of

God itself. Through this book God speaks, giving us an understanding of reality that transcends anything that can be envisioned by the human mind alone. The Bible, written by men but *through the inspiration of the Holy Spirit*, gives us God's *eternal* perspective on the world — truth not bound by any time or place (2 Timothy 3:16 – 17).

This is why Christians defend the Bible with their very lives. And since the Bible calls followers to an allegiance higher than the state, tyrants seek to destroy it.

Christians find that the Bible's authority, its textual integrity, its historical accuracy, and its transformative power attest to its unique status as God's Word.

By the Power of the Holy Spirit

When you understand the Bible's origins, you understand why Christians through the ages have trusted their lives to it. Many Christians today, especially evangelicals, have little understanding of Church history. Many imagine that the Bible came into existence when God gave His Word to a group of scribes who bound and published it in a first-century publishing firm.

But remember, Jesus and His disciples were well versed in and abided by the Old Testament, the ancient law that had been handed down by God to the covenant people and meticulously recorded and maintained. It was their first "Bible." The apostles recognized that Jesus' teaching did not abolish but fulfilled these sacred Jewish texts. As time went on, however, the apostles recognized they needed to maintain authoritative accounts of the life and teachings of Jesus, as well as the implications of Jesus' life and teaching for Christian doctrine and life. Within twenty years of Jesus' ascension this process began and the end result is what we now know as the New Testament. The story of the New Testament's creation is a remarkable and faith-affirming account, detailing the meticulous way in which the written Scripture was documented and preserved.

This was possible only with the inspiration of the Holy Spirit. Remember that before Jesus' resurrection, the disciples were caught up in their own longings for an earthly messianic kingdom. And even after the resurrection, in the moments before Jesus' ascension into heaven, the disciples asked, "Will you now restore the Kingdom to Israel?"

But at Pentecost human reason was elevated so that men could truly grasp the truth of God. Within *moments* of the holy fire falling upon them, the apostles fully understood the implications of Jesus' statement: "Those who have seen me have seen the Father." The apostles, led by Peter, rushed out into the marketplace to declare the truth of the risen Lord to all.

The opening chapters of Acts proclaim the heart of the Christian faith only forty days after the shattering event of Jesus' crucifixion. Thereafter, the apostles obeyed Jesus' commission to "go and make disciples of all nations, baptizing them in the name of the Father and of the Son and of the Holy Spirit, and teaching them to obey everything I have commanded you" (Matthew 28:19–20). From the first there was a specific propositional content to this faith—a declaration of God's nature. God had spoken and His Word was knowable.

For the remainder of the first century, the fledgling Christian Church was taught directly about the faith through Peter, Paul, and the other apostles, although martyrdom soon began thinning their ranks.[6] Leaders like Timothy, Clement, and Polycarp would take their leaders' batons. The direct transmission of the faith from one church leader to another continued with meticulous care.

The Canon

The young Church first embraced the written records from Paul's careful explication of Jesus' teaching. Paul's letters to individual churches were copied and exchanged among all church communities. Not long after his death in AD 66 or 67 every new center of the Church had a set of the most recognized letters of Paul. In the same way, manuscripts with the four Gospels, Matthew, Mark, Luke, and John, circulated and were copied by the churches and were quickly accepted as authoritative.[7]

Soon, many other accounts of Jesus' life and Paulinelike letters claiming apostolic authorship began appearing, which often included false teachings like Gnosticism—the idea that salvation comes by way of a higher knowledge rather than surrendering the will to Christ. The leaders of church communities needed criteria by which to distinguish authoritative writings from heretical texts.[8] The major standard employed was whether the documents faithfully communicated the apostles' teaching, even — as in the case of Luke — where the texts were not written by apostles.[9] This was called the "rule of faith." Strict adherence to the apostolic witness decided what writings should be accepted as authoritative and thus "handed down" as approved for the worshiping community.[10]

By the end of the second century nearly 90 percent of what came to be known as the New Testament was accepted by Christians as apostolic and divinely inspired, and hence authoritative. Discussions surrounding the remaining books continued in the third and fourth centuries alongside the debates that led to the formulation of the ancient creeds of the Church — the Apostles', the Nicene, and the Athanasian.[11] Following the example that began in New Testament times, when Peter, Paul, and James met with leaders in Jerusalem to adopt ethical guidelines for new Gentile converts (Acts 15),[12] the early Church leaders met together for prayer, reflection, and decision making.

The Church continued this participatory practice as debates ensued about what books should be included in the New Testament, with the major centers of the new church, Rome, Alexandria, Jerusalem, and Antioch, each contributing their own lists. The Christian Bible, it is important to remember, was assembled over four centuries of the most painstaking study, open debate, discussion, and research. Remember, too, that the early New Testament scholars who participated in these discussions were close in time to the events of the New Testament, many having been taught directly by the apostles or their immediate successors.

Out of these deliberations important understandings could be achieved that continue to guide us to this day. The early Church scholars, for example, recognized that the four Gospels presented Jesus' life in different sequences with different audiences in mind; but this was seen not as a conflict or a liability, as argued in the current wave of anti-theist books, but as a strength, because the diversity in the accounts gave a fuller understanding of the faith and served to guard against narrow, misleading interpretations.

From the hand of Athanasius came the first extant list that included exactly the twenty-seven books we have today in the New Testament. Athanasius was also the theologian who did so much to secure our understanding of Christ as fully God and fully man. Jerome, the translator of the Bible into Latin, led the synod that in AD 382 confirmed this list.

Similarly, the Old Testament canon derived from the same kind of lively debate and intense scrutiny. It came from two main sources, the Hebrew Bible as it existed in Jerusalem, and a translation of the Hebrew Scriptures into Greek known as the Septuagint produced by scholars in Alexandria.[13]

By the time the New Testament canon—the official compilation of books—was accepted by all Christians, the Christian Bible was the most studiously examined proclamation of a faith ever compiled. Understanding how carefully the consensus, guided by the Holy Spirit, was reached explains why still today in discussions among Protestants, Catholics, and the Orthodox, so many common affirmations can be made; we after all rely on the same history, the carefully maintained records of the first five centuries of the Church's life, known as the Patristic Era. This era enjoyed the purest understanding of the Christian faith and the greatest unity and thus, according to many scholars, provides the most reliable resource for fully understanding biblical revelation.

This laborious and careful process also explains why the Bible has proved so enduring. Over the past fifteen centuries the text has been translated into innumerable languages and, apart from an occasional word or phrase changed for clarity, has remained essentially unchanged. Neither persecution nor so-called enlightened skeptics have shaken confidence in it. This is why thousands have been willing to lay down their lives for the Bible, from the Scillitan martyrs to the persecuted Church today. All true Christians affirm that *God has spoken*; that the Bible is the Word of God.

Archaeology

Believers can also point to mounting archaeological evidence that consistently confirms the Bible's accuracy and sheds additional light on its historical context. The weight of scholarship, one eminent scholar has noted, began to shift dramatically in support of Scripture in the early decades of the twentieth century as technology, travel, and funds permitted widespread archaeological digs.[14] For example, excavations by French archaeologists uncovered over 20,000 cuneiform tablets, dating from the fifteenth century BC, that corroborate the cultural and legal background of the stories of Old Testament figures like Abraham and Moses.[15]

Or consider that early in the twentieth century, secular scholars dismissed the Hittite empire because there was no evidence of its existence other than the biblical references. Then archaeologists discovered the ruins of the Hittite empire in what is today Turkey. It turned out to be an advanced civilization, so much so that today a dictionary of the Hittite language has been published by scholars at the University of Chicago.

Then there is the crucial discovery of the Dead Sea Scrolls. The Dead Sea Scrolls revealed that Psalm 22, which predicted Christ's crucifixion, was indeed dated well before the Maccabean era. For several generations, Bible scholars had believed Psalm 22 could not have been written before the Maccabean era because the practice of crucifixion, which it had referred to, had not been invented.[16]

Before the end of the 1950s, no less than 25,000 biblical sites had been substantiated by archaeological discoveries;[17] there has been no discovery proving the Bible false. No other religious document now or in history has ever been found that accurate. The Book of Mormon, for example, talks about a civilization in North America in 400–600 BC. Not a single artifact of that civilization has ever been discovered.

Archeological evidence, often discovered in strange ways, continues to confirm the biblical account. In modern day Israel a helicopter flying over the beach detected a great circle suggesting that an ancient city had once occupied the site. An archaeological dig found Caesarea Maritima, and signs honoring Pontius Pilate.

There is so much archaeological evidence for the Bible's historicity that two professors at a leading seminary have published a Bible that is fully annotated with archaeological discoveries.[18] Paul Johnson, the great British historian and popular author, says it is no longer the men of faith but rather the skeptics who should fear the course of further discovery.

Textual Integrity

Beyond the archaeological discoveries, the truth claims of the Bible are supported by the uncanny coherence and unity of the Bible itself. It consists of sixty-six books, or seventy-three, as in the Catholic tradition, written over 1,500 years by forty people in three different languages, and yet there's a remarkable harmony and consistency in the overarching story. The ancient manuscripts possess an astounding consistency and integrity.

Scholars have a wealth of documents to work from, far more than are available with ancient manuscripts that no one challenges. For example, in the case of Aristotle, there are forty-nine ancient manuscripts, the oldest of which was copied 1,100 years after Aristotle's death. In the case of the Bible, there are 14,000 manuscripts of the Old Testament alone. No other book even comes close. The next closest is Homer's *Iliad* with 600. The devotion of Christians to their Scriptures ensured their transmission to future generations.

And the continued discoveries confirm the biblical accounts. Some extreme critics used to argue that the Old Testament couldn't be trusted because there was a 1,300-year gap between the originals and existing copies. Up until the time of the Dead Sea Scrolls the oldest manuscript available was from AD 900. But as noted, the Dead Sea Scrolls were discovered, and the oldest scrolls dated from the first century BC—a thousand years earlier. Far from challenging the accuracy of the later copies, the Dead Sea Scrolls gave us tremendous confidence that we can reliably know the sense and wording of the texts as they circulated in antiquity.

In the case of the New Testament alone, 24,947 ancient manuscripts have been discovered written in several different languages, the oldest copy dating back to AD 150 or earlier.[19] By studying the subtle variations in these manuscripts and doing a lot of hard thinking, contemporary scholars have come closer to reconstructing the original texts. We have more reason to believe in the accuracy of our New Testament now than ever, and every small issue as to their accuracy has been examined in exhaustive detail.

Why are the manuscript copies of Scripture so accurate? Jewish tradition provides one answer. According to Hebrew practice, only eyewitness testimony was accepted; and when copying documents, the Jews would copy one letter at a time — not word by word, not phrase by phrase, not sentence by sentence.

Transforming Power

Even beyond this impressive historical evidence, the Bible is unique in the remarkable impact it has had on countless lives and widely differing cultures over these thousands of years. Think about all of the books that have been written just in the last fifty years — from Dale Carnegie's formula for influencing other people to Anthony Robbins's *Personal Power*. But how many of them changed anyone's life or are even remembered today?

At the end of 2006, many magazines and newspapers devoted substantial coverage to how to change your life in the coming year. (The popularity of this theme suggests something about the human yearning for transformation.) This advice, like most New Year's resolutions, did not last beyond its time in print.

Think too of all the mystics that have arisen in recent centuries, who offer us a chance to be transported to a higher state. Most of these simply rise to the surface, become celebrated, attract the gullible (incidentally making small fortunes), and then pass quickly into oblivion. What has become of the teachings of the Beatles' guru, Maharishi Mahesh Yogi, or Timothy Leary's pal Baba Ram Dass or Helen Schucman of "a course in miracles" or the theosophist Madame Blavatsky? Few even know what these people taught any more.

But for two thousand years, the Bible, often unaided by any human intervention, has transformed—and many times dramatically so—the lives of those who read it. St. Augustine is a good example. For most of his life he was a famed academic in the Roman Empire, a successful rhetorician by trade—one of the noblest professions of his day—but he lived a thoroughly dissolute, self-indulgent life. There came a time when he began to consider the claims of Christianity, which were then fast spreading in the empire.

He was alone in a garden one day when he heard a child singing out a line from a game: "Pick it up and read, pick it up and read, pick it up and read." He turned to his copy of the Scriptures, which was opened to Romans 13. His eyes were drawn to the following words: "Not in orgies and drunkenness, not in sexual immorality and debauchery, not in dissension and jealousy. Rather, clothe yourselves with the Lord Jesus Christ, and do not think about how to gratify the desires of the sinful nature" (13–14). Deeply convicted, he surrendered to Christ, and the Roman rhetorician went on to become bishop of Hippo, the greatest theologian after Paul, and one of the most formidable intellects of Western civilization.

Or consider St. Anthony of Egypt, the founder of monasticism. He heard the Gospel text, "If you want to be perfect, go, sell your possessions and give to the poor" (Matthew 19:21) and straightaway went and did what Jesus' interlocutor, the rich young ruler, refused to do. Anthony sold all his property and goods and from then on devoted himself exclusively to prayer—and counseling the thousands who eventually trooped into the desert after him.

Reading Paul's letter to the Romans freed Martin Luther from the scrupulous tangle of pious works into which his religious life had fallen. One day this devout monk, close to despair because he could not be sure of his salvation, was deeply moved by the words of Paul: "The righteous will live by faith" (Romans 1:17). Luther wrote, "I felt myself to be reborn and to have gone through open doors into paradise."

In the years I've been a Christian I've known thousands who have read the Bible and been transformed for good. I remember hundreds of convicts like one particular repeat offender, known as the most incorrigible inmate in the California prison system—who read the Bible, gave his life to Christ, and after his release from prison spent the last ten years of his life counseling at-risk kids, keeping them out of prison.

The transformative power of the Bible affects people from all walks of life. One man, for example, who was born a Jew, received a good education, but fell into great depression. One night he slit his wrists, attempting suicide, but was miraculously spared. A counselor later suggested he read the Bible. So this young man did, starting with Genesis. By the time he reached Isaiah 53, "But he was pierced for our transgressions … and by his wounds we are healed," he realized that he had come to faith in Christ. It was clear to him how much the Old Testament anticipated the New. He has gone on to be an effective and articulate preacher of that very same Bible.

The latest wave of atheist literature of the Dawkins-Hitchens-Harris genre ignores the centuries of careful scholarship and evidence; taking verses and sections out of context, these authors argue that the Bible is a dreadful book filled with violence and war, and reflects a mean-spirited God who represses people—a "celestial dictatorship," in Hitchens's words.[20] (The principles of interpretation these authors employ have been scorned even by secular peers.)

I would ask Hitchens, Harris, Dawkins, and company, if this book is so evil, how has it survived all of these years? Why has it been the bedrock of forming the most humane civilization in history? How does it continue, if it is mean-spirited, to spread love around the world and turn hard-hearted criminals into gentle lambs? How could reading it have resulted in such people as Augustine and St. Francis? Why would the Chinese, in the midst of atheistic madness, turn to it as their refuge?

The Bible has, amazingly—no doubt with supernatural grace—survived its critics. Thirty to sixty million copies are produced annually. The harder tyrants try to eliminate it and skeptics dismiss it, the better read it becomes. Voltaire, for example, who passionately sought to erase the Christian influence during the French Revolution, predicted that within a hundred years no one would read the Bible. When his home was later auctioned off after his death, it was purchased by the French Bible Society. As one pastor said, the Bible outlives its pallbearers.[21]

———

Simply put, the Bible is the rock on which the Church stands or falls. It is the ultimate authority for all Christians—Protestants, Catholics, and Orthodox alike. It is revealed propositional truth. The texts were written by men under the inspiration of the Holy Spirit, and thus are *revealed* to us. It is *propositional* because it makes a series of claims. It is *truth* because it is from God, and thus must certainly be true; God could not have spoken something that is not true because that would be contrary to His nature. This is why all true Christians take the Bible as their ultimate authority—and why no Christian should ever be intimidated in defending it.

I was at a Religious Heritage dinner some years ago to receive an award, and one of the other awardees was sitting next to me. He was from a mainline church, and he quickly let me know of his degrees and advanced studies. During the dinner he looked at me with real sympathy. "You're an Ivy League graduate, Mr. Colson, and very well read and educated. Certainly you don't believe in all this fundamentalist stuff about the Bible, do you?"

I looked at him and smiled. "Do you mean do I believe the Bible is true?" He nodded as he was chewing his filet mignon. I drew back in my chair and said simply, "Of course I do, don't you?"

Christians have no reason to be intimidated. The evidence that God has spoken is overwhelming.

CHAPTER 4

TRUTH

Knowing *God is* and *He has spoken* enables the Christian to affirm that there is truth, an ultimate reality that begins with God and extends throughout His creation. The Christian believes that humankind can know truth—that is, the way things really are—through the Bible and in at least three other ways.

Truth in the book of nature. In the North Carolina mountains I saw God communicate through creation; as one twelfth-century saint wrote, "For this whole visible world is a book written by the finger of God."[1]

Truth through reason. Also, we can reason about creation's significance. Christians believe that by being made "in the image and likeness of God" (Genesis 1:26) we are given a free will and the capacity of logical thinking. Christianity does not consist of a hidden body of teachings disconnected from everyday realities, nor does it insulate itself in a realm of subjective notions that cannot be disproved.

In fact, by reason we can test how other religions, philosophies, and other worldviews compare to Christianity in practice, as we will in the chapters that follow. We can observe which worldview conforms to the way the world really works—to what is true. Honest comparison leads to only one conclusion.

Truth through conscience. Morever, God reveals truth through our conscience. We can distinguish the good from evil because we have a moral sense bred into us. This is what Paul meant when he said humans both obey God's law and know themselves in violation of it by virtue of the law "written on their hearts"(Romans 2:15). Remember, we accept that the conscience is written on the heart not because the Bible makes it so by saying it, but because the Bible reports that God made humans this way. Human experience teaches that there has been from the beginning of time a moral law that *all* people and all cultures can know.

For example, the Code of Hammurabi, which contains moral teaching, was written seven hundred years before the Mosaic Law. Confucius preached a high morality, with a view to heaven. The ancient Greek Penandros said that "a good conscience" was true freedom. Almost every religion in history has embraced some form of the Ten Commandments. This idea of a universal moral law that God implanted in humans preceding propositional revelation is what C. S. Lewis, in his book *The Abolition of Man*, called the "Tao."

But our understanding of the universality of the moral law and of our consciences' abilities to understand it has been compromised by today's cultural relativism. This is why many young people, even Christian young people, blanch when I ask them if they believe there are any moral absolutes. But then when I ask them whether it would be right for someone to steal their wallet or to kill someone because they were a Jew or to push an old lady crossing the street into traffic, there is often an "Aha!" moment. Though they have been conditioned to suppress their conscience, educated out of their innate moral sense by postmodern relativism, they instinctively know that those things would never be right.

Similarly, young children know right from wrong. A child can walk down the street, find a toy, and keep it, like the old children's rhyme "finders keepers, losers weepers." But snatch a toy from another child's hands and the "loser" doesn't weep — he demands his toy back. "That's mine!" he says, "and you can't take it!" Even at that early stage they have the primal knowledge that there is a law we all live by — a moral law.

There is even now scientific evidence that this law is written on the heart. One Harvard scholar has discovered that the brain contains "a circuit specialized for recognizing certain problems as morally relevant." The brain incorporates, he says, a "universal moral grammar, a tool kit for building specific moral systems."[2] The professor, though an agnostic, concludes that morality is grounded in our biology, or as the Bible puts it, the law is written on our hearts (Romans 2:14–15).

The Question of Truth

The question of truth—of a common and knowable reality that exists independently of our perception—is the great fault line of Western culture today. The dominant point of view dismisses the idea. The fastest way to provoke scorn from most university professors is to use the words *reality* and *truth*.

Why does this word *truth* breed such animosity? Because rebellious human nature resists truth's claims. If something is really true, it must be true not just for the person saying it but for the person hearing it. And the fact is, we don't want to obey a higher authority from any quarter—especially what purports to be from God—for fear it will impinge upon our personal autonomy. We cling to the idea that we create our own truth.

———

This conflict was at the heart of Pilate's confrontation with Jesus—a pivotal moment in the New Testament in which the willful blindness of human pride turns decisively against God's Son. During his encounter with Jesus, the Roman procurator wants to know if Jesus is a king.

Jesus acknowledges he is a king, but not of an earthly kingdom. "For this I came into the world, to testify to the truth. Everyone on the side of truth listens to me."

"What is truth?" Pilate asks (John 18:38). Every translation of the Bible makes this a question, but Mel Gibson, in his film *The Passion of the Christ*, proved to be a better theologian: the subtitle of the spoken Aramaic puts an exclamation mark to Pilate's reply "What is truth!" Not waiting for Jesus to answer was to dismiss the very possibility of knowing truth.

For educated Romans like Pilate, as with many of today's intellectuals, religion was only an expression of culture and a means of securing political allegiance. Imagine his reaction to this pretender to the Jewish throne, this Jesus who claimed to have cornered the market on truth. How presumptuous, and what a threat to Pilate's pretension. Pilate no doubt believed above all else in the truth of the Roman garrison — in skepticism's refuge, power.

What Jesus teaches is that reality is not what we subjectively make of it, or what our culture may believe. There is objective truth, and we are able to apprehend it with our senses. We are not a dream in the mind of God, an illusion, as Eastern religions and some New Age philosophies teach. Nor is reality so much programming that has been downloaded into our minds as in *The Matrix*, the film once so wildly popular on American campuses. Jesus is *the* ultimate reality.

———

We encounter Pilate's dismissal of the truth everywhere today. Richard Dawkins was asked in an interview with *Time* magazine whether good and evil have no meaning. Dawkins replied, "Even the question you're asking has no meaning to me. Good and evil — I don't believe there is hanging out there anywhere something called good and something called evil. I think that there are good things that happen and bad things that happen."[3] The attacks of 9/11 are not intrinsically evil, and bringing relief to tsunami victims is not intrinsically good? Preposterous.

But Dawkins is a brilliant man; he knows what he is saying. If good and evil were acknowledged as something more than personal value judgments, that would imperil his atheistic worldview. It was the existence of a moral law known to all that caused the then-atheist C. S. Lewis to convert to Christianity.

But the Dawkins mentality has gripped our culture; 63 percent of Americans deny the knowability of moral truth, as do 53 percent of evangelicals. Among teenagers, the next generation of leaders, only 8 percent acknowledge there is moral truth.[4]

Even serious Christians are being taken in. A public school teacher in the Bible Belt, a graduate of Prison Fellowship's Centurions worldview program, presented, at a voluntary Christian club meeting in her middle school, a thirteen-week worldview course for teenagers. Out of 275 seventh-graders, 43 signed up. When she came to the tenth lesson, comparing Islam, Buddhism, and Christianity, the kids, in her words, "went nuts" over the claim that Christianity was true. Seven of the eight serious Christian students she had chosen as group leaders refused to teach it. After a heated discussion, the teacher adjourned the session, asking the group leaders to consult parents and youth pastors. When they met again some days later in preparation for the next week's session, all eight leaders informed her they had consulted their parents and some their youth pastors. One youth pastor said one can never be sure about truth; it is "all perspective." Another said God is bigger than this narrow view. And the parents were alarmed their children might offend other students. One girl had stayed up all night writing a paper on why we shouldn't hurt other students. Our Centurion teacher argued to no avail; all seven of the objecting students remained adamant, so she canceled the lesson.

If this is any indication of the state of the Church and Christian families, we are in deep trouble. The Church, remember, is "the pillar and foundation of the truth" (1 Timothy 3:15). But if we, even in so-called conservative churches, are intimidated by political correctness and have swallowed the myth that all religions are alike, who will defend the truth? This lack of courage means the end of a vital faith wherever it appears. If we do not take truth seriously, we will not take God seriously.

The Church and the Truth

The drift away from the truth of the historic Christian faith in European and mainline American churches is even affecting serious, orthodox believers. Questions are being raised by younger evangelicals associated with the emerging church movement, or "postmodern Christianity." Younger leaders have become impatient with churches that have so many resources and yet little impact. They see evangelical congregations as more and more falling into the trap of "cultural Christianity." Too many of us, they say, believe Christianity consists in intellectual assent to the plan of salvation as a means of securing our own eternal destiny followed by a lifetime of church attendance. This is truly the faith without works that James pronounces dead—younger evangelicals are absolutely right about this and we can learn from them.

Emerging church leaders want to recover a truly biblical vision that understands God's role in history as the redemption of the entire creation. Jesus, through His ministry, death, and resurrection, announces the reign of the eternal Kingdom of God. The Christian life demands not merely the acknowledgment of Christ's significance but our willingness to join Christ in carrying out His mission. On this point I agree strongly.

But here's the rub. These evangelicals are ministering to young adults who have been formed by our postmodern age. Because of postmodernism's foundational belief that we can never know the truth, today's young adults resist direct presentations of the Christian faith and its ethical implications. So some younger evangelical leaders have resorted to emphasizing experience and indirect means of witness; their worship services are characterized by storytelling, visual (often multimedia) presentations, contemporary music, and an open invitation to join the conversation. This, in itself, is not troubling; in thirty years traveling the prisons of the world, I've seen the Gospel presented in every imaginable way and circumstance.

But understanding the way an audience thinks does not mean converting to the way that audience thinks, especially at the expense of truth. Within the largely constructive emerging-church movement is a group know as the "emergent community."[5] Some of its leaders, I fear, have become captives of postmodernist skepticism themselves. They see traditional apologetics as too much aligned with "modern"—or Enlightenment—thinking, and nothing but "dry, dusty doctrines." Some believe the Church should give up on doctrinal teaching—and even on the Bible, according to certain emergent church leaders—for the sake of presenting Christianity as a big-picture story in which all of our individual stories and experiences can find their meaning.

This conception of church life and the failure to teach doctrine do nothing less than institutionalize agnosticism—the inability to know the truth—within churches themselves. It also conveniently excuses us from saying some of the hard things love must sometimes say.

There are other potentially bad effects. When the life of the Church is restricted to an ongoing conversation, church leaders quickly become cult leaders because they are the only ones empowered to attune the conversation to their own agendas. When the faith is based on truth, on the other hand, anyone can call a leader to account.

While "cultural Christianity" throughout the evangelical world is indeed a scandal, postmodern Christianity's diagnosis of the problem is off the mark. Christian doctrine becomes dry and dusty only for those who don't believe it with the lively faith that takes action. That God became man in Christ is, on the face of it, an outrageous claim. The resurrection is either the greatest hoax ever foisted on humankind or the unique, boundary-bursting, death-defying event that Christians believe it to be. As Dorothy Sayers writes, "It is the dogma that is the drama."[6] If evangelicalism has fallen into the trap of cultural Christianity, replacing truth with therapy and creating a feel-good belief, it is no surprise it has lost the drama of the greatest event in human history. The answer isn't to discard doctrine, however; it is to revitalize it.

This distaste for doctrine has led some postmodern Christians to adopt the mantra "We want deeds not creeds." But wait a minute. For over thirty years, the movement known as Prison Fellowship and I have been taking the Gospel into the prisons, demonstrating the transforming power of Christ to turn the most reviled sinners into saints. No one would argue that these have not been worthwhile deeds. But if the creeds I believe in are false, then my efforts have been totally misplaced; I cannot be sure that my deeds, however noble, are really good. It is the creed that makes me carry out the deed—that keeps me going into the most rotten holes in the world—and gives me the message I preach. The same is true of any Christian movement based on the faith.

In my ongoing dialogue with younger evangelical leaders, I have many times raised the question of truth, to which they have responded that truth can be known once we experience truth incarnate, that is,

Christ Himself. But without the apostolic teaching and the Bible, we cannot know who this Jesus we've experienced is.

Nor is there a dichotomy. When the great theologian Timothy George sits at his desk, if he looks to one side he'll see a portrait of William Tyndale, the great martyr who fought to bring the Bible to the public, and on the opposite wall he can see a beautiful portrait of Christ on the cross. Timothy points to the portrait of Christ as the Word Incarnate, and then to the portrait of Tyndale as the defender of the written Word. But as he is quick to point out, they are the same Word. We cannot separate Jesus from God's spoken revelation.

When Jesus becomes the captive of private experience, He rapidly degenerates into a vague, mystical figure who approves our own wishes. To present Jesus without doctrine is to present a disembodied savior, a moral teacher perhaps, but with no more authority than Confucius. This is why I believe that the question of truth and its knowability is the most important single issue for the Church and perhaps for the culture today.

Why Truth Matters

Truth Matters Because the Heart of What We Believe Is at Stake

The path of postmodern Christianity bears some chilling resemblances not only to early church heresies (such a Montanism) but to the theological liberalism of the last century, which led some Protestants to abandon the basic propositions of Christian doctrine. A late defender of theological liberalism, Deane William Ferm, writes,

> What are the motifs of liberal Protestantism? Perhaps the most important one is the priority of firsthand personal experience as the authority for one's religious beliefs. All doctrines must be extracted from "the inward experience of Christian people."

In the last line, Ferm is quoting famed German philosopher Friedrich Schleiermacher, nineteenth-century progenitor of twentieth-century Protestant liberalism.[7] Doesn't that sound hauntingly like the arguments we hear today?

The great conservative leader, Princeton professor J. Gresham Machen, resisted this trend heroically early in the last century, arguing that when doctrine and truth are abandoned you don't get liberal Christianity, you get another religion altogether, which he called liberalism. We saw how this led to the decline of mainline churches in the last century, and conservative churches are at risk of the same thing today.

Without Truth the Gospel Is Perverted

Weakening our commitment to the truth allows us to undermine the Gospel without arousing even a protest. When Katherine Jefferts Schori became presiding bishop of the Episcopal Church of the U.S., *Time* asked her for her prayer for the Church. She answered, "That we remember the centrality of our mission is to love each other. That means caring for our neighbor. That does not mean bickering about fine points of doctrine."[8] But as we have seen, right doctrine leads to the love of neighbor Schori would like to see practiced. And without first loving God, the first commandment she ignored, we can't love our neighbor with the consistency and stamina this world demands. (Bishop Schori's answer reveals that the current fracturing of the Episcopal Church is not primarily over gays being ordained, but over the authority of Scripture.)

The mission of the Church is perverted as well. When truth is abandoned, therapy takes its place. We learn how to cope with our problems instead of curing them.

Rejection of Truth Results in Biblical Illiteracy

Abandonment of the truth shows up in widespread biblical illiteracy. Pollster George Barna has discovered that most churchgoing adults reject the accuracy of the Bible, the existence of Satan, and the sinlessness of Jesus. Many see no need to evangelize and believe that good works are one of the keys to persuading God to forgive their sins. It would be humorous if it were not so tragic that the most widely known Bible verse among adult and teen believers is "God helps those who help themselves," which is not in the Bible—it's actually a quote from Ben Franklin's *Poor Richard's Almanac* (1757). When given thirteen basic teachings from the Bible, only 1 percent of adult believers agreed with or accepted all thirteen. I encountered the same thing in my personal survey. This is why Barna describes this as "an age of spiritual anarchy ... [while the] Church is rotting from the inside out, crippled by abiblical theology."[9]

Rejection of Truth Leads to Ethical Confusion

Denial of the truth of God's revelation undermines any attempt to deal with contemporary ethical questions, particularly in regard to sexuality, which plays a major role in all of our lives. It's often the place where we want to make up our own rules.

At a prayer breakfast in the Midwest some years ago, I met a doctor active in a good Bible study and a strong evangelical church. The subject of homosexuality came up, and he told me that as a doctor he believed homosexuals have a natural instinct and desire that needs to be satisfied, so how can we as Christians deny them the same pleasures heterosexuals have?

It's an argument I've heard many times — one that evokes some sympathy; no one wants to denounce anyone's desire for sexual pleasure. Christians who do are viewed as being bigoted. But I pointed out to my new friend that homosexuality is contrary to God's design, the natural order, and the truth about God's creation, as he could read in Romans 1.

It is important to understand the context in which Paul wrote in order to grasp how we understand moral truth. In the first part of Romans 1 he tells us that God's eternal power and divine nature are plainly seen from His creation. So "men are without an excuse"; though they knew God "their thinking became futile and their foolish hearts were darkened" (Romans 1:20–21). Paul then uses homosexuality as a prime example of the consequences of denying the obvious: "Therefore God gave them over in the sinful desires of their hearts to sexual impurity ... their women exchanged natural relations for unnatural ones ... [and] the men also abandoned natural relations with women and were inflamed with lust for one another" (Romans 1:24–27).

Now why did Paul single out homosexual behavior? Because he thought it was the most obvious example of defying the self-evident created order. On *Larry King* one night, Rick Warren answered the question plainly: stand a naked man and a naked woman together, he told Larry, and you can see how God has designed us. (King was, for once, speechless.)

There is a self-evident connection between God's created physical order and the corresponding moral order that enables our behavior to "fit" the physical. I have found whenever I've explained this it takes much of the sting out of what appears to be God's "puritanical" desire that people have no fun and explains why Paul used this one particular sin (which is no more grievous than heterosexual sin) as the most obvious example of defying the creation.

It also answers the charge, which many younger people raise, that Christians are homophobic to the extent we all must repent. But the charge is wrong, I believe. I've worked lovingly with hundreds of prisoners stricken with AIDS and have witnessed many Christians doing the same. Catholic Charities, after all, runs most of the AIDS facilities in America.

The Rejection of Truth Undermines Cultural Development

From the time of the Church's emergence during the Roman Empire, the Christian faith, and the reason that relied on it, built the greatest society in human history. During the eighteenth-century Enlightenment, however, nonbelieving philosophers and scientists argued that since God wasn't necessary for explaining creation, He wasn't necessary to explain the moral order either. Reason alone would govern.

The problem was that reason without revelation lacked authority, which leads to chaos and tyranny.

The history of the twentieth century, particularly World War I, World War II, and the Holocaust, were horrifying testaments to this. German philosophy had culminated in the fascism that nearly destroyed civilization.[10] Another godless philosophical newcomer, communism, was already ravaging the world and would continue to do so.

But in the aftermath of World War II, Western intellectuals did not renounce the formative influences of fascism and communism and return to the authority of faith. Instead, they despaired of any true understanding of the world—of both faith and reason, ushering in the postmodern era.

We see the effect of this everywhere in the West. Without a basis for morality, no moral consensus can be reached, which is why we are in an ongoing and increasingly strident culture war. Human rights and the law, once seen as God-given, now lack their former authority. Instead of being based on "Nature and Nature's God," as our founders wrote—"rights" are determined subjectively. If Dawkins is right that there is no good or evil, we shouldn't have tried the Nazi war criminals at Nuremburg. And the culturally powerful can do what they like with us, from euthanasia and cloning to engineering babies. Ethics become utilitarian—that is, we do what produces the maximum happiness, rather than what is objectively right. This is why liberal churchmen were in the vanguard of the eugenics movement before World War II, which led to Hitler's gruesome medical experiments.[11]

These circumstances jeopardize the very existence of Western democracies. If people are not guided by conscience and self-restraint, government inevitably becomes increasingly coercive to stave off chaos. That's why our laws are proliferating as never before. This is even more obvious in Western Europe, where laws have been elaborated to an almost unimaginable extent to protect people's rights. Yet overwrought legalism cannot be sustained. It leads to repression and then tyranny. It all comes back to the lack of a basis of authority in the truth.

Rejecting Truth Leads to False Gods

When the God of the Bible is rejected, people choose a new god. The postmodern age has anointed secular tolerance as its god. Tolerance once meant listening respectfully to all points of view, freely discussed in our common search for the truth. But the creed for the new god of tolerance is that knowing truth is impossible. So everyone is free to think and act as he likes, with one exception: those who have the audacity to believe that they know the truth, particularly if they think God has revealed it to them, are not tolerated. The result is that those who crowned the new god of tolerance have become the absolute arbiters of culture. The new god of tolerance becomes, in the guise of liberalism, an absolute tyrant.

Public endorsements of secular tolerance have now become a new public ritual. I watched a debate in the 2006 elections in which a supposedly conservative candidate for governor said he was pro-life. But he quickly assured the questioner that he would not seek any changes in the law. He would not want to "impose his personal views on others," he explained. That's the logical equivalent of saying, "I believe it is wrong to molest a child, but I'm not going to try to prevent anyone from doing so." Why would you want to be governor if you could not seek, through the proper legal means, to prevent moral injustice? In a commentary not only on the politician but on the people, he was handily elected, having succeeded in offending no one at the expense of abandoning his professed convictions.

The only thing the god of tolerance hates more than Christians making truth-claims is Christians proving them. Beginning with a facility in Houston, Prison Fellowship now runs residential programs, "spiritual boot camps," within prisons in locations scattered across the country. This is called the InnerChange Freedom Initiative — or IFI. We have, since the beginning, contended that these demonstrate the truth of the Gospel in transforming lives. In 2003, the first peer-reviewed academic studies validated our claims. University of Pennsylvania researchers reported that IFI graduates had an 8 percent re-incarceration rate versus 20 percent in a comparable control group (and 67 percent nationally). Prison officials were astounded.

It was the first empirical evidence that this faith-based approach to corrections works — in other words, that the Gospel is true. And that's when Barry Lynn of the Americans United for Separation of Church and State decided to sue.[12] To prove our truth-claims proved an outrage that tolerance could not abide.

Why does truth matter so much? Because the Church simply can't be the Church without being on the side of truth. Jesus came as the champion of the truth and of those on the side of the truth. Without understanding this, the Church cannot even present the Gospel. Without truth, it resorts to therapy and has patients, not disciples.

Much of Christianity's retreat from the truth or tempering of our witness in the West has been motivated by good intentions — not to offend or be judgmental, the desire to feel more personally connected to God and to make Christianity more relevant and culturally acceptable.

The history of Christianity, including the faith's surge in the Third World today, shows the reverse to be the case. While we always want to be sensitive to other cultures, we cannot be co-opted by them. The early Christians who treated plague victims certainly weren't embracing the pagan culture. Nor were they trying to make Christianity more relevant and win over the hearts of an empire; they were simply carrying out the truth of their faith — that every person is made in the image of God and therefore possesses dignity.

—

The task of this generation — as it will be in every generation — is to understand Christianity as a complete view of the world and humankind's place in it, that is, as the truth. If Christianity is not the truth, it is *nothing*, and our faith mere sentimentality.

CHAPTER 5

WHAT WENT RIGHT, WHAT WENT WRONG

"God so loved the world . . ." begins everyone's favorite Scripture. God loves the world—that's the first, great, and inexhaustible premise of Christian thinking. Human reasoning about truth, God's existence, and God's revelation leads to this summit from which everything else must be seen.

The Faith is the Great Romance, the Divine Comedy, all the way to the end. Jesus points to God's care for lilies, for swallows, even for the green grass that thrives one day and is gone the next. "You are so much better!" Jesus says. "Can't you see God loves you?"

Originally, God's creation was unspoiled; the Garden of Eden was an earthly paradise for our first parents, Adam and Eve. Their story is rendered figuratively but orthodoxy teaches that these are historical events.

Adam and Eve knew God intimately, recognizing the sound of His footsteps. They were invited into God's reign over the earth, as Adam named the animals God had created and Eve joined in his stewardship of creation. They could offer to God what no other creature could: praise. They were not only free from pain but immortal, enjoying perfect and effortless self-control.

But something terrible happened to disrupt this earthly paradise. The world came under the influence of Satan, as a province in revolt against God, as anyone can plainly see—with wars, strife, tsunamis, and deadly diseases.

The Bible teaches that human history is actually a subplot of a larger story—the cosmic war in the heavens between God and

Satan, good and evil. Satan rebelled against God before the world began, which rebellion God put down, throwing Satan and his followers out of heaven (Isaiah 14:12–15).[1]

So the war in heaven continued on earth. Satan, in the form of a serpent, approached Eve in the Garden of Eden. His first words raised doubts about God's word (the same challenge we hear today). "Did God really say, 'You must not eat from any tree in the garden'?" the serpent asks (Genesis 3:1).

Eve knew the truth. God had said, "You must not eat from the tree of the knowledge of good and evil, for when you eat of it you will surely die" (Genesis 2:17).

" 'You will not surely die,' the serpent said to the woman. 'For God knows that when you eat of it your eyes will be opened, and you will be like God, knowing good and evil'" (Genesis 3:4).

Tragedy then enters human history. Faced with the ultimate temptation to be like God, Eve doubts God's word and eats. Adam soon joins her in the sin. As the serpent predicted, they do know, in a new way, the difference between good and evil, because now they are ashamed and guilty; they realize they are naked, and sew fig leaves together to cover themselves (Genesis 3:7).

This is what Christians call *original sin*, rebelling against God. God, being righteous and just, must then carry out His judgment — the promised consequences of death. He takes away Adam and Eve's earthly immortality, providing a fixed term to their shame. God also demonstrates His loving nature by providing animal skins as protection against a world that has grown immeasurably harsh. Adam and Eve then go into exile from Eden and the human race with them (Genesis 3:23–24).

Creation itself suffers the consequences of their rebellion, its harmonious weave fouled and crossed by willfulness. God says to Adam. "Cursed is the ground because of you; … It will produce thorns and thistles" (Genesis 3:17–18).

In this way the human race inherited a legacy of sin, both in the world itself and in human nature. Adam and Eve set the pattern for the whole human race; human nature was thereafter bent toward sin.

We are born as sinners. Everything from the time of Adam, including the human soul, has been stained and corrupted by forbidden fruit.

The Problem of Evil

But why would God bring a world into existence that would be characterized by such evil and suffering? What about "acts of God" like hurricanes, tsunamis, floods, and famine? Humanity is afflicted with cancer and a thousand other diseases. Can all the evil of the world be attributed to humankind's failings? Is God truly innocent? He put Adam and Eve in a situation where He knew, if God is omniscient, or all-knowing, that they would fail.

This is the question Sam Harris and other atheists have raised. It is called the problem of evil. Theologians and philosophers have wrestled with this question from the beginning of time — and will continue to. How could a good God allow all the sin and suffering in the world?

A generation ago, some Catholic scholars believed they could "help" God out of the problems created by the problem of evil. How could a good God allow suffering? These theologians answered that the whole universe must be evolving and God evolving with it, which became known as "process theology." Author Rabbi Harold Kushner adopted this idea for his hugely popular book *Why Bad Things Happen to Good People*. Don't blame God for sin and suffering, Kushner said; He doesn't have that kind of absolute power, but we should love Him anyway.

But trying to argue that the God who spoke the universe into being is less than all-powerful is a self-refuting assertion. The real reason for sin and evil is that God created us in His image and gave us a free will, which means we have the capacity to reject God and prefer our will to God's. Pride — "I can do it my way" — will always separate us from God.

Knowing that humankind could sin, should God have created us as free creatures? Was this worth the untold suffering of human history?

As we ponder this question, consider whether we enjoy being free-willed creatures. Would we rather exchange our place in the creation for that of the finest among the other animals, say a dolphin, a lion, or an eagle? Would we choose to live only by instinct? We certainly want the blessings of free will, even if we don't like the consequences of our evil choices, which we often perversely blame God for. But of course we can't have it both ways.

Never was this clearer than in the case of Comair flight 5191 when it attempted to take off at Lexington, Kentucky's Bluegrass Airport on the morning of August 27, 2006. There was one operator in the control tower that morning. It was still dark. And as flight 5191 taxied out, the controller instructed its pilots to go to Runway 22. There was construction on the main runway, which knocked out its distance-remaining lights and caused confusion. The usual taxiway to the main runway was also closed. The pilots should have received Notices to Airmen (or NOTAMs) about both these developments through prerecorded messages from the control tower.[2] But these were not available. As a result, James Polehinke, the copilot, taxied on Runway 26 instead of Runway 22. Runway 26 was only 3,500 feet long, not enough for a Canadian-built Bombardier CRJ–100 to take off.

According to investigators, Polehinke and the senior pilot, Captain Jeffrey Clay, failed to do a compass verification of the direction of the takeoff, which would have alerted them that they were on the wrong runway. Their flight manual required them to do this, and to verify it with the controller. A series of human errors committed, the plane raced down the short runway, smashed through the airport's perimeter fence, and into trees on the neighboring farm. Forty-nine people died in the ensuing crash.

Copilot Polehinke was the sole survivor. He remained in a coma for more than ten days (and eventually had a leg amputated). When he regained consciousness, his first words were, "Why did God do this to me?"

This was a tragedy of immense proportions and a terrible burden that James Polehinke will have to live with. But should a person who got wrong instructions from the control tower, and then failed to verify his heading, blame God? Should God have taken away the copilot's free will that early morning? (If God always removed the consequences of our errors and sins, we wouldn't really have a free will.)

Are We Responsible?

The question of evil and suffering will no doubt continue to haunt us. But in today's enlightened world, do we really believe that all the evil and suffering we see is traceable to the original human decision to disobey God, that sin is therefore *our* responsibility? Aren't people basically good, corrupted by society, or broken by disadvantages? This is what sociologists, psychologists, and most academics say.

I asked this question on the source of evil while visiting the California Rehabilitation Center in Orange County. The prison is located on the outskirts of an urban area in a flat, arid, and dusty part of California. Huge rolls of concertina barbwire surrounded the complex. A line of one-story buildings, like so many chicken coops, fanned out in a V from the central, two-story, flat-roofed administrative buildings.

The institution is the state's primary correctional drug rehab facility. Year after year we are packing more and more people away in such prisons—over 2 million today. I stopped when I arrived, surveyed the dreary site, and asked myself a question I've asked countless times: How is it in this, the richest, most powerful nation on earth, that we have to pack so many human beings in these dreadful places?

I spoke to between three and four hundred excited inmates jammed in the chapel that morning, many apparently serious believers. Five minutes into my talk I asked them the question that had struck me that morning, "Okay, now, you fellows that are in here, you are the experts. Why is it that we as a nation are filling so many prisons?"

Dozens among the guys sitting there in their blue denim uniforms began shouting out, "Sin!" The word became a ringing chorus. "Sin!" I was stunned. I can't imagine any other audience where, if I asked that question, I would get that answer. These men have lived it, though. They know the truth.

When asked the same question I asked the inmates, "What's wrong with the world?" G. K. Chesterton, a delightful British writer, answered, "I am." The problem is sin! My sin. The biblical account is true. The evils we do—theft, murder, adultery, greed, arrogance, folly—all of these evils come from inside and make a man unclean. The problem of sin is not what goes into us but what comes out of us. All of these things, Jesus said, come from inside and make a man unclean (Mark 7:14–16).

But, remember, it is inside us—and not always obvious. I was in prison with an inmate who had been a Mafia hit man. He had twenty-six notches on his barrel and ice water in his veins. I asked him once how he could live with this. "Chuck, you were in the Marines. You were trained to kill people. I was in the service of the Cosa Nostra, and I was hired to kill the enemy." I never saw the slightest suggestion that this man's conscience was in any way troubling him.

I know about rationalization from my own life. I know it also from the hundreds, perhaps thousands of normal-looking human beings in prison, many of whom have committed unimaginably horrific acts, but have justified them and feel no remorse. And they look and act normal. The most terrifying truth I have discovered in life is the banality of evil; the most ordinary people are capable of the most horrific sin; it is in us all.

Denial and the Blame Game

Our culture's refusal to accept the truth of original sin has created a mentality of wholesale denial. We find the judgment in the word "sin" a far greater offense than the failings to which it's applied. When our own behavior might be described as evil or sinful, we compartmentalize our thinking, profess ourselves victims, or find ourselves genuinely astonished that any such darkness could have emerged out of us.

Making excuses is part of human nature. Eve, after all, when God chastised her, blamed the serpent; and Adam blamed Eve. But the intellectual fashions of the past two hundred years have provided a slew of new excuses. First came the Romantics with their belief in the individual's essential goodness. Only the corrupt influences of society were responsible for turning innocent, dewy-eyed children into hate-filled monsters. The pervasive influence of Darwinian evolution then led people to see murderous and even genocidal behavior as the unfortunate remnant of our survival-of-the-fittest past. Freud personalized the struggle, centering it in repressed sexual desires and proposing therapeutic answers. Marx then saw people as being the products of how their societies made money. Behaviorist psychology taught us about positive and negative reinforcement, which direct our lives in this view like rats through a maze. Sociobiology, updating Darwin, sees human behavior as driven by the imperative of our genes to replicate in future generations.

These various theories of behavior contradict one another except in one thing: they all treat human responsibility as an illusion. The underlying reason for this is their dismissal of God. Because they get God wrong, they also misunderstand human nature.

Because of our philosophically emboldened excuse making, we now live in a society filled with victims and nonjudgmental authorities. Each of us, by turns, learns to play both roles: we are the victims of our families, friends, neighbors, poverty, coworkers, religious and political leaders; our friends must be as well, so when they tell us their tales of victimization, we know not to judge them.

So a friend will say, "I'm breaking up with my wife because I need more than Judy can give me." Then he'll specify the various ways in which Judy has proven incompatible — all no doubt a complete reversal from how she acted during their dating life.

We'll then ask, "Are you sure?" Then we might propose a series of therapeutic solutions, cultivating other helpful friendships, finding new interests, redirecting energy into work pursuits. But in the end we feel compelled to agree that everyone has his needs. Needs can pulverize the best will in the world! We find it impossible to respond: *Who cares what you need? That would be wrong. You are responsible.*

We cannot even hold a terrorist fully to account, let alone friends or neighbors. Look at what happened when Zacarias Moussaoui was tried as a conspirator in the 9/11 attack on America. Moussaoui was convicted by the jury. But the jury, after long deliberation, decided to sentence him to life in prison instead of the death penalty. When the jurors were surveyed after the verdict, nine of the twelve explained the lesser sentence by noting that Moussaoui had a troubled childhood. A dysfunctional background excuses someone for knowingly taking part in a plot to kill thousands of innocent civilians? As *Newsweek* correctly bannered on its cover about the same time, "Freud is not dead."

Theodore Dalrymple, who worked for years as a doctor among prisoners and in hospitals with England's lower class, tells in almost comical accounts how this therapeutic mindset has distorted our system of justice. Non-Christian criminals now see themselves as victims of circumstances beyond their control.

One prisoner told Dr. Dalrymple that he had become depressed after "his trouble came upon him again." His "trouble" was breaking and entering into churches, stealing their valuables, and then burning them down to destroy the evidence. The doctor wondered whether this "trouble" had come about because the prisoner had been forced in his childhood to attend too many church services by a hypocritical family. "Not at all; it was because in general churches were poorly secured, easy to break into, and contained valuable objects in silver." The man blamed his actions on lax church security. The prisoner thought this only reinforced his compulsion to steal.[3]

Dalrymple's fine books are filled with such hilarious and sad examples. He talks about the wanton neglect of children brought on by sexual license, where many among the Britain's lower class accept that they are the victims of their sexual drives, ensuring that their children certainly will be.

Over the thirty-three years of my ministry I have discovered the bankruptcy of the sociological explanations for the cause of crime. As studies in the 1970s and 1980s showed, the cause of crime is not, as we have been led to believe, a bad environment or an unfortunate upbringing. We are not victims, as liberal politicians told the poor and minorities (thereby encouraging more antisocial behavior). The cause of crime is wrong moral choices, the lack of moral training during the morally formative years.[4] The inmates in that California prison got it. As Christians, they knew the truth.

Self-justifying thieves, the Moussaoui trial, and our reticence to speak of "sin" in regard to crime are only glints off the shield with which we hide our own behavior. We flinch at the judgment even of a mass murderer because we don't want our materialism, our craving of status, our lust for power, our shady business ethics, our neglect of our children, our abortions, and our drug and alcohol addictions held up for scrutiny. We live in the land of no fault divorce, as if there could ever be such a thing.

Satan's Best Work

As we've seen, Satan practices his deception not only on individuals but on whole cultures. He uses false religions and false ideas to ensnare cultures in evil. If he can turn a whole people toward worshiping a false god, he can compromise millions of consciences at once.

The most tragic instances of this phenomenon come in the form of otherwise decent men and women carrying out crimes against humanity. Hitler was a monster, but the Nazi war machine and the Holocaust death camps were run by thousands upon thousands of "normal" Germans. Ordinary people also carried out the Turks' genocide against the Armenians, ran the Soviet Gulag and China's Cultural Revolution, Pol Pot's Killing Fields, and the Rwandan genocide. Those who are currently killing people by the hundreds of thousands in Darfur or blowing themselves up in the Middle East are as human as we are. In our own country slavery turned otherwise good Christians' hearts to stone, which continued to manifest itself in segregation and today's racial divisions.

"Did God really say ... ?" "What is truth?" With questions like those, a thousand devils have been let loose upon us, and we have danced along. We take our cues from Adam: "The woman gave it to me," he says; "it's her fault." It's *always* someone or something else's fault.

But the truth is we are responsible. All true Christians affirm that humans, given the gift of a free will from God, disobeyed Him. Our original parents' sin is thus our legacy.

—

It is critical to understand why Christians believe this. Besides the biblical witness, the history of civilization along with our own experience attests to it. And why does it matter? Get this wrong and you get life wrong. Human responsibility is misunderstood, chaos results, and human hubris leads to tragically flawed utopian experiments. And you get God wrong because without human responsibility there is no need for a Savior. These questions are critical to understanding life and reality.

So can we once again embrace the truth and take back our world for God? How? When nations are occupied, other countries mobilize great invasions of the occupied territory and set the people free. This has happened throughout human history, from the Greeks to today. My generation saw it up close. Much of the world was under the oppressive rule of Hitler's brown shirts. But the West mobilized and invaded the enemy-occupied territory. God invaded our world as well, if in quite a different way.

CHAPTER 6

THE INVASION

In the summer of 1954, I was a Marine infantry platoon commander stationed at Camp Lejeune, North Carolina. Once, in the middle of the night, I was awakened by a call at my quarters ordering me to report to the base in two hours, seabag packed. Our battalion had been ordered on a top-secret mission, and several hundred men were herded onto a troopship, the USS *Melette*.

A few days later we were cruising off the coast of Guatemala, close enough that anyone on shore could see us.

The officers were briefed in the wardroom in preparation for a landing, ostensibly to protect American lives and property. The planned invasion was labeled "Hard Rock Baker"—a covert plan to restore the Guatemalan government to its pro-American leaders. The CIA was directing the operation against the newly installed leftist-leaning government of President Jacobo Arbenz Guzmán—a classic case of gunboat diplomacy. We listened on the shortwave radio to Radio Moscow and Pravda denouncing the American "invasion" in Central America, while President Eisenhower and his secretary of state, John Foster Dulles, denied Americans were anywhere in the area. "Hard Rock Baker" was not publicly disclosed, in fact, until the mid-1990s.

At dawn the second morning I walked out on the deck of the troopship and saw one of the most impressive sights of my life—a flotilla of warships, including an aircraft carrier with Corsair fighter bombers taking off, cruising over the beach, circling, and landing. It was a deliberate and provocative show of force. I watched and took part in the tremendous preparations for what would have been a relatively minor military action. Our troopship was filled with live ammunition; two of the support ships brought along enough resources to sustain the action. Huge logistical preparations were required for an invasion even of a small Central American country.

As it turned out, we did not have to land. Arbenz fled and his Communist supporters melted away.

What I experienced off the coast of Guatemala pales in comparison with the invasion of Normandy on D-day, June 6, 1944, the largest seaborne landing in history. The invasion of Normandy was the first successful opposed landing across the English Channel in nine centuries. Movies like Saving Private Ryan and Band of Brothers, as well as books like The Longest Day and The Greatest Generation, have taught young people not only the horror and carnage of war but the tremendous courage displayed by American, British, Canadian, Polish, and Free French troops during this pivotal moment in World War II.

More than 150,000 troops were committed to the initial invasion, employing 6,900 vessels, 4,100 landing craft, and 12,000 airplanes flying 14,000 attack sorties. A thousand of these airplanes were transports that parachuted troops behind enemy lines the night before the invasion in order to thwart counterattacks.

Preparations for the Normandy invasion began in earnest in March of the previous year. The Allies designed armored vehicles for the assault that included "swimming" Duplex Drive Sherman tanks, mine-clearing tanks, bridge-laying tanks, road-laying tanks, and a company of British engineers equipped with large-caliber mortars for destroying concrete emplacements.[1] The invasion demanded two artificial Mulberry Harbors be towed across the English Channel and placed at the beach outside the French town of Arromanches and Omaha Beach. Within two weeks the British landed an additional 314,547 men, 54,000 vehicles, and 102,000 tons of supplies at Arromanches, while the Americans put ashore 314,504 men, 41,000 vehicles, and 116,000 tons of supplies at Omaha. An underwater pipeline called PLUTO was constructed to deliver fuel from Britain to the invading forces.

Ten thousand tons of bombs were dropped on the German defenses, and the French resistance was given orders to sabotage key bridges, railway lines, telephone exchanges, and electricity substations.

Despite the Allies' air superiority and hours of heavy bombardment against the beach defenses by the warships' guns, the German's batteries of 155 mm and 75 mm guns, as well as machine-gun nests, pillboxes, and the beach's sea walls, remained intact as thousands of brave men in the landing craft motored toward shore. Once the bow ramps of the Higgins Boats dropped open for their complements of thirty-six men to race forward, nothing stood between these troops and the German guns but the morning air. At Omaha, Gold, Sword, Juno, and Utah beaches, the troops' only chance was to run, swim, and crawl up the beach to the sea walls, where they could reassemble for assaults on enemy gun positions. In the first hours at Omaha, more than 2,400 died. The first wave of troops at Juno suffered casualties of 50 percent, many in the hail of bullets as the boat ramps were lowered. Blood, gore, flying limbs, and floating corpses made it a living hell for the first waves of men out of the boats. Over the next weeks, as the battle progressed inland, the U.S. would eventually lose 29,000 men and more than 100,000 wounded and missing. The British gave up 11,000 of their finest; Canada 5,000.

The preparations and costs in terms of human lives of this military action were enormous, but the invasion of Normandy settled the outcome of World War II in Europe. Once the Allied forces had established a beachhead in Europe, the die was cast and the final outcome of the war was no longer in doubt. The Battle of the Bulge and other potentially catastrophic reversals were still to come, of course, but the invasion of Normandy was so massive and successful that it allowed the Allies to turn every counterattack into another victory. As if preordained, the outcome was clear: the evils of Hitler and fascism would be conquered.

The Incarnation

In one sense, the great invasions of history are analogous to the way in which God, in the great cosmic struggle between good and evil, chose to deal with Satan's rule over the earth—He invaded. But not with massive logistical support and huge armies; rather, in a way that confounded and perplexed the wisdom of humanity.

It was a quiet invasion. Few people understood what was happening. Mary, the mother of Jesus, knew that she was with child, but she also knew that she had never been with a man, not even Joseph, to whom she was engaged. She had learned of her pregnancy and what was to be a virgin birth when an angel told her that she was pregnant with the Son of God.

For many, including Joseph, the doctrine of the Virgin Birth is hard to accept. But the God who could speak the universe into being, who could create human life, could certainly choose to make Himself known by the power of the Holy Spirit through a virgin. And it was essential He do it this way. Jesus could never have been the Savior of humankind if He were born into sin, because then His death on the cross would be for His *own* sins, not for *ours* alone. Only a totally sinless savior could take our sins upon Himself, which means God, and only God, could be His Father.

Most of the people in Palestine at the time of Jesus' birth were expecting a Messianic invasion like we saw at D-day—conquerors in armor bringing a sword to set the people free from oppression.

Jesus only added to the bewilderment of the people who knew Him when He announced: "The time has come.... The kingdom of God is near. Repent and believe the good news" (Mark 1:15). This was the time the Jews had waited for so long? Liberation? And who was this ordinary Nazarene carpenter to say he was bringing in the Kingdom of God?

———

Sometimes I think Jesus' humble announcement of the liberation of the people and the coming of the Kingdom of God is as badly misunderstood in churches today as it was by the Jews of His time. He was bringing in the reign of God on earth—first through His own ministry and then by establishing a peaceful occupying force, His Church, which would carry on God's redemption until Christ's return in power and glory at the Kingdom's final triumph. In the cosmic struggle of good and evil, Jesus' inauguration of the Kingdom was more decisive than D-day or any other invasion in human history.

But one place Jesus' announcement is understood clearly is in the prisons where I have preached for more than thirty years. Put yourself in the place of a prisoner. Imagine if you had been caught in some of the bad things you've done. Remember your youthful indiscretions, the jealousy that you may have harbored, the false statements you've made, your anger against enemies, the person that was once close who you cannot forgive (that's a prison in itself). What if you hadn't escaped injury that day you were driving drunk or had been caught in that lie to governmental authorities? Or what if you had pursued to the limit the murderous hatred we all feel when angered and you actually took revenge? Most of us stay out of jail, but few have not experienced moments in their lives when they were capable of just about anything. Remember such a moment and let the nightmare of its consequences play out imaginatively. You've been caught, tried, and imprisoned for twenty years, perhaps.

Now imagine looking at bare concrete walls for as many as twenty-three hours a day, eating what passes for food, fending off the fights, rapes, and gang violence. Your family's gone; the only real hope you have is that someday you might get out of prison. But who will want you then? If you do get a job, you may be among the one-third who aren't rearrested and cast back in. Try to feel the desperation, the fear. Then maybe you'll be able to hear the message of Jesus as you've never heard it before.

When I speak to prisoners, I read Jesus' inaugural sermon, when he went into Nazareth's synagogue and read out from the scroll of the prophet Isaiah. "The Spirit of the Lord is on me, because he has anointed me to preach good news to the poor. He has sent me to proclaim *freedom for the prisoners* and recovery of *sight for the blind*, to *release the oppressed*, to proclaim the year of the Lord's favor" (Luke 4:18–19, Isaiah 61:1–2, emphasis added).

Wherever I read that passage in a prison, I experience an instantaneous connection with the inmates. Often they raise their arms and cheer as if they were at a football game. Jesus' message means freedom! It means victory for those who once had no hope.

Can you hear the Kingdom message as it's meant to be heard: good news to the poor and *freedom* for you, for me? In foreign countries, when those words are translated, I can see eyes brightening. They're prisoners; they're blind; they're oppressed. They understand that Jesus came to proclaim *their* freedom. They understand that the Kingdom of God turns the order of society upside down — the poor inherit the Kingdom of God, while the wealthy have their reward already.

As I recount the story of Jesus to prisoners, the identification gets stronger and stronger. He was followed by a ragtag bunch of powerless disciples, preaching this amazing message to set free the prisoners and the poor and the oppressed. It was such a radical message that the people who heard Him in Nazareth that day tried to kill Him. For this radical message Jesus was later arrested, or as we inmates would say, "busted."

I ask, "You know what it's like to be busted?" The prisoners nod they do.

I also ask if they know what it is to be betrayed. There's a chorus of affirmation, and I tell them the story of Judas betraying Jesus — Jesus had a snitch among His friends.

"Have you ever had a chance to plea bargain?" Their heads nod; their hands shoot up.

Jesus was called before the Roman governor and asked if He was the King of the Jews. Had He said no, He would have been set free. But He couldn't "cop a plea," as inmates say, because He had come as King of God's Kingdom, which He could not deny.

Jesus was, of course, fully God because He was God incarnate, but He was also fully human. His humanity was clear that night in the garden when even His closest disciples let Him down; there He asked God to "let this cup pass" if it was the Father's will. But Jesus, as we see throughout His ministry, knew exactly what God had said; that He would be the "man of sorrows." He knew exactly the mission He was on. And though in His humanity He would have chosen to avoid the cross, He knew that He must be condemned. And so, as I tell the inmates, an innocent man, the gentlest man who'd ever lived, thirty-three years old, was condemned to die and sat on death row alone, utterly rejected with the cries of the crowd's "crucify Him—we have no king but Caesar!" ringing in His ears.

Here then is the scandal. God chose to invade planet earth in the person of His Son, what Christians call the Incarnation—God made flesh. He did so to rescue fallen humans. He became human so we could become holy.

God appeared not with trumpets sounding and the hoofbeats of horses, not with great armies at His command, but in the person of Jesus, who had nothing. When He was born, He was born in a borrowed manger—a feeding trough. When He rode into town in Jerusalem in fulfillment of Scripture, He rode on a borrowed donkey. And when He was buried, He was buried in a borrowed tomb. He was a true radical with His message for the poor. He kicked over the tables of the money changers in the Temple, signaling that the old system of sacrifice associated with the Temple was now out-of-business. He was not a white Anglo-Saxon, so commonly pictured in the West; He was an olive-skinned Semite born in the Middle East—a man for all seasons, a suffering servant, not ashamed to call the despised His brothers and sisters, nor to bear the sins we keep secret.

The revolutionary nature of God's invasion of our world is far more significant than all the other invasions of history taken together. This one established the possibility of the rule of God in every human heart and began the reclamation of our world as God's own.

The Cross: Jesus Dies for Us

When you understand, as inmates, the poor, and the marginalized do, the radical nature of Christ's message, it's no wonder that those opposed to God's rule ordered Him crucified. He was a dangerous threat to the evil world order.

So Jesus was taken from death row, His robe torn off Him—He was strip-searched, I remind the inmates, just as they were. He was beaten, scorned, and mocked, a crown of thorns pulled down upon His head until the blood ran. Then He was forced to carry His own cross to Golgotha, the "place of the skull," which was littered with the bones of the crucified. And there, He was nailed to a cross to hang between two thieves, common criminals. Golgotha was at a cross-roads where everyone coming to and from Jerusalem would see this shameful and agonizing sight—and thus be deterred from following, Him. Prisoners know all about the deterrent theory of punishment. The judge's gavel still rings in their ears.

If you can still imagine yourself as a prisoner, think about what the scene at Golgotha reveals. Being nailed to a cross was an invention of the Romans, considered the most painful death imaginable, with prolonged suffering often lasting hours. None of us can get out of our minds the grisly portrayal of the crucifixion in Mel Gibson's film *The Passion of the Christ*. Watching that film was one of the most sobering and convicting experiences of my life. Prisoners can really relate when they realize that Jesus went through that horrific experience for them, as He endured it for all of us. I see the truth register in their expressions: Jesus suffered like this *just for me?*

While hanging in agony on the cross, Jesus, the Son of God, watched as Roman soldiers cast lots for His clothing. They taunted Him by saying, "If you're God, come off that cross and save yourself." (But any display of His power would have aborted His mission; and had He done so, He wouldn't have saved us.) Then He saw so many others, standing, watching, doing nothing, seemingly not caring—the sort of indifference so many have today in our self-absorbed culture.

Jesus was accompanied in His greatest moment of trial by two thieves, common criminals hanging on either side of Him. The first thief, called in tradition Gestas, looked over and said, "You're supposed to be God. Well then, save us. Get us out of here." That's the prayer we all pray. Even atheists cry out to be saved when facing a frightening experience. But why should He save us?

The second thief, known in Catholic tradition as St. Dismas, understood what the first thief didn't. Dismas rebuffed Gestas: "He's innocent. We're getting what we deserve." He then looked at Jesus and said, "Jesus, remember me."

To which Jesus responded, "Today you will be with me in paradise" (Luke 23:43).

I ask inmates to put themselves in the place of the good thief and to pray just as He prayed, "Jesus, You're innocent. You're holy. I'm guilty. Remember me." The good thief's understanding of his own sin, his repentance, and his desire to be with Jesus made it possible for him to be saved—for Jesus to answer his prayer. Repentance and the desire to be in Jesus' company are the crucial elements of any sincere conversion.

Thousands of times around the world I have seen the power of God work in the most remarkable ways through such simple prayers, whole groups of inmates and the poor praying out loud, individuals weeping, many responding with open confessions of faith. I have seen some of the hardest, toughest, meanest looking convicts dissolve in a flood of tears. In some prisons, I have literally been mobbed afterward by weeping convicts. They get it.

Repentance and acceptance of Christ's saving work bring with them a new understanding of one's own worth that at first may seem paradoxical. However gravely I have sinned, Christ still thought I was worthy of His sacrifice. That's grace, indeed; that's love! One inmate in a Florida prison looked like thousands I've met; missing teeth, tattooed, his face scarred by dissipation and a depraved life. In tears he said to me, "All my life people have told me I was no good, I would never amount to anything. For the first time in my life today, I feel like I'm worth something." Another inmate in one of the maximum security prisons in America, who turned out to be a Mafia leader, fell to his knees crying. "Until this day I have never felt any good," he sobbed. "Now I know I can be forgiven and be decent. Now I have a reason to live." As the Scriptures say, "While we were still sinners, Christ died for us" (Romans 5:8).

These men came to understand the central truth of the Gospel message, that the Son of God actually hung on a cross and died the most agonizing death in order to take upon Himself the sins of mankind—all of us, rich and powerful, poor and helpless. You and me. This is why at the heart of every orthodox confession of faith is the atoning death of Christ, which is the supreme outpouring of God's love for us. This is the wellspring of grace, God's unmerited favor, His salvation.

Never forget the second thief on the cross. He did nothing but repent and respond in faith to the Christ being crucified beside him. For this he was promised a place in heaven, the only place in all Scripture where an individual is given such a promise.

Everyone is like the first thief or the second, or perhaps one of the crowd, standing around with their hands in their pockets. Remember that great Negro spiritual "Were You There When They Crucified My Lord?" Well, you are. This central event in human history is replayed, moment by moment, day by day, as we contemplate the question of who Jesus is. Everyone must confront that question. Not to do so is to make a choice, the wrong one.

This is why the cross is the symbol of Christianity. It marks the dividing line between man's futile efforts to achieve God's righteousness and God's gracious act in sending Christ to redeem all who will follow. It represents the most decisive moment in history, when God answered the great human dilemma that we have all sinned and yearn for forgiveness: God took upon Himself our sins to set us free. It is where justice and mercy meet. It is scandalous, for as Paul wrote, Jesus "cancelled the written code ... that stood opposed to us; he took it away, nailing it to the cross" (Colossians 2:14). He made the very instrument of what the authorities calculated would be a shameful defeat into the sign of God's victory. As Paul further writes, "Having disarmed the powers and authorities, he made a public spectacle of them, triumphing over them by the cross" (2:15).

This is the heart of Christianity. It is why we can say that Jesus' invasion of Satan's territory assured that the victory will be completed on Christ's return.

When I was in Moscow in 1990 preaching at the Moscow Baptist Church, just blocks from the Kremlin, I told a packed crowd of worshipers that all through human history, as far back as recorded time and doubtless before, kings, princes, tribal chiefs, presidents, and dictators have sent their subjects into battle to die for them. Only once in human history has a king not sent his subjects to die for him, but instead, died for his subjects. This is the King who introduces the Kingdom that cannot be shaken, because this King reigns eternally. Within months of that day in Moscow, the great Communist behemoth fell, and the crowds in Red Square raised the cross high, chanting "Christ has risen! He is risen indeed."

The Resurrection

When Jesus died, His body was taken to a guarded tomb and buried. His disciples were crestfallen. They were weak as well. As I ask inmates, "Do you know what it is to be betrayed?" Peter insisted he did not know the man, cursing for emphasis.

The death and burial of Jesus was not the end of the story, though. On the third morning, Mary Magdalene and Mary, the mother of James, went to the tomb to sprinkle spices on the body of Jesus wrapped in its burial cloths. The tomb was empty. Two angels appeared and told them, "He is not here. He has risen."

And this is the second part of the story, which explains why it is truly "good news" — the best news ever for all humanity. The story doesn't end at the cross or the tomb. For Christ was bodily raised from the dead by God, and He lives and reigns today, seated at the right hand of the Father. The ugly crucifixion, the most hideous symbol of death and shame ever devised, was converted in that instant into the holiest of holy symbols. All true Christians believe that Jesus Christ has been bodily raised in victory over death. This is why Patty and I, sitting in St. Paul's, could join in that great victory chant, "Christ has died. Christ is risen. Christ will come again!"

And this is why the resurrection of Jesus has been subject to greater challenge and scrutiny than any other event in human history. The Jews and the Romans feared that the disciples would hide the body and claim Jesus had risen. For centuries the idea of a "Passover Plot" has been widely held by skeptics.

Doubts continue to be raised even in the Church. Some years ago, the Anglican bishop of Durham, David Jenkins, publicly announced that he did not believe in the physical resurrection, that it was merely a "conjuring trick with bones."[2] I was in Sri Lanka shortly after his widely publicized statement and was told by an Anglican priest that the Buddhists and Senegalese and Muslims were using the statement to lure believers away from Christianity.

Of course they would. Without the resurrection, Jesus is no different than any other prophet or Buddha. This is why the central attack on Christianity has always been against the scandal of the cross and the empty tomb.

Still, many who call themselves Christians today share Bishop Jenkins's skepticism, embracing the argument that many have made through the centuries that Jesus' followers simply played upon the ancient myths about a god rising from the dead, hid Jesus' body, and then created the Passover Plot. It is true that many religious groups in ancient times believed such myths. (Even the Jews expected a messiah who would be resurrected, as recent scholarship establishes.[3])

But does this prove that the early Christians adopted the resurrection story to fulfill the myth? Or does the existence of the myth or belief indicate a reality, common to all those who are born with the image of God in them? This goes to the point C. S. Lewis often made — does the yearning for heaven within us presuppose the existence of something we are made to yearn for? I would argue that the deep-seated beliefs, that go way back in time, that God would come and be resurrected from the dead mean that this truth was written in the human heart. Jesus is God's sovereign plan fulfilled.

This is the great choice every human being has to make: Is the resurrection account true or only a myth? If the latter, it is an abomination, taking away any validity to the Christian claim. Believing that the resurrection was merely symbolic doesn't create liberal Christianity or a more enlightened version of our faith as many argue; it reduces Christianity to something utterly vain, a belief system like paganism. For if we were to believe Christ was not bodily raised, then Christianity would rest on the belief in a human sacrifice — offering an innocent man to die for our sins. This is not enlightened thinking; it is barbaric. It is why so-called liberal Christianity is untenable, no better than paganism.

The apostle Paul put this question to rest once and for all. "If Christ has not been raised, your faith is futile; ... [and] we are to be pitied more than all men" (1 Corinthians 15:17, 19). All the apostles recognized that if the resurrection was not a historic fact, there could and should be no such thing as Christianity.

My personal experiences in the Watergate scandal convinces me of the historic proof of the resurrection, as I've written elsewhere.[4] I was charged with being part of the conspiracy to cover up the Watergate break-in. What most Watergate buffs have failed to note, however, is that the conspiracy succeeded for less than three weeks. It wasn't until March 21, 1973, that John Dean, the president's counsel, advised Richard Nixon of precisely what was happening. His words were, "Mr. President, there's a cancer growing on your presidency." At that point, for the first time, the president and several of his aides fully understood what was happening. But by early April, John Dean went to the prosecutors to make a deal, as he wrote with refreshing candor, "to save his own skin." When he was granted immunity, others followed suit. The conspiracy unraveled soon thereafter. And from then on, Nixon could only delay the inevitable.

Think of it: the most powerful men around the president of the United States could not keep a lie for three weeks. And you'd have me believe that the twelve apostles — powerless, persecuted, exiled, many martyred, their leader Peter crucified upside down — these common men, gave their lives for a lie, without ever breathing a word to the contrary? Impossible. As we are seeing with Islamic radicals today, people will die for something they believe to be true; but men will never die for something they know to be false. Human nature destroys the idea of the Passover Plot or any cover-up conspiracy.

For two thousand years the historicity of Christ's crucifixion and resurrection has been challenged on many grounds. But no one has ever produced evidence of the kind that brought President Nixon down — "a smoking gun," that is, evidence that could contradict the biblical account. Is that not evidence of its veracity? Can you think of any other event in history that has been so thoroughly examined, has not been disproved, and yet some still disbelieve it? The consistent eyewitness testimony of the apostles and earliest believers to the reality of Jesus' bodily resurrection, given among those hostile to the claims of Jesus, clearly points to the resurrection as a historical reality.

The Ascension:
Christ Lives and Reigns for Us

Following His resurrection, Jesus spent forty days with His disciples, teaching them. Then He gathered them together, explaining that they were to remain in Jerusalem and wait for the Holy Spirit to come in His place. While the apostles were watching, before their eyes, Jesus ascended in a cloud that hid Him from their sight. Once again, two men dressed in white appeared. They told the apostles that Jesus had been taken into heaven but would return. This is what Christians call "the ascension."

Jesus' ascension is a crucial event in God's redemption of creation—God's reclaiming of the world from Satan. The ascension is a preview, in many senses, of God's ultimate victory, as the angels who explain Christ's ascent into heaven also prophesy that in the same way—in glory and power—Christ will return to the earth (Acts 1:11). In the ascendant Christ we see what we shall one day be—persons with immortal bodies who are brought into God's presence. It has often been remarked that Jesus' flesh was the first bit of this earth to be fully redeemed. Our own flesh will one day be similarly transformed (1 Corinthians 15:53), as will all of creation.

Christ's ascension also ensured that the Holy Spirit would be sent as our advocate and comforter, through whose indwelling presence believers have continuous access to Christ, who is now seated at the right hand of the Father. He continues to act on our behalf, as the Scriptures tell us, putting His enemies under His feet, plundering the household of Satan, and preparing a place for us. He is upholding the universe and everything in it by the power of His Word.

The Scriptures go so far as to say that even now we are seated with Christ at God's right hand (Colossians 3:1). With Christ's mission completed, we can be assured that the Son is pleading our cause to the Father, for the human experience itself has become God's own. This is a mystery beyond human understanding, but it's on this basis that the apostle John assures us "we have one who speaks to the Father in our defense, Jesus Christ the Righteous One" (1 John 2:1).

God the Father created us and sent His Son Jesus to die on the cross for us, and we were then promised that when Jesus ascended into heaven He would be succeeded by the Holy Spirit.

But wait a minute — haven't we raised a confusing question in all this? Are Christians asked to believe that God is one in three persons? What kind of god would give us three gods?

Knowing the answer to that question — the nature of God Himself — is critical, for the Trinity is actually one of today's most contentious issues.

CHAPTER 7

GOD ABOVE, GOD BESIDE, GOD WITHIN

God is all powerful, all knowing, the ultimate source of all reality. Serious Christians must understand the nature of this God in His fullness, particularly God's Trinitarian nature and God's sovereignty. Both are crucial to the *freedom* of the Christian life.

The Trinity: One God in Three Persons

The Trinity — Father, Son, and Holy Spirit, one God in three persons — is often considered to be mysterious at best, self-contradicting at worst. Everyone would acknowledge that the idea of a triune God — three in one — is the most difficult of all Christian doctrines, which is why so many neglect it or even write it off.

But this is tragic. As St. Caesarius of Arles said in the sixth century, "The faith of all Christians rests on the Trinity."[1] While the Trinity transcends the bounds of human understanding, this doctrine is at the heart of Christian spirituality, and in the life of faith we experience its truth at every turn. Understanding the doctrine of the Trinity is especially timely because it figures in today's titanic clash of civilizations.

———

An Islamic evangelistic campaign, funded by often-extreme Wahhabi influences in Saudi Arabia, is spreading across America today, particularly on university campuses. Recently, Sheikh Yusef Estes gave a lecture on Islam and Christianity at Louisiana State University.[2] Now known as a Muslim chaplain and scholar, Estes was once a Christian minister, raised in Texas by strong Christian parents. In a beguiling fashion, Estes began by describing areas of agreement between Islam and Christianity. Both Christians and Muslims believe Jesus is a messenger of God who was born supernaturally, he said. Islam also agrees with Christianity that Jesus was the Messiah predicted in the Old Testament. Muslims, like Christians, accept the importance of Jesus Christ, as well as major figures in the Old Testament like Adam, Noah, and Abraham. "But while Christians believe in the Trinity of God—the Father, the Son and the Holy Spirit—Muslims believe there is no Trinity, only one God with one message, whom they call Allah."[3]

Similarly, James P. Dunlap gave a lecture at Middle Tennessee State University describing his journey from Christianity to Islam. His tone was welcoming and inclusive. "The Bible is a book of God, a word of God," he said. "There are many beautiful, true and Islamic things in the Bible. We do not believe that all other religions are wrong. We feel like we have added some things to the other religions. We feel like every people have their message that brought them the truth."[4] He went on to explain the main difference between Christianity and Islam: "We believe that the Trinity falls under 'shirk,' worshiping something as God that is not God." To maintain the doctrine of the Trinity is idolatrous, the worst sin in Islam.

Dr. Jane Smith, a scholar of Islam at Hartford Seminary, explains Islam's appeal to converts through its strict moral code, its similarities to Judaism and Christianity, and its well-defined steps for practicing the faith. "Muslims' straightforward message about God," she said, "is a lot less complicated than trying to figure out the Trinity."[5]

The lectures of Estes and Dunlap and hundreds like them were sponsored by the Muslim Student Association (MSA), which is spearheading the campaign on campuses. Muslim activists hand out little tracts showing pictures of three separate gods and tell students Christians are blasphemous in worshiping these three gods. The MSA boasts 150,000 Muslim students and over 600 chapters on university and college campuses. Activists are moving into high schools as well, often under the pretext of teaching about minority religions and diversity.

The MSA is manipulative in its attack on the Trinity, some publications representing it as Father, Mother, and Son. The idea that God the Father married a woman to produce the son Jesus was a Christian heresy widely spread during the time of Muhammad, who obviously seized upon it. I have seen this clever but totally misleading evangelistic effort used in the prisons over the years. Muslims say they are simply "correcting" false Christian teaching.[6]

A friend attended—and secretly recorded—an all-day seminar held on a campus by the MSA on how to convince "someone to become a Muslim." The principle thrust of the day's teaching hammered home that the Trinity is irrational and blasphemous.

The danger to one's faith that Islam's attack on the Trinity represents should not be underestimated. Even people who should recognize the danger are taken in, like a young couple who live in Maryland: Idris and Nafia Abdur-Rahim. They were impressed by a charismatic young man named Said Regeah, who presided over a radical Islamic mosque. Although Nafia was raised in the home of a Southern Baptist preacher, she and her husband were converted from Christianity to Islam because of their doubts about the Trinity.[7] The Abdur-Rahims remain committed to their new faith despite being a part of a Muslim community among whom several of the September 11 perpetrators once mingled.

Response to Attacks on the Trinity

How would you or I respond to this attack on the Trinity as a form of idolatry? Is Christianity a form of polytheism—the worship of more than one God—in disguise? Can you state what Christians mean when they speak of the Trinity? Do you know what the biblical evidence is that led Christians to affirm that God is one but three persons, equal in all respects? And why is this central to our worship as Christians? Most Christians and even some pastors do not know.

Critics point out that the doctrine of the Trinity is never explicitly spelled out in the New Testament. Because of this the Trinity will always be a focus of anyone who wants to recast Christianity. America's journey to secularism began in earnest, for example, when Ralph Waldo Emerson and other transcendentalists decided they could no longer accept the Trinity. Emerson and company gave birth to the Unitarian Church, in which Jesus became a moral teacher, God the Father dissolved into the Universal Mind of pantheism, and the Holy Spirit registered, if at all, as the bonds of community.

Though the Trinity is not explicitly defined in the New Testament, it is made abundantly clear. Jesus explained the Trinitarian nature of God to His disciples at a time of crisis, when late in Jesus' ministry His followers remained confused about His mission. They feared being rounded up at any moment, imprisoned, and executed. They looked to Jesus for reassurance, asking that He show them the Father so that they could feel secure in their commitment.

In response Jesus says that those who have seen Him have seen the Father (John 14:9). "I and the Father are one" (John 10:30). Jesus also promises that "the Father ... will give you another Counselor to be with you forever — the Spirit of truth ... the Counselor, the Holy Spirit, whom the Father will send in my name, will teach you all things and will remind you of everything I have said to you" (14:16 – 17, 26). The Father and Jesus would come to dwell within them through the Holy Spirit and they would know true peace. Jesus used the Trinity to reassure His disciples.

The biblical revelation discloses the Trinitarian nature of God in a long-prepared historical sequence: God the Creator in Genesis, Jesus the Son at the beginning of the New Testament, and the Holy Spirit in Pentecost's confirming of the Church. The New Testament is clearly Trinitarian in its witness.[8] Jesus' great commission to His followers to make disciples of all nations includes the instruction, "baptizing them *in the name of the Father and of the Son and of the Holy Spirit*" (Matthew 28:19, emphasis added). This baptismal formula might be called Christianity's first creed, for it anticipates the classic summaries to come, the Apostles', Nicene, and Athanasian Creeds. It also has many echoes in the New Testament, including Paul's benediction to the Corinthian church, "May the grace of the

Lord Jesus Christ, and the love of God, and the fellowship of the Holy Spirit be with you all" (2 Corinthians 13:14).

The Record from the Early Church

Ever since the time of Christ, people have puzzled over how the Father, the Son, and the Holy Spirit could be one God, a particularly difficult concept for the Jews, steeped as they were in a monotheistic understanding of God. Admittedly, the Trinity is a mystery, the foremost example of God's revelation giving us information beyond what we can know or imagine. But far from being the product of speculation by theologians, the doctrine of the Trinity emerged from what Jesus had taught His followers and the exhaustive deliberations of the apostolic era.

The early Church affirmed its belief in one God, strenuously countering any teaching to the contrary.[9] God was, in the words of the Nicene Creed, "one God, the Father Almighty, maker of heaven and earth." The one God was known as "Father." (The ancient prayers of Judaism never addressed God as "*Abba*" — an intimate term, and later on, Islam would develop ninety-nine names for God without ever calling God Father.)[10] As in Judaism, this one God was holy and just, but He had come closer to us, having been revealed by Christ as intimately concerned with redeeming His creation.

As the early Church grappled with Jesus' testimony and how His mission should be described, they attempted to strike the right balance between His humanity and His divinity. On the one hand, everyone understood that the oneness of God had to be maintained. But how could God be one and the sacrifice of Jesus truly be the sacrifice of God? What did Jesus mean when He identified Himself with the Father?

A school of theology, the Sabellians, put forward the idea that Jesus could not have been truly distinct from the Father. They thought the one God merely appeared or revealed Himself in three different modes or methods: God the Father became Jesus Christ and then the Holy Spirit. But if that were the case, then Jesus praying to the Father would have been nothing but a show. Jesus' radical dependence on the Father comes through everywhere in the Gospel. Also, if Jesus only appeared to be a man, could His experience of human existence, and particularly His suffering, have been real? The Scriptures state that Jesus was tempted to sin like any other man and underline His suffering at every opportunity.[11]

Others proposed maintaining the oneness of God by teaching that Jesus was not fully divine but only a superior created being—a righteous man or a demigod. Arians of the fourth century nearly persuaded the Church of this proposition. But the great Church Father Athanasius heroically stood against this, and the Church recognized that if Jesus had only been a man He could not be humankind's Savior. Only if Jesus was fully man *and* fully God could His death and resurrection be the work of God, reconciling humankind with the Father.

This is why the Church confessed in the Nicene Creed that Jesus was "true God from true God ... of one Being with the Father"; and at the same time, "He came down from heaven, and was incarnate by the Holy Ghost of the Virgin Mary, and was made man."

The early Church also considered what the apostolic witness taught about the Holy Spirit. Was the Spirit fully a person or an indefinable force sent from God? The Church Fathers relied on the Scriptures to answer this question. In John's Gospel, Jesus refers to the Holy Spirit five times by the emphatic pronoun "he."[12] Both Jesus and the apostles speak of the Holy Spirit as possessing the three chief characteristics of personhood: mind, feeling, and will. In Romans, Paul writes of the "mind of the Spirit" (8:27)—the same mind that Jesus promises will "guide you into all truth" (John 16:13). We know that the Spirit possesses feeling because we are counseled not to "grieve the Holy Spirit" (Ephesians 4:30). And the Spirit chooses what gifts to give each believer "just as he determines" (1 Corinthians 12:11).[13] The Spirit then was not a metaphor for inspiration but as much a person as the Father and the Son.

For these reasons the Nicene Creed calls the Spirit both "Lord" and the "giver of Life." As Lord, the Holy Spirit is fully God. As the "giver of life," the Holy Spirit restores men and women's fellowship with God and transforms believers into people capable of doing God's will. The Spirit is the one who makes us holy, sets us apart for God; it is through His power that we are enabled to live the Christian life.[14] Through the inspiration of the Holy Spirit we receive the words of life found in the Bible and by the power of the Spirit are raised to new life.[15]

The early Church's complete understanding of the Trinitarian nature of God was settled by the end of the fourth century. The whole Church professes one God in three persons. These persons are distinct from one another, and their distinction lies in the relationship of each to the other. Each fills a different role, each complementing the other. Yet in each of these three persons, Father, Son, and Holy Spirit, the fullness of God resides.

How Can We Really Understand?

So the three persons of the Trinity are distinct, but God is one.

Even as we understand the logical reasons by which the Church arrived at this doctrine, we find it baffling. But many concepts we encounter in life are baffling and yet valid. Just think of higher mathematics and the complexity of very advanced physics. Since we are talking about the nature of God, how could a true understanding not present similar difficulty?

Many analogies have been offered for the Trinity. The Church Father Gregory of Nyssa, for instance, compared the Trinity to a rainbow, which breaks a single beam of light into different colors, each blending seamlessly into the other.[16] But none of these analogies fully captures the infinitely greater complexity of persons that are distinguished in their relationship to one another yet one. If pressed too far, in fact, these analogies usually lead into error. Ultimately, the deepest source we have for understanding or verifying the Trinitarian nature of God is encounter. God meets us in the Trinity in the way that every human heart demands. Every person wants to know that his particular life is connected to the source of all life — as a creature I long to know that I am connected to the Creator. Every man and woman also wants to be assured of the good and loving character of this Creator God.

Only the Trinity of the Christian faith satisfies these yearnings. The Creator God of Christianity is not a distant, unapproachable, judging God as in Islam. Neither is God so diffuse within creation as in Eastern religion that God cannot be found. The Father is close beside us in the Son, as we encounter this God in the person of Jesus: "God with a human face," as Pope Benedict likes to say. Further, through the power of the Holy Spirit this God comes to dwell within us—God gives us His life. The Holy Spirit enables us to live out God's will with its heroic demands.

———

We shouldn't ever find ourselves on the defensive regarding the Trinity, as many do today. To the contrary, when properly understood and explained, it accounts for the biblical data about God as one God, existing in three equal persons, Father, Son, and Holy Spirit. The Trinity also answers the deepest needs of the human heart, offering a depth of spirituality unknown in any other religion. And far from being a vulnerability exposing us to Islamic proselytizing, it can, when winsomely presented, bring Muslims to Christ.

Take the case of "Farid," originally a nominal Muslim who came to the United States in 1993 to study. He fell under the spell of the MSA and soon joined their ranks, evangelizing. In debates with Christians, he contended that the Trinity was idolatry, or, as Muslims call it, "*shirk*." But in those same debates, he found his own position weak when he was forced to argue that Jesus didn't die on the cross, only appeared to, as Muslims believe. Although he was warned against investigating the topic, Farid began to study the history of the first century. He went to the original sources, just as we have advocated Christians should. He was struck by the thoroughness of the apostolic teaching, the care with which the Bible was prepared, and the certainty of the apostles and their followers.

Farid soon gave up his evangelizing on behalf of the MSA, continuing his search more deeply into Christian theology. He came to see that far from rejecting the Trinity, it "was the only logical explanation of what is reported in the New Testament, and [it] was logical and non-contradictory, just as a wave-particle duality principle in physics was the only plausible yet unbelievable and seemingly contradictory way to explain the world."

Eventually, Farid's search brought him to the point of exhaustion, where, in his imagination, he lay outside the gates of the City of God. At this point he cried out to God to rescue him, if God would. "I felt a strange feeling of God's love, as if he was telling me that I am his, and that he will love me and take care of me for the rest of my life and after." This experience led to Farid committing himself to a new life as a Christian. He no longer saw God as Allah, a remote being who watched over his life, weighing his good and bad deeds. Rather, God became Farid's eternal Father, "an infinite being who cares about me personally, and who wants me to be fully committed to him."

The Trinity and Christian Spirituality

Not only does the true understanding of the Trinity and the nature of God lead honest, truth-seeking Muslims to Christ, but it enables you and me to live far more fulfilling and meaningful lives. The Trinity enables us to better understand the scriptural teaching that God is love. Love cannot exist without someone to love, which is why Allah and any unitary understanding leads to a cold, impersonal god. The essence of the God of the Bible is His intertwined triune nature of Father, Son, and Holy Spirit. The three continuously pour out love to one another and receive love in return. The Trinity exists as a perfect community of self-giving. In this life, Christians enjoy participation in this community through the indwelling of the Holy Spirit, and in the world to come we will be united with the Godhead in perfect love. The Trinity sums up our final hope. What could be more central to our faith?

Our experience of the Trinity is actually a common part of everyday Christian experience. We invoke the Trinity every time we recite the Lord's Prayer. Our heavenly Father supplies our daily bread, through Jesus Christ the Father forgives our sins, and by the power of the Holy Spirit we can overcome temptation.[17]

This is why knowing doctrine is so important. Understanding the Trinity radically changes our view of the world and of God's character. We are able to know God intimately without diminishing His transcendent character as Creator.

God's Sovereignty over All

Next, we need to examine the implications of God's role as Creator.

Note that all three persons of the Trinity play key roles in creating and sustaining the world. The Father speaks the world into existence through His Word, which is carried out by the Holy Spirit. We glimpse the Holy Spirit in the creation account brooding like a dove over the waters of the unformed abyss.

The apostle Paul pays particular attention to how Christ sustains the world. "For by him all things were created: things in heaven and on earth, visible and invisible, whether thrones or powers or rulers or authorities; all things were created by him and for him. He is before all things, and in him all things hold together" (Colossians 1:16–17).

The phrase "all things hold together" in Christ is striking. He is essentially the glue of the universe, the binding force of the created order. Scholars like John Polkinghorne, a noted physicist and former president of Queens College, Cambridge, now an Anglican priest, argue that Christ is the animating force that keeps the universe in order and existence. Think about it this way: He is the information —the *Logos*, as we noted—behind all the carriers of information like DNA.

This gives new meaning to God's rule, God's power, and God's understanding—all of which are infinite. God's sovereignty over all of creation cannot be denied. No wonder Abraham Kuyper, the great Dutch theologian, said, "There is not a square inch in the whole domain of human existence over which Christ, who is sovereign over *all* does not cry out: 'Mine!'"[18] And, I would add, if Christ cries out, "Mine!" then the obligation of Christian people in the Church is to look at all of creation and cry out, "His!" Jesus is Lord over every aspect of life—how we spend our spare time, what we read, how we form our families, the way in which we build neighborhoods, the law, politics, science, music, medicine, and on and on.

When you grasp this, you see why I have been disappointed when I've asked serious believers what Christianity is. Some say a religion, most simply say a relationship with Jesus, and a few will talk about the Church. While all these answers are true, they are reductionist — only part of a much larger truth. As noted earlier, the correct answer, clear from Scripture, is that Christianity is a way of seeing all of life, every aspect of reality; it is a worldview.

This means that we have two divinely authorized commissions. The first is well known, the Great Commission, to make disciples and baptize them (Matthew 28:19). But the second is equally important. It is to bring the righteousness of God to bear on all of life, to take dominion, to carry out the tasks we are given in the first chapters of Genesis, to bring a redeeming influence into a fallen culture. I call this the Cultural Commission.[19]

————

Why is it so important to understand the nature of the triune God who is outside of time and space, the source of all that is, and thus sovereign over every aspect of creation? Grasping the enormity of this, in the way theologian Timothy George brilliantly teaches, fundamentally alters how we see our own existence.[20] Take, for example, how differently we as Christians see our lives lived out in time. Our society thinks of time as moving along a straight line, the clock ticking off seconds, the calendar dropping away days and years. We treat time like a commodity to be consumed. There's a part of our lives we've used; there's a part we're using now; there's a part we can look forward to — that is, if there is a future for us. And as we do this we experience a tyranny of sorts. The bottom of the hourglass is filling up, so we make nervous jokes about middle age, and later about the "golden years," all the while aware that this mortal flesh is decaying. At some point, everybody waits for the doctor's diagnosis: "You have six months left to live. Put your affairs in order. And by the way, here's the number for your local hospice." And then seconds, hours, and days really speed up.

I've seen people approach their deaths in a state of utter despair. The end is generally a time of melancholy, and for many, great bitterness. I knew one ninety-two-year-old man who had lived a full, rich life; still, he became jealous and angry over his grown children's attentiveness to a newborn grandchild. The Christians I've known, on the other hand, have usually faced death with serenity, almost anticipation.

Living in time is one of life's great tensions. We are nostalgic for the past, which lives only in our memory, in the midst of a disappearing present, while our hopes for the future can never be assured. Time measured from one end point to another is painfully elusive, as George puts it, and a source of unending anxiety.[21]

This notion of time as linear began with the Greeks. But much later in the nineteenth century, Friedrich Nietzsche, who pronounced God dead, saw time only in terms of "that which was." In other words, time is a closed door on all hopes and dreams.[22] It was this frustration, humankind's inability to change the past or control the future, leaving only the present to be enjoyed, that gave rise to the school of existentialism and the West's "live for the moment" mentality that has done so much to undermine our moral traditions.

But for the Christian, this is a false and despairing view of time. No one captured the full meaning of the biblical texts better than St. Augustine, who argued that time itself is God's creation. As Augustine wrote in Confessions, "You precede all past times in the sublimity of an ever present reality. You have made all times and are before all times."[23] Eternity in the view of Christian thinkers thereafter, Aquinas and others, was that time has no beginning and no end, no parameters, no margins, no boundaries outside of God Himself. Time was willed and created by God. Thus we can see that time and the world were created together and have no existence apart from each other. So, in the words of George, "Time is not a receptacle, it's a relationship."[24] A critical distinction.

While theologians understood Augustine's writings, scientists only came to realize their truth hundreds of years later. Albert Einstein announced, to the astonishment of the world, his theory of relativity: time and matter form a continuum and change relative to their velocity. Writers about Einstein's theory noted that this radical idea had first been advanced in Western thought some 1,500 years earlier by Augustine. Augustine came to this insight, not by mathematics or formulas or observations of the Hubble telescope, but by reflecting on the doctrine of the incarnation. Once again we see that the Bible anticipates what scientists later discover to be true.

What does all this tell us about life? It tells us that as Christians we do not need to live oppressed by the ticking clock — the tyranny of the urgent. Life's value doesn't depend upon where we are in time; whether we are young, middle aged, or old. We see life, all of life and all of the time that God created for us, as a gift. The greatest time of our life, then, may occur at any point in our lives. Maybe the most important insight we'll ever have or the greatest contribution we'll ever make is in our dying words or in a youthful experience of learning. Maybe it will come during our most productive years. But the point is we are not restricted. Each moment of life is a gift open to the possibility of eternity, and so what we do now matters for eternity. The gift of time enables us to prepare ourselves for an everlasting relationship with God. This is what gives significance to every one of our actions.

—

How does this doctrine, unique to the Christian worldview, affect us? Why does it matter? Once you see the triune God as dwelling apart from time and space, in what we can only imagine as an eternal present, God's liberation from every circumstance, even the losses of time, acquires rich new meaning. We live in an entirely new way. For good reason the Scriptures celebrate the "glorious freedom of the children of God" (Romans 8:21).

PART II

THE
FAITH
AND LIFE

CHAPTER 8

EXCHANGING IDENTITIES

To live as Christians, we must first understand exactly what occurred on the cross when the good thief expressed faith in Christ and Christ promised him eternity. It was an exchange of identities. Christ comes to the cross to die, giving His righteous life for us; we in turn come to the cross to die, surrendering our old sinful life for Him. Thereafter Christ lives in us (Galatians 2:20).

This is the heart of Christian conversion. It is what we mean by the term *salvation*, or what Christians frequently speak of as *being saved* or *born again*. Our past sins are not only forgiven, but we are transformed to live a new life with God's power and grace.

The New Testament makes it clear that this gift of salvation, becoming righteous, or exchanging identities comes by faith—not works—or any merit of our own (Ephesians 2:8). I helped to organize a group called Evangelicals and Catholics Together (ECT), which underlined the agreement of both communions on this central question in a remarkable 1997 document, affirming what the Reformers meant by *sola fide*—or faith alone!*

---

*"The Gift of Salvation," *First Things* (January 1998), 20–23, also at *www.firstthings.com/article.php3?id_article=3453&var_recherche=gift+of+salvation*. "We agree that justification is not earned by any good works or merits of our own; it is entirely God's gift, conferred through the Father's sheer graciousness out of the love he bears us in his Son, who suffered on our behalf and rose from the dead for our justification. . . . Faith is not merely intellectual assent but an act of the whole person, involving the mind, the will, and the affections, issuing in a changed life. We understand that what we here affirm is in agreement with what the Reformation traditions have meant by justification by faith alone (*sola fide*)."

Because understanding how we are saved is so central to the Christian faith, an analogy may be helpful: Paul writes that "God credits righteousness apart from works" (Romans 4:6). Think of the term *credit* in this way: God treats Jesus' substitutionary, atoning death as provision of the righteousness that is, in a sense, deposited in the bank. Your act of faith is to believe that God has done this, whereby that righteousness is credited to your account. From then on you begin drawing on it and as you live a new life you invest it by producing good works

Today's ECT understanding reflects a return to the unanimity that once existed among the early Church Fathers. Though many serious disagreements continue, we have, in at least one key area, leapfrogged over centuries of contention and dispute, even wars, to recover the basic rule of faith embraced by the apostolic teaching, which I refer to frequently in these pages. This presents an extraordinary opportunity for Christians to join together in proclaiming and defending the simple truth of the Gospel.

The Free Gift

Since the Gospel seems so clear and inviting, why do so many resist the Good News? Part of the answer is that salvation, being a free gift from God, sounds too easy. Certainly God wouldn't just let us into heaven because we embraced Christ's saving message, without regard to our own past behavior. That's counterintuitive.

We also like the good things we do, and we think we ought to get credit for them. We'd prefer to save ourselves, a preference that stems from pride. The sin of the Garden of Eden is the very thing that still condemns us.

How often have you challenged people to come to Christ and had them say, "But I'm not good enough." That seldom happens to me in prisons, but it happens to me half the time outside. This is yet another form of pride — our lurking suspicion that one day we *will* be good enough.

People also resist the Good News because they fail to take sin seriously. If we're really not sinners, they seem to think, then all we need is a little self-improvement. But when we do take our sin seriously —as I did for the first time the night Christ came into my life in 1973 in a flood of tears in my friend's driveway—when we realize we have been rescued from a hopeless condition—dead in our sins and trespasses—then we rejoice and in gratitude join God in reclaiming the world He loves for Himself. We'll want others to know about this incredible free gift as well.

What Is Saving Faith?

But many wonder if a mere profession of faith is genuine. Does it satisfy God? A young woman whom I knew to be mature in the faith once asked me whether she should be rebaptized. She explained that she received Christ when she was young, having grown up in a family of strong believers, but she hadn't understood her childhood commitment as a total surrender of her life.

I assured her she need not be rebaptized, that the Lord accepted her faith as sincere, even though she only grasped its meaning as any child would. Still, I took it as a sign of her spiritual health that she raised the question.

"Just what is saving faith?" is a good question for us to ask in today's culture, where everything is a subjective choice. "Making a decision for Christ" may be an unhelpfully vague description of what faith entails. Were we really repentant? Did we intend to cooperate with God in His work and our transformation? God alone knows the heart and whether our surrender at the cross and our commitment to the Lordship of Christ is genuine.

In a sincere conversion, however, we will soon experience changing affections and habits. Things that used to seem appealing no longer do; things that weren't appealing now are. If your faith is alive, you will experience increasing discontent and conviction over sins of the past and will respond with a genuine desire to turn away, to be changed. If you do not experience "hatred of sin and love of holiness," Charles Spurgeon said, God has "done nothing in you of a saving character."[1]

Sadly, in today's self-obsessed culture many see "being saved" as the ticket to a nice, comfortable, blessed life. Period. Some people go from conference to conference, marveling at the speakers, reading all the books that flood the market telling us how to "get more out of" the Christian life. These people will tell you that they are fulfilled personally, and in one sense they are.

The problem is, Christianity is about a lot more than what God can do for you. Rick Warren got it right at the beginning of his extraordinary book *The Purpose Driven Life*: it's not about you; it's about God. Changing affections and Bible study must inevitably cause us to be restless, not to get more out of the faith but to give more back to God. The more we learn about Him, the more we want to be like Him.

And this will drive us to act like Him. Jesus, remember, emptied Himself of the godhead's glory in order to call us brothers (Philippians 2:5–7, Hebrews 2:5–18)—and we are called to imitate His humility in putting ourselves at others' service. It was this realization that compelled me to start going back to prison after my own sentence was complete. Nobody likes going into these rotten places. I still smell the smells, still see the depth of suffering. But I sensed this was what God wanted me to do. Out of gratitude, I could do no less.

Before my conversion, I never thought about prisoners; but after my conversion, I began to see the men around me not as bank robbers and drug dealers but as brothers in need of help. In the thirty-two years that I've been going back into prisons, I have experienced a deepening love for these battered and bruised men and women there. I no longer consider it a chore or a responsibility; I find it a joy to give myself to them, sharing the Gospel, even holding people dying of AIDS in my arms.

This is why I believe it is so essential for Christians as part of their conversion process to assess their gifts and discover how they can do the greatest amount of good for others—and then go do it. A friend in my church had a successful landscape business but felt drawn to the mission field, taking several trips a year to India, Pakistan, and Bangladesh. Finally, God's call became clear to him. He sold his business, put his money into ministry, and is now in fulltime mission work, training missionaries abroad. I can think of fifteen or twenty people in my own church who have done similar things.

These people have discovered that while the Bible tells us our salvation is by faith alone, it is not a faith that is alone. (Too many people stop after reading Ephesians 2:8 – 9; verse 10 tells us we are saved "to do good works which God prepared in advance for us to do.") We are known by our fruits (Matthew 7:16). But this is where it gets costly to believe, for true Christianity is countercultural. It means death to self, giving up self-control — and personal autonomy, as we know, is the thing postmodern thought prizes more than anything else. True faith means putting the cause of Christ and the needs of others ahead of self and doing the gospel.

So salvation is a free gift — but it costs everything. A young German pastor once wrote that when Christ calls, He bids a man to come and die. This pastor discovered this truth for himself in the midst of one of the most evil eras in human history.

Costly Grace

Dietrich Bonhoeffer's arrival in New York on June 2, 1939, seemed providential. Already an internationally known theologian, the thirty-two-year-old Lutheran minister was a leader of the German resistance against Hitler. Dismissed from teaching at the University of Berlin, prohibited from public speaking, banned from publishing, Bonhoeffer had been under constant surveillance by the Gestapo. Over the radio he had declared "leaders or offices which set themselves up as gods mock God," only to have his microphone cut off.[2]

Three months before his arrival in New York, Bonhoeffer received notice of his being called into the armed forces. Conscription meant pledging allegiance to the Führer, as dishonest an act, Bonhoeffer felt, as sacrificing to a Roman emperor.

So to save Bonhoeffer, church authorities arranged for him to leave the country. With Bonhoeffer's landing in New York, Protestant circles around the globe rejoiced that this charismatic young leader's life had been saved.

Bonhoeffer was given the "prophet's chamber," a suite of rooms at Union Theological Seminary. He brought to Union not only the finest credentials but tried-by-fire experience as a Christian educator. Along with Martin Niemöller and others, Bonhoeffer was a leader of the Confessing Church, the orthodox remnant in Germany.[3] When the Confessing Church was expelled from state-run institutions, Bonhoeffer founded an independent seminary, which went underground after the Gestapo closed the first campus.[4] Bonhoeffer's students knew him as a personable mentor who took them out on long walks to discuss their hopes and dreams. With a fair complexion, he had a thinning sweep of blond hair across a high forehead, blue eyes under rimless glasses, boyish cheeks, and full lips. At someone's greeting, his expression brightened and became eager like a friendly spaniel's. In conversation he spoke quickly and loved to tell a joke that could clinch — or diffuse — an argument.

Bonhoeffer was comfortable in almost any circumstance — a gift that would later seem almost otherworldly. At Union Seminary in the summer of 1939, however, Bonhoeffer was profoundly uncomfortable, experiencing a homesickness he had never before known. He spent his time in the prophet's chamber feverishly writing at a desk, smoking cigarette after cigarette as he tried to understand the unease that had come over him.

Bonhoeffer's contacts in America were rapidly making plans for lecture tours and teaching. They presumed he would not be returning to Germany for the duration of the expected war. Bonhoeffer knew about the lecture-tour plans, which brought home to him that in his friends' minds he had chosen exile. Was this his intent?

His friend Paul Lehmann wrote, "I do know that it is unthinkable that you should return before America shall have had the fullest opportunity to be enriched by your contribution to its theological hour of destiny."[5]

Dietrich Bonhoeffer had made the most important journey of his life nearly a decade before, in 1931, when he went from being a theologian and pastor to being a Christian. Reading the Bible as the authoritative Word of God, rather than as an object of intellectual inquiry, brought a decisive change.

For the first time I discovered the Bible.... I had often preached, I had seen a great deal of the church, spoken and preached about it — but I had not yet become a Christian.... I turned the doctrine of Jesus Christ into something of personal advantage to myself.... I pray that will never happen again. Also I had never prayed or prayed only very little. For all my loneliness, I was quite pleased with myself. Then the Bible, and in particular, the Sermon on the Mount, freed me from that.... It became clear to me that the life of a servant of Jesus Christ must belong to the church, and step by step it became clearer to me how far that must go.[6]

The people around Bonhoeffer could not help but notice the change. One student recalled Bonhoeffer saying, "Every word of Holy Scripture was a love letter from God directed very personally to us, and he asked us whether we loved Jesus."[7]

In the summer of 1939, Bonhoeffer was trying to figure out how he might best serve Christ. In the prophet's chamber Bonhoeffer could not stop thinking about Germany and longing for news from his friends. He began roaming the streets of New York as he tried to shake his anxieties. On Sunday, June 18, he visited the liberal Riverside Church and heard a sermon on the philosophy of the pragmatist William James. Thoroughly dissatisfied, he went that evening to the Broadway Presbyterian Church where Dr. John Hess McComb, whom his friends considered an "arch-fundamentalist," preached on "our likeness to Christ." This was far more what he needed to hear.

Try as he might, he could not escape the conclusion that his vocation compelled him to share in his countrymen's fate as they suffered the Nazis' evil. He explained his decision to the sponsor of his flight to America, Reinhold Niebuhr:

I have made a mistake in coming to America.... Christians in Germany will face the terrible alternative of either willing the defeat of their nation in order that Christian civilization may survive, or willing the victory of their nation and thereby destroying our civilization. I know which of these alternatives I must choose; but I cannot make that choice in security.[8]

Bonhoeffer was on his way back to Germany, and, as he knew, very likely the cross.[9]

Dying to Self

Upon his return to Germany, Bonhoeffer underwent another transformation, one that he considered morally ambiguous: he became a double-agent, ostensibly spying for the Third Reich while working for its downfall. From the beginning of Hitler's rise to power, Bonhoeffer had spoken out against the Nazi party's anti-Semitism. Though he had renounced violence, he now came to see the use of force on behalf of the innocent as among the demands of love. Christians must commit themselves "not just to bind up the victims beneath the wheel, but to halt the wheel itself."[10]

The husband of Bonhoeffer's sister Christine, Hans von Dohnanyi, in reality a secret member of the German resistance, worked for Admiral Canaris at the Abwehr, the counterintelligence office of the Nazi High Command. Canaris and Dohnanyi soon became key players in the efforts of select military leaders to assassinate Hitler.

Dohnanyi provided a way for Bonhoeffer to help in halting the wheel. He made him an agent, a spy, of the Abwehr. Bonhoeffer was supposed to collect information for the Third Reich from his church contacts in England, Switzerland, and elsewhere — that was his cover story. In reality, Bonhoeffer traveled outside of Germany to inform the Allies of the plans to assassinate Hitler and to plead for help. Dohnanyi, Bonhoeffer, and others also used their positions to smuggle Jews out of the country under the code name Operation 7.

The German resistance to Hitler made several attempts on the Führer's life, planting two ineffective bombs and one that barely missed killing Hitler. As the plots unfolded, the Gestapo came ever closer to uncovering the treasonous activities of Dohnanyi and Bonhoeffer in the Abwehr. On April 5, 1943, Bonhoeffer phoned his brother-in-law's home, and an unknown man answered. He guessed that his coconspirator had been arrested and he would soon be arrested himself.

His fears can only be imagined. He admitted to colleagues that he questioned whether he could endure torture. He wrote to his brother

Karl-Friedrich, "Certainly none of us is eager to go to prison. However, if it does come to that, then we shall do so—hopefully, anyway—with joy since it is such a worthy cause."[11]

At four o'clock in the afternoon two men came looking for Bonhoeffer. Without any official documents, they searched his room and then insisted he come with them. Bonhoeffer walked out to their car carrying only his Bible.

He was taken to Tegel Prison—Berlin's facility for political prisoners—and tossed into solitary confinement. His cell was cold, but the blanket on his cot was so greasy and smelly that he found it unusable. He listened to the screams of prisoners and the angry retorts of guards through most of the night and awoke in the morning to a crust of bread for breakfast.

Bonhoeffer's total isolation continued for the first twelve days, and he thought of ending his life. Soon enough, though, Bonhoeffer managed to live more vibrantly in prison than most do outside. I found his example invaluable during my incarceration, as I read his most influential book, *Letters and Papers from Prison*. Instead of sleeping away his confinement, as many prisoners do, Bonhoeffer set himself a rigorous schedule. He took a cold shower early each morning to wake himself up, then dressed and exercised, ate breakfast, and immersed himself in the Scriptures. Then the day's writing and reading began. His family was allowed to bring him weekly packages that included food, tobacco, and books. He turned to the works of the early Church Fathers, Tertullian, Cyprian, and others. Their experience struck him as like his own as they had contended for the faith in a world dominated by hostile paganism—cults of race and blood to which Nazism was a return.[12]

It wasn't simply activity that distinguished Bonhoeffer's life in prison but how his piety affected those around him. He became known to Tegel's guards as a man who could be depended on for wise counsel. They also noted Bonhoeffer's generosity as he constantly shared the contents of his family's weekly care packages with those around him.

When the Allies began bombing Berlin, and Tegel's inmates were rushed to the basement to withstand the bombardment, everyone noticed that Bonhoeffer hardly flinched when the old prison rocked like a capsizing ship. One of Bonhoeffer's fellow inmates said, "Bonhoeffer ... always seemed to inspire an atmosphere of happiness, of joy in every small event of life, and of deep gratitude for the mere fact that he was alive.... He was, without exception, the finest and most lovable man I have ever met."[13]

For most of Bonhoeffer's time in prison he and his coconspirators kept to their cover story of Abwehr agents working on behalf of the Third Reich. But on July 20, 1944, the final attempt on Hitler's life failed, and many of the conspirators were exposed.

Bonhoeffer was transferred from Tegel to the dungeons of Gestapo headquarters in Berlin, and from there, with the other conspirators, he was moved to a basement lockup in an SS barracks that stood just outside the gates of the concentration camp at Buchenwald. He was interrogated repeatedly and denied contact with his family. On April 5, by direct order of Hitler, Bonhoeffer was condemned to death.

Bonhoeffer was eventually moved by a circuitous route to the death camp at Flossenbürg. He was first taken with some prisoners who would eventually be released to Schönberg, where Bonhoeffer led a worship service. Bonhoeffer spoke on the texts "By his wounds we are healed" (Isaiah 53:5) and "Praise be to the God and Father of our Lord Jesus Christ! In his great mercy he has given us new birth into a living hope through the resurrection of Jesus Christ from the dead" (1 Peter 1:3).[14]

Soon thereafter, the pastor was summoned. He parted from his companions, saying, "This is the end—for me the beginning of life."[15]

At Flossenbürg, Bonhoeffer was reunited with five other conspirators, including Admiral Canaris, Dohnanyi's superior. On the morning of April 9, between five and six o'clock, their executions were carried out.

The camp doctor remembered the manner in which Bonhoeffer went to his death.

Through the half-open door in one room of the huts I saw Pastor Bonhoeffer, before taking off his prison garb, kneeling on the floor praying fervently to his God. I was most deeply moved by the way this unusually lovable man prayed, so devout and so certain that God heard his prayer. At the place of execution, he again said a short prayer and then climbed the steps to the gallows, brave and composed. His death ensued after a few seconds. In the almost fifty years that I worked as a doctor, I have hardly ever seen a man die so entirely submissive to the will of God.[16]

Dietrich Bonhoeffer's death came three weeks before the liberation of Berlin.[17]

Suffering and Redemption

Bonhoeffer's consecrated life is a model for us all—a total giving of self to Christ. Most of us will not be tested in this way, but he has set the standard for us.

Now, of course, this kind of consecration doesn't happen all at once. New converts seldom become Bonhoeffers. The young woman who asked me if she should be rebaptized realized that she had grown a great deal. We must not be impatient. Give God time to lead. George Müller, the fabled evangelical leader of the nineteenth century who started orphanages for children off the streets of London, acknowledged when he was ninety that he had not come to the point of total surrender of his heart until four years after his conversion. It was only then that he realized his love of money, prominence, position, power, and worldly pleasure was gone. "God, and He alone, became my all in all," he said. "In Him I found everything I needed and I desired nothing else."[18] Like Müller, we will never truly know how real our faith is until it is tested.

But there's one thing you can be sure of: you *will* be tested. New believers and mature believers alike need to understand, contrary to what popular books tell us, the Christian life is not without pain, difficulty, and suffering. When I was released from prison after my highly publicized conversion, a number of friends wanted to avoid me, confiding to others that they weren't as concerned about associating with a former convict as a strange-talking religious fanatic. You will soon discover this soft hostility in the workplace, perhaps at home, certainly in your social circles.

More serious challenges will come because of your newfound concern for others; you won't be able to ignore people's needs or injustice as you might have earlier. That's why so many contented middle-class folks I've known have, after coming to Christ, become involved in prison ministry or helping neighbors or volunteering at a hospice. This can be a joy, as I've discovered working among prisoners, but it can also exact a heavy price.

When Mother Teresa was being investigated for beatification, investigators discovered her writings about her periods of depression and doubt. Mother Teresa depressed? One of the most admired women in the world, whose life was filled with great works—how could that be? Mother Teresa suffered by taking on the grief and pain of others. Friends of mine who spent time with her said that she constantly grieved about the children being aborted in the West and those dying close by for whom she could not care. Dying to self and caring more about others is not a gentle death. (That she persevered against all hope [Romans 4:8] trusting Christ through the darkness, is in fact the strongest evidence of her faith.)

There's another cost few people talk about. You may, for example, find yourself in a mission for God that seems to bear no fruit. Impatient Americans quit quickly. But Christians can't. I have known missionaries who have worked for years and years with extreme deprivation and with only tiny churches to show for all of their efforts. I'm always comforted by Hudson Taylor's experience. When he left China after a lifetime of work, he left only a handful of churches behind. Most thought that Taylor's Chinese spiritual heirs must have died out during Mao's Cultural Revolution. But today, by some estimates, 120 million Chinese are Christians. We don't always see the fruit of our labor.

Sharing in Christ's Suffering

We may find the account of a life like Bonhoeffer's thrilling, but no doubt his sacrifice also makes us cringe. We ask ourselves whether we could handle the suffering. Suffering is, Bonhoeffer teaches us, the cost of discipleship, the title of one of his books.

No one wants to suffer. Instinctively we do everything we can to avoid it, unless, of course, you're a stoic, like one of my former White House colleagues, Gordon Liddy, who once held his hand over an open fire to prove he feared nothing. Or some have martyr complexes and go looking for suffering; but you don't need to — it will find you. It's a consequence of the fall, an effect of the curse. Sometime in your life you will lose a loved one or find yourself rejected. I have met very few who in the course of life have escaped serious medical problems. Nobody gets through scot-free.

More fundamentally, suffering belongs to our calling as Christians. After their first arrest, the apostles left the Sanhedrin's court "rejoicing because they had been counted worthy of suffering disgrace for the Name" (Acts 5:41). It was a *privilege* to share in His work. In many places today Christians are called to suffer persecution for the sake of the Gospel. In India, North Korea, Myanmar (Burma), and scores of other countries, Christians risk their lives by even professing Christ — something most of us in the West know little of.[19]

This is why easy-believism, the prosperity gospel, is so abominable: it sets a person up for a terrible fall when the first hardship comes, as it will. Whatever glimmer of faith the person might have had may well be snuffed out.

So the real question is not whether we will suffer but how we will react to adversity when it comes. We can see it as a miserable experience to be endured, or we can offer it to God for His redemptive purposes. This is the great truth Christians know: God will always use what we suffer for Christ's work of redemption if we let him.

I went through a difficult time going from the White House to prison. A Christian friend wrote me to say I should welcome adversity as a blessing. Okay for him to say, I thought, but I was the one suffering. And yet today I look back deeply grateful to God that I went to prison. If I hadn't, thousands of other inmates who have found Christ and a new life and been able to resettle in their communities or be reconciled with their families would perhaps never have done so. My suffering was trivial compared to what God has done in creating a ministry that is now circling the globe reaching "the least of these."

The way Christians endure suffering can be, in fact, our most powerful witness. The radio pastor Steve Brown once quipped that whenever a pagan gets cancer, God allows a Christian to get cancer as well so the world will see the difference in how we handle it. This is every Christian's witness. As the Church Father Dionysius wrote of the heroic nursing efforts of the Christians in Rome, they drew "on themselves the sickness of their neighbors and cheerfully accepting their pains ... transferred their death to themselves and died in their stead." True Christianity is made most visible in the midst of suffering and death.

But it's not just a witness. Suffering is redeemed in yet another way — in developing character. As one devotional writer put it, in the same way steel is the product of iron and fire, great character is made not through luxurious living but through suffering. And character is the only thing we carry with us beyond this life, because it shapes our soul and deepens our faith.

This is why a well-known pastor once famously said no one is fit for the pulpit who has not been broken. Being broken enables us to understand the needs of others. Our suffering equips us to help others when they suffer.

Suffering is rightly called "the school of faith," for it is only through trouble, difficulties, and setbacks that we are brought to the end of ourselves. The normal human tendency, particularly for strong-willed people, is to rely on our own strength and resources. But when those are not available to us, when everything has failed, when we have to abandon every other hope, we are forced to trust God alone. Martin Luther's wife said, "I would never have known the meaning of the various psalms, come to appreciate certain difficulties or known the inner workings of the soul; I would never have understood the practice of the Christian life and work, if God had never brought afflictions to my life."[20]

The devotional writers speak of

a divine mystery in suffering, a strange and supernatural power in it which has never been fathomed by human reason. There has never been known great saintliness of soul which has not passed through great suffering. When the suffering soul ... does not even ask God to deliver it from suffering, then it has wrought its blessed ministry; then patience has its perfect work; then the crucifixion begins to weave itself into a crown.[21]

No wonder so many believers, from the apostle Paul to the persecuted Church today, have said that they long for "the fellowship of sharing in [Jesus'] suffering" (Philippians 3:10). Hebrews tells us that the "author of our salvation," Jesus, was made "perfect through suffering" (2:10). Why then should we expect, if we are going to draw ever closer to Christ, that we should be exempt from suffering? Would not God use suffering in our lives for the same purpose He used suffering in the life of Christ? Was this not the message of John Paul II as he lay dying, in terrible agony but with complete transparency, so that the world would see that a saint gladly experiences what his Savior experienced?

It is often said that suffering is the distinguishing mark of the true Christian. There was a popular story in the Middle Ages about Martin of Tours, the saint for whom Martin Luther was named. As the story went, Satan once appeared to Martin in the guise of the Savior Himself. Martin was about ready to fall to his feet and worship him when he suddenly looked at the palms of the apparition's outstretched hands and exclaimed, "Where are the nail prints!?" At that, the apparition disappeared.

Where are the nail prints? These are the marks of true faith. People should find the nail prints in the lives of true Christians.

CHAPTER 9

RECONCILIATION

At the cross Christ reaches out to us, reconciling us to God and calling us to be reconciled with one another. This invitation to reconciliation is universal, applying to all nations and all peoples, to rich and poor, bound and free. It's an unconditional welcome to each of us.

Forgiveness, which makes reconciliation possible, is the centerpiece of the biblical account. When practiced, forgiveness is life changing, even world changing. And it often plays out in the most dramatic and unexpected ways.

His Wife's Assassin

In February of 1995, when Jésus Amado Sarria was given his cell in Medellín's Itagui Prison, he burrowed in, posting his own guard at the door. So many people wanted to kill him that for months Sarria never ventured into the prison's common areas.

Like most of Colombia's prisoners, Sarria was being held on a drug charge, specifically, shipping 5.9 tons of cocaine to El Salvador, which was no doubt ultimately bound for the U.S. Shipping enough cocaine to keep Los Angeles high for a week might seem reason enough to put someone in prison, but Sarria's case was far darker and more complicated.

Sarria's working life began as a guard in Colombia's version of San Quentin. From there Sarria went into the army, ascending to the rank of sergeant major while privately commanding a paramilitary force allied with the Cali drug cartel. As "Minister of Defense" for the Cali cartel, Sarria fought a running war against leftist guerrilla groups, as well as the rival Medellín cartel, and the government's drug interdiction efforts. This meant bribing and intimidating those who could be bribed and intimidated—and killing those who could not. It was said of Sarria that he ordered an execution before every meal. The Cali cartel often directed its reprisals not only against enemies but against their own families, and this kept Sarria's network of assassins—his *sicarios*—plenty busy.

I saw the violence in Colombia firsthand after I met on April 30, 1984, with Colombia's minister of justice, Rodrigo Lara Bonilla, a fine Christian, a Harvard-educated lawyer, and a great supporter of Prison Fellowship. Minister Bonilla had recently ordered a spectacularly successful raid on the Tranquilandia complex—a huge cocaine manufacturing operation in the Colombian jungle. At the end of our meeting, I gave him a copy of my book *Life Sentence* in Spanish.

That evening Minister Bonilla got in the backseat of his chauffeured Mercedes limousine and began the drive home. Several motorcyclists came up alongside the car. When the driver wouldn't pull over, they opened fire with submachine guns. The car was brought to a halt, and Bonilla was assassinated with a spray of bullets. The next day I opened the newspaper to find a picture of the blood-spattered backseat where a copy of my book lay open.

Victims like Rodrigo Lara Bonilla, whom Jésus Sarria and others had executed, were real, and their numbers were not exaggerated. Death was a way of life in Colombia.

Like many highly placed members of the drug cartels, Sarria developed legitimate business interests, including restaurants and a string of luxury hotels in Colombia's most fashionable resorts, which were useful in laundering money and as additional profit centers. He married a famously beautiful and intelligent woman, Elizabeth Montoya de Sarria, and together they became prominent in Colombian society. For twenty years the insatiable desire of *norteamericanos* (North Americans) for cocaine had brought so much money into Colombia that its traditional society had virtually been restructured. Members of Colombia's oldest families—the class Colombia's press referred to as the "oligarchy"—and members of the government now rubbed shoulders with newly rich, if shady, figures like Sarria. The Sarrias were particularly adept at making friends among politicians.

In the early 1990s the Cali cartel made its most ambitious attempt to turn Colombia into a "narcopolis"—a drug kingdom. They began funding political candidates, and they weren't choosy as to party affiliation, often backing rival candidates for the same post. The money was there for anyone who would take it. The Cali cartel made particular inroads into the Liberal Party. During the presidential election of 1994, the cartel succeeded in placing their candidate, Ernesto Samper, in the nation's highest office. They backed him with 6 million dollars of drug money, much of which Sarria and his wife personally funneled into the campaign's accounts. The Sarrias were the go-betweens from the Cali cartel to Samper's campaign.

After the election, the Samper campaign's treasurer, Santiago Medina, who had fallen out with his former boss, began revealing the newly elected president's ties to the cartel. The first disclosures put Sarria in prison, as President Samper and his Liberal Party tried to dissociate themselves from their former backers. Sarria thought of himself as a "political prisoner"—if exporting cocaine were truly a crime, in his view, the whole nation would have to be locked up.

This being Colombia, Sarria's wealth allowed him to make his "cell" relatively comfortable. His quarters were actually a suite of rooms that included a living room–office and a bedroom and bath. A door off the living room led to a terrace. There was a tile-topped table where he worked and took his catered meals. He was able to use his cell phone, a laptop and printer, and a copying machine. He had a good Sony television set brought in and a new toilet installed. A maid offered coffee or tea to his visitors.

His quarters at Itagui Prison served as his command post as he kept in contact with his lawyers, his paramilitary forces, his business associates in the cartel, and his business interests. Sarria had all the major papers of Colombia brought to him each morning, each of which had its own view of the case. And he watched the news on his Sony television with the intensity of a man whose life is being played out by the media, as his was.

In recent days Sarria's circumstances had become of less immediate importance as his wife, Elizabeth, grabbed the headlines. A taped phone conversation between his wife and President Samper had been released. During this call his wife promised to bring a diamond ring to Samper's wife and used diminutives like "Ernestico" that emphasized her intimacy with Samper. At one point she said, "Whatever, I love you." Samper called her by a pet name, "Mona," which earned Elizabeth the nickname "The Divine Mona" in the newspapers. His wife's seductive ways hardly surprised Sarria; as a couple, they practiced Satanism and witchcraft and the Black Mass. Theirs was a marriage that had passed from tenderness to the mutual pursuit of power: Macbeth and his Lady doing a political *rumba*.

This phone conversation was included in what became known as the infamous "narco-cassettes"—tapes of conversations between President Ernesto Samper or his agents and go-betweens for the Cali cocaine cartel.

In the days before the release of these recordings Elizabeth Montoya de Sarria had agreed to testify against Samper, although keeping such a promise was another matter. The Sarrias had lived for years under death threats—there was a 2-million-dollar contract out on Sarria at that moment. Never before, though, had Sarria had such an acute sense that his wife's life hung in the balance. She had been contacted by the U.S. authorities about their witness-protection program. They were considering other forms of exile, which, if Sarria had been free, he might already have chosen for his family. For the immediate future, Sarria had directed his wife to cut off communications with the government and disappear into one of his safe houses. She should not even try to contact him. No one could be trusted at this point but her longtime bodyguard Humberto Vargas.

Four days after Sarria's last communication with his wife, he was watching the evening news when the program switched to a live report. He heard his wife's name called and then her press nickname, "The Divine Mona." A gurney was being wheeled from a Bogotá apartment building to a waiting ambulance. The emergency technicians virtually ran with the gurney from the apartment's door to the vehicle. The little clip of their dash was shown over and over again.

Finally, the video was frozen where the camera had been able to come in closest. Sarria caught sight of his wife's curling dark hair, the tip of her sharp nose; her eyes were closed and the white sheets around her ran with blood. She had been shot at least twelve times, the reporter said. The spectacular violence signaled their enemies' intent to slaughter anyone and everyone who talked. The camera then refocused on the apartment building, showing a stucco wall pockmarked by bullets. Her bodyguard, Humberto, had been gunned down as he tried to flee. Sarria hardly moved but kept staring at the television set long after the station cut away from his wife's murder.

Elizabeth and he had three children; they might be next.

———

Most stories at this point would turn into a revenge drama. We have all seen enough movies to anticipate what should come next: Sarria escapes from prison and then tracks down his wife's killers, simultaneously exposing the corrupt political leaders who ordered her execution. That's the story we want told because we want revenge when someone inflicts violence on those we love. But God desires a different outcome. He acts in the world so that revenge might become reconciliation.

The guard whom Jésus Sarria hired to watch his cell turned out to be a Christian. He talked with Sarria about his faith and gave his employer a New Testament.

The guard's act may have been a simple one, but it showed great courage. Think for a moment of the hardened people you know — those least likely to respond positively to a Christian gesture. This was a man for whom murder had become a way of life. But his guard trusted that God's Word is more powerful than any destructive force and can soften the hardest of hearts.

Reading the New Testament began the process of Jésus Amado Sarria's coming to Christ. His conversion was part of a great flowering of the Gospel within the prisons of Colombia.

Five years before, in 1990, Prison Fellowship's Colombia director, Lacides Hernandez, and an extraordinary OMS missionary named Jeannine Brabon, along with a host of volunteers, began working in another prison in Medellín called Bellavista. At that time Bellavista, with a population of 4,300 inmates, was the most violent prison in Latin America, averaging one murder per day. Lacides and Jeannine began with a few Bible classes. In time a church sprang up with inmate leaders, whose reach extended to thousands through family members visiting on weekends. A live daily radio program proclaiming freedom in Christ began airing from the prison chapel. The early study courses turned into a full-fledged Bible institute, whose graduates now number in the thousands.

The change this witness brought about at Bellavista was unmistakable. Instead of one murder per day, the prison has averaged one murder *per year* since Colombia's Prison Fellowship Ministry took hold. From Bellavista, Christian influence radiated outward, as newly converted inmate leaders were transferred elsewhere and started churches in more facilities.

Today, Jésus Amado Sarria is a free man — one whose liberation goes far beyond his release from prison. Although Colombia was never able to convict President Ernesto Samper of any crime, disclosures of drug money flowing into his campaign motivated Samper to crack down on the drug trade. Sarria did his part, cooperating with American authorities to convict extradited Colombians, which necessitated his children going into the witness-protection program. Then Sarria reformed his business network, ridding it of drug influence. He also began a ministry as an evangelist, particularly among prisoners.

Not too long ago he crossed a last threshold in his new life. He had commissioned his own investigation in his wife's murder. He ascertained to his own satisfaction that police officials had carried out the hit, but he had never been able to find out who the actual triggermen were.

When Sarria visited a Colombian prison as an evangelist, a leader of the ministry asked to speak with him privately. One of his wife's assassins, the leader said, would be in Sarria's audience that day. This man had become a Christian too. The man wanted to know whether he could meet with Sarria and ask his forgiveness.

At first Sarria thought the request out of the question. There's a limit, after all, to what anyone can endure. He thought of how angry the plea would have made him in years past and the ruthless means he would have employed to exact his revenge. The man was lucky enough that Sarria had changed. He felt on the verge of erupting with the old anger. "I don't know," Sarria said, trying to put the petitioner off.

The ministry's leader stayed in front of Sarria, waiting for another answer. Sarria was still trying to control his anger when he felt an unexpected dread come over him. He swallowed hard. How could he do this? This man had killed Elizabeth, the mother of his children, taken away from her the chance to live—to live the way they had truly wanted as Christians, if only they had known it.

But then, that was the secret of this new life, wasn't it? "Forgive us our debts as we forgive our debtors." How many times had he sent wives and mothers and children as well to death? When he had been giving these orders, he felt almost nothing. No, the crushing weight of the evil he had perpetrated had only become clear to him when he accepted the possibility that God might forgive him. Still, he wasn't sure how he would react—whether he could manage it. And yet, how could he refuse? The chance to be part of Jesus' work in lifting guilt from the man's shoulders might be worth the cost.

So he told the ministry leader that he would meet with the man. What he experienced was as complicated as he had feared and as cherished as he could hope. "Because we both have given our lives to Christ," Sarria says, "I was able to go to him, and give him my hand, hold him, and hug him, and cry with him about his sin; to give him my forgiveness and to ask him to forgive me. It was a very painful moment, but it was a pain that was totally separated from revenge, from anger, from anxiety. I'm sure that is the kind of pain the Lord Jesus Christ suffered on the cross for all of us."[1]

The Curse of Unforgiveness

As centuries of broken armistices, peace accords, and treaties attest, the secular world has no way to accomplish the kind of reconciliation witnessed in Colombia—a man forgiving another man who murdered his wife, and both finding themselves bound together as brothers. In contrast, the cycle of violence begetting violence and evil perpetuating evil in today's world seems almost unbreakable as vividly demonstrated in the brilliant but graphic Steven Spielberg film *Munich*.

Munich is the story of the Palestinian terrorist attack that killed eleven Israeli athletes at the 1972 Olympics. The film opens with a meeting of the Israeli war cabinet. The Israelis knew that not responding would only embolden the hostile Arabs surrounding Israel, inviting yet more attacks.

The cabinet recruits a young Israeli intelligence officer, Avner Kaufman, to lead an assassination team against the eleven Palestinian terrorists responsible for the Israeli deaths. Prime Minister Golda Meir sets the policy: "We say to these butchers, you don't want to share this world with us—and we don't have to share this world with you."

Avner, whose wife is about to give birth to their first child, crisscrosses Europe, successfully eliminating Palestinian terrorists one by one. As the Israelis exact their punishment, the Palestinians counterattack, sometimes shedding the blood of innocent civilians. There are moments of poignant dialogue portraying the dilemma of an eye for an eye and a tooth for a tooth: Arabs killing Israelis, Israelis killing Arabs—but to what end?

When Avner's cover is blown, he realizes that the cycle of violence will not be ended until someone kills him; and even if no one does, the violence is destroying his humanity. He flees to New York, seeking refuge with his family. He is driven deeper into guilt by his mother, who tells him that he was justified because Jews must do "whatever it takes." Finally, his Israeli superior arrives and confronts him; Avner tells him, "There is no peace at the end of this" and refuses to return to Israel, his way of breaking the cycle.

The viewer comes to see Avner not as a coward, but as someone wracked by guilt and futility. At the same time, the viewer sees the horrible dilemma: any nation is bound, in a fallen world, as Americans discovered after 9/11, to wield the sword, signaling to its enemies that such an attack will not go unpunished. But the response only perpetuates the violence.

Breaking the Cycle of Violence

So how do people find reconciliation and peace in a broken, often evil world? We must first recognize that alienation is the consequence of the fall; we are alienated from God and from one another — which opens a great divide between nations and ethnic groups, within families, between friends, and even in the ranks of believers.

Still, the desire to make things right, to repair damaged relations, is part of our nature. The *imago Dei* is in all of us, so we sense the need to right wrongs, to seek justice. We want to be freed from guilt's burden. This is why most of the great religions of the world, and many secular therapies, recommend forgiveness.

For the Buddhist, forgiveness is prescribed because it prevents harmful emotions that disturb one's "mind karma." This is beneficial teaching, but it lacks moral force. Hindus are urged to forgive, since it is characteristic of one born of a divine state, as one teacher describes it.[2] But Hinduism has no concept of grace; what you have done in this life will inevitably be done to you in the next, which perpetuates the evil cycle.

Both the Old Testament and the Quran teach forgiveness. But Judaism and Islam are religions of works, where one must earn God's forgiveness and favor. Islam is especially problematic: whether God's will to forgive applies to everyone is questionable, and evil done against the unrighteous can become virtuous. God has a double standard in Islam when it comes to forgiveness that introduces a potentially deadly relativism into Islam's ethics.

Only in Christianity does God sacrifice *Himself* to pay the debts of humankind. This is the basis of the compulsion that uniquely directs the Christian toward moral behavior: if Christ lives in me, and Christ has died for my sins, and the sins of others, how can I be unforgiving of someone who has hurt me? Forgiveness is not an option. It is a mandate, and failure to forgive is disobedience to the One who died for us.[3]

In comparing Islam on the one hand and Christianity on the other, look at two events from recent history. In the Middle East today, Shiites are killing Sunnis, Sunnis killing Shiites, and this has been going on since Muhammad's followers quarreled over who should succeed him—for some 1,300 years. Neither side in this senseless bloodshed can appeal to a common source of authority for reconciliation.

But consider what occurred in South Africa when the transition took place from white minority rule to full enfranchisement and a government reflective of the black majority. A Truth and Reconciliation Commission was established under the leadership of Bishop Desmond Tutu. Through telling the truth about the misdeeds of the former white government and requests by tainted officials for forgiveness, South Africa, miraculously as it now seems, was able to avoid bloodshed. There followed a peaceful transfer of power. It was a clear case of people drawing upon the rich Christian tradition all South Africans, white and black, enjoyed.

The key to reconciliation, as in South Africa, is the ability to forgive. Christians pray "forgive us our debts, as we also have forgiven our debtors" (Matthew 6:12). We are also commanded to "not repay anyone evil for evil" (Romans 12:17), to "love our enemies" (Matthew 5:44), and "if your enemy is hungry, feed him" (Romans 12:20). This is the incredible power of the Gospel to "overcome evil with good" (Romans 12:21) This is why no other religious system in the world has ever had or can ever have the transforming impact on culture Christianity has.

Challenge to the Christian Community: Unity

We as Christians are given this great gift, the ministry of reconciliation (2 Corinthians 5:18). The first step, if Christians are to be faithful ministers of reconciliation, is to repent of our own failures to practice this consistently. As critics are quick to point out, the history of Christianity is replete with examples of the Church's unholy alliance with the state, resulting in the forced conversion of Jews in Spain, the Fourth Crusade's sacking of Constantinople, religious wars in the sixteenth and seventeenth centuries, and the persecution of Christians within the body of Christ. In many people's minds, especially the current critics, Christians have done no better than atheists in providing peace and reconciliation.

The typical Christian defense, which I have frequently used, is that even though Christians have failures in our past, it's nothing compared to the horrors of twentieth-century atheism, such as the Holocaust, Stalin's Gulag, and Pol Pot's Killing Fields. But that answer, while verifiably true, is wholly inadequate. Too often Christians simply miss the mark, which is what caused John Paul II on Ash Wednesday of the millennium year to lead the Catholic Church in a day of collective repentance. Against the advice of many, John Paul acknowledged the violence, abuses of power, material corruption, anti-Semitism, and other abuses practiced by the Church's sons and daughters. This historical precedent was only possible for a faith that recognizes the world's need for justice and humanity's helplessness if not for grace. Has any other religion ever — *ever* — engaged in such an exercise?

By honestly facing up to our own weaknesses, we acknowledge that as Christians we fail to live up to the teaching of the One who gives us life. Through repentance, we are saying we want to do better with God's help.

The place to begin as the repentant people of God is right in our congregations, where we have the clearest of biblical commands to be of one mind and one heart, to bear one another's burdens, to be reconciled with one another, to be one body with one faith and one baptism (Ephesians 4:1–6).

But often we have trouble loving those in our own church who have offended or slighted us or those who have a different idea about the music program. I've sometimes seen more bickering in Christian groups than I can remember in the secular world. Reconciliation within the Church requires a surrender of pride and a willingness to put God's interests over our own interests. Peacemaking within the congregation should be a high priority.

And it works. I've helped mediate differences between believers and found that whenever the Bible is applied, it succeeds. In thirty-four years as a Christian, I can think of only one case in which a person whom I apparently offended refused to give forgiveness and come to final reconciliation.

Divisions can be dangerous. Remember Paul's warning to the Corinthians about communion. "I hear that when you come together as a church, there are divisions among you, and to some extent I believe it" (1 Corinthians 11:18). Then Paul writes that whoever eats "in an unworthy manner will be guilty of sinning against the body and blood of the Lord" (11:27). I shudder at that thought and never receive communion until I have examined my conscience and asked to be forgiven for unresolved issues with other believers.

This is the thing that was on Jesus' heart the night before He was crucified when He prayed for all who would believe, "that all of them may be one, Father, just as you are in me, and I am in you." He continued: "May they also be in us so that the world may believe that you have sent me" (John 17:21). In the midst of his passion and suffering, knowing that He was to go to the cross the next morning, these were His very last pleas to the Father. In the light of these Scriptures, can a true Christian ever seek to perpetuate disunity?

This is why the early Church made such a heroic effort to be of one mind and one heart. In the apostolic era, there were brutally divisive debates over whether Jesus was fully God and fully man, over the Trinity, over faith and works. Yet through the conciliar process, through open debate and discussion, unity was achieved.

Across the Confessional Divide

Christians must see across the confessional divides—the valleys that keep denominations separate, and keep Protestants and Catholics apart—and seek unity within the body of Christ. The first major split in the Church was between East and West, when the Eastern Church, now known as the Orthodox Church, established its own identity in Constantinople. The second great division occurred with the sixteenth century's Reformation. As a result, there are three major divisions today: Orthodox, Roman Catholic, and Protestant.

Even some Roman Catholic scholars agree that the Protestant Reformation was helpful in correcting excesses and abuses within the Church. But the rancorous divisions led tragically to wars and bloodshed, and these divisions have continued for centuries, even after many of the reforms were accomplished. When we rejoice over our divisions, rather than experiencing them as a cause of grief, we place ourselves in the position of the Pharisee who thanks God that he is not on like the common run of sinners (Luke 18:10–14). Can we listen to Jesus' prayers for unity and maintain such an attitude?

There is a consistent pattern of people on both sides reaching across the Reformation divide. In 1541 some Reformers met at Regensburg, Germany, with Cardinal Cantorini and a bevy of Catholic theologians; among them was a young aide by the name of John Calvin, who later wrote that the participants came very close to an agreement on justification by faith, the issue at the heart of the Reformation. Shortly after the conference, Cantorini died, along with the Vatican's apparent willingness to agree.

Calvin, and to a lesser extent Luther, remained anxious throughout their lifetimes to resolve the differences. Calvin never ceased seeing the Church in its totality; he did not make a Protestant confession a requirement for fellowship. According to one historian, he freely admitted that "some churches" and persons within the Roman communion are within the true Church.[4]

In the seventeenth century, a Puritan pastor, Richard Baxter, believed that there was a "core of orthodox Christianity that Puritans, Anglicans, and Catholics could all affirm … that should have been a source of peace among them." He urged that participants come together as "mere Christians," the phrase later made famous by C. S. Lewis's book *Mere Christianity*. Though a nonconformist and rejected in many circles, Baxter's argument remains valid today. By "mere Christianity," Baxter, like Lewis after him, meant the nonnegotiable, irreducible fundamentals of the Christian faith, understood clearly from the apostolic era onward. This remains in our time the greatest hope for at least the partial fulfillment of Christ's prayers for unity.

Continuing Efforts Toward Unity
Following the Reformation

Even throughout the centuries that followed, deep though the differences remained between Protestants and Catholics, efforts were consistently made to work together. At the end of the nineteenth century, evangelicals, feeling increasing pressure from the forces of the Enlightenment and the erosion of Christian influence in culture, reached out to Catholics. After all, the attack on Christianity of modern times, like today, was not limited to one denomination.

One good example is Dwight L. Moody, the great evangelist. Moody, to the consternation of his followers, helped build a Catholic church in his hometown of Northfield, Massachusetts. When he was challenged, he said, "If there are Roman Catholics it is better that they should be good Roman Catholics than bad. It is surely better to have a Catholic Church than none."[5]

During that same period, Abraham Kuyper, a hyper-Calvinist and evangelical theologian, led a movement in Holland to unite Catholics and evangelicals in a common social cause. They formed a political party, which Kuyper later led to power, becoming prime minister. He pleaded in his writings for greater understanding between evangelicals and Catholics. "What we have in common with Rome concerns precisely those fundamentals of our Christian creed now most fiercely assaulted by the modern spirit," he wrote. "... If Romish theologians take up the sword to do valiant and skillful battle against the same tendency that we ourselves mean to fight to the death, is it not the better part of wisdom to accept the valuable help.... I ... am not ashamed to confess that on many points my views have been clarified through my study of the Romish theologians."[6]

In the beginning decades of the twentieth century, J. Gresham Machen, whose classic book *Christianity and Liberalism* distinguished true Christianity from its liberal counterfeit, pleaded for common ground among true believers, whatever their denomination. The division between Rome and evangelicals was great, he argued, but it "seems almost trifling compared to the abyss which stands between us and many ministers of our own Church."[7]

What one theologian has described as the "ecumenism of the trenches" has often brought Christians together across denominational divides. When I visited Eastern Europe as communism was falling, I found repeated instances of evangelicals and Catholics who had been working together, praying together, even worshiping together in the face of their common enemy, the communist oppressors. One priest in the Czech Republic told me that his best friends and closest fellow prayer warriors were evangelicals.

This is exactly what Catholics and Protestants, picketing together side by side at abortion clinics, discovered here in America, bridging the gap in ways that hitherto might have been impossible.

At a meeting of Catholic and evangelical scholars in New York in 1992, we discussed the near-open warfare between our churches in South America. Many of us were convicted—we believe by the Holy Spirit—to continue those discussions and seek increased harmony. This was the beginning of Evangelicals and Catholics Together (ECT), an informal gathering of Catholic and evangelical leaders. The effort, once hugely controversial, has become much less so as progress has been achieved. In the succession of papers released was one (referred to earlier) on justification by faith alone, which agreed precisely with what the Reformers meant by *sola fide*.[8] ECT has been guided by the famous formulation: "In essentials, unity; in non-essentials, liberty; and in all things, charity."

Why is this so important? Remember Jesus' prayer that His followers might be one as He was one with the Father *so that the world would know God sent Jesus into the world* (John 17). Without an effort to be one with each other, we undermine our own evangelistic efforts. The modern apologist Francis Schaeffer wrote a booklet called *The Mark of the Christian*, describing the importance of our unity and love for one another. Bitter division, Schaeffer wrote, gave the world the right to disbelieve the Gospel.[9] That is our scandal.

Admittedly, ecumenism has a bad name for many because it is associated with liberal attempts to reduce Christianity to its lowest common denominator. Orthodox ecumenism today, however, seeks only unity in the service of truth. And the truth of the great fundamental creeds—mere Christianity—can be affirmed by all true Christians, even as in our separate denominations we are, as I am, committed to our distinctives.

Our common stand can powerfully affect our culture. Catholics and Protestants working together for twenty-five years have begun to reverse the culture of death; the U.S. Supreme Court's affirmation of a ban on partial-birth abortion represents a historic shift.

Even in Northern Ireland, long the black eye of Protestant and Catholic relations, where open warfare has been waged in the streets, I have seen brave Protestants and Catholics working successfully for reconciliation. I have visited Northern Ireland many times and have seen the worst and the best of the "troubles," as they were euphemistically known. In the late 1970s I witnessed homes exploding. I even stayed with a Protestant family who were openly contemptuous of Catholics.

Prison Fellowship, however, was working even then with both Catholic and Protestant prisoners, and in 1983 our ministry staged an unforgettable conference at Queens University, Whitlow Hall. A former IRA member, Liam McCloskey, and Protestant paramilitary member, Jimmy Gibson, who were on furlough from prison, told the stories of their Christian conversions and their union in Christ. "Before, if I had seen Jimmy on the street," Liam said, "I would have shot him. Now he's my brother in Christ, and I would die for him."[10] Eight hundred people erupted in tears and applause.

Inspired by the conference, I agreed to accompany Father Neal Carlin to Londonderry, a Catholic stronghold, where the first violence erupted in 1972, to meet with a group working for reconciliation.

As we started off in Father Carlin's car, I realized with more than a little alarm that he was wearing his collar, which would make us a target all along the dangerous road. We passed through checkpoints where British soldiers stood at the ready with submachine guns. The guards scanned the undercarriage for bombs with a mirror on a long pole.

Londonderry was a drab industrial town, under a gray sky, with street after street of tenements and row houses, some with walls pockmarked with bullet holes, huddled in the long shadows of dusk. The streets of the Catholic section, decorated with radical IRA and Sinn Féin graffiti, were totally deserted, as if an air raid siren had gone off and everyone was hiding inside.

Father Neal pulled the car into a square with a small war monument on one side. "We're here," he told us. "Follow me. Walk, but walk briskly."

He led us down an alley between two industrial buildings to a warehouse. I felt like we were meeting foreign agents at a secret location.

When the warehouse door opened, we heard raucous gospel singing. The warehouse was ablaze with light, filled with people smiling for joy, clapping, and singing. The crowd included a host of Catholic charismatics, local Protestant leaders, and our own prison volunteers.

I spoke about the reconciling work of Christ — the crying need of Northern Ireland! Every time I made a point the place would erupt with foot stomping, clapping, and shouts of "Amen!" The Irish are notoriously dour at worship, but not this night.

As I write this, Northern Ireland seems to be completing its long journey to reconciliation, with Protestants and Catholics having agreed to a coalition government. Catholics have disarmed and agreed to pursue their aims only through political means. The Protestant leadership foresees sharing appointments in the executive branch with Catholics — nearly unthinkable a decade ago. How much credit historians will give to the reconciling efforts of faithful Christians remains to be seen. But from what I saw, such efforts played a key role, demonstrating that there is an answer to the futile cycle of violence portrayed in the film *Munich*.

———

If forgiveness and reconciliation are at the heart of the Gospel, if Christ can reconcile murderers with their victims' loved ones and even bring about peaceful settlements of religious wars, what then do we say about division among true Christians? We must repent of it. The scandal to the world must be the cross, not our division.

In a world where Christianity is being assaulted on all sides, true believers must stand together in common defense of the faith. It is the challenge of the Church to work toward this, imperfect though our efforts may be, as we profess one Lord, one faith, and one baptism.

CHAPTER 10

THE CHURCH

On the cross, Christ not only reconciles us to Himself but incorporates us into His body, the Church, which consists of all those who have accepted Christ's offer of salvation—what the early Church called the *communio sanctorum*, the community of saints. As individual Christians, we are also called to be part of a specific confessing body, or local church, where our spiritual duties and disciplines can be fulfilled.

This is the community God had in mind before time itself began (see Romans 8:29). We cannot understand the Church without seeing her as part of the sweeping story the Bible tells, and we cannot be faithful Christians without affirming God's central role for the Church—the living body of Christ. The Church is a reclamation project, reestablishing God's rule in the midst of a world still mostly under Satan's sway.

This is much different in character and purpose from the common perception. Today we see churches as big buildings, sometimes with steeples, where worship services are held. These places also conduct Sunday schools, host youth groups, sponsor choirs, open their basements to AA meetings, and so on. In other words, we tend to form our ideas about the Church on the basis of what churches do. We ask each other, "Do you go to a good church?" We want to know whether the preaching is lively, whether the music program suits our tastes, whether there are activities for our kids.

Local churches care about getting people interested in them and go to great pains to make themselves attractive, as I discovered one Sunday in our own wonderful church when we had a visiting pastor preach about why Christians should join the church. He was a very successful senior pastor, widely known and justifiably respected. I looked forward to his message.

His rhetorical skills did not disappoint us. Within the first few minutes he had people comfortable, attentive, and ready to learn. The text he chose was Psalm 84, and his message would have done his homiletics professor proud.

We need the church, the pastor intoned in his reedy drawl, "because it is such a lovely place," referring to verse 1. He went on to laud the beauty of our church's campus. The church ought to be a beautiful place, he said, so that people will be drawn to it, find it welcoming, and want to participate.

The church was a "loveable" place as well because of the sweet fellowship that we experience there. He spent the next several minutes explaining how relationships are nurtured inside a church, which is what church surveys tell us people most want.

He continued, describing the church as a "living place," an allusion to the references in Psalm 84 to the living God. It's the place where you encounter the living God and can be born again. That's true; I joined in the "amens."

Halfway through the sermon, however, I began to get uncomfortable. This man was saying that we should join a church because it is good for us. It is, of course, but that's not the reason we join. We gather with our fellow believers in order to express our love for God. Worship is about God, not us.

Even great pastors, like this man, are caught, it would seem, in the grip of our consumer-driven culture. Albeit unwittingly, the Church is seen as the conveyor of various commodities, a spiritual retailer, God's Gap. But God is not a divine vendor and we are not God's customers.

Christians need to change our whole vocabulary. We can't talk about the Church as a building or a place we go. The word used in the New Testament for the Church is *ecclesia*, the same word used in the Greek Old Testament as "the assembly" of God's people.[1] *We are the Church.* Catholic, Orthodox, and Protestant doctrine all teach this. (One of the most exciting churches in America, Redeemer Presbyterian in New York City, doesn't even have a building!) We are the bride for whom Christ, the Bridegroom, gave Himself (Ephesians 5:25). Think about that scriptural analogy—Christ shed His blood for the Church; shame on us when we trivialize her. The Church is the gathering of saints and angels in holy festival, as described in Hebrews 12, which takes place even on earth as we enter into worship.*

We worship God because God is worthy of our worship. The Church glorifies God on earth, and this is a primary means by which we participate in God's life. When Jesus said the gates of hell cannot stand against His Church, He was foreseeing the people of God, drawn into unity with God and each other through worship, spilling out of our meeting places to spread the Gospel and righteousness. How else could we assault the gates of hell? You won't confront them in your comfortable sanctuary. Have we forgotten this? We worship God in our churches so we can follow Him in the world.

Classic Marks of the Church

The Church always has the same identifying marks.

The Word

Foremost among the marks of the Church is the preaching of the Word. The Church proclaims the Gospel, not only to bring in unsaved people but to edify and strengthen and deepen the knowledge of the faithful in the Word of God. In Paul's closing words to his protégé Timothy, written from prison when Paul believed he would never see Timothy again, he instructs him: "Preach the Word; be prepared in season and out of season; correct, rebuke and encourage—with great patience and careful instruction" (2 Timothy 4:2).

In every confession of the Church, the Church has been guided first by Scripture and then by its own tradition in interpreting that

*"But you have come to Mount Zion, to the heavenly Jerusalem, the city of the living God. You have come to thousands upon thousands of angels in joyful assembly, to the Church of the firstborn, whose names are written in heaven" (Hebrews 12:22–23).

Scripture. This has sometimes led to controversy in the entire Christian Church. Protestants in the Reformation argued that they were guided by *sola scriptura*, or "Scripture alone"; the Catholic Church has emphasized tradition. But as we agreed in another ECT statement, both sides of the Reformation divide are guided by tradition, but both sides see the primary authority as Scripture. Tradition only helps us understand and elucidate it.

The Sacraments, or Ordinances

The second mark of the Church, as all confessions would agree, is the administration of the sacraments. A sacrament is simply a mark to the world of the presence of God—an outward sign of an inward and spiritual reality. Every church practices at least two sacraments, although some, including my own, call them ordinances. The first is the Lord's Supper, the Eucharist, when we share the body and blood of Christ. For me this is the most intimate moment in a church service. It's the one I most look forward to in my church because I find myself drawn into a deep intimacy with God. And ever since Gibson's *The Passion of the Christ*, I have realized through the memories of its graphic scenes how great a sacrifice my Savior made for me. I am overwhelmed with emotion and gratitude as I often hold that cup and wafer in quivering hands.

Something happens when we truly come into communion with Him in this way. A number of years ago I took former Secretary of the Treasury Bill Simon into prison with me. Bill had experienced an intimate encounter with Christ late in his life and took on a Eucharistic lay ministry for the Catholic Church. This day we were on death row in a Texas prison. I went from cell to cell, greeting the men, sharing Christ with them, offering them the hope or encouragement of the Gospel. Bill Simon followed along beside me and, to every Catholic inmate, offered the Eucharist. I will never forget the moving picture of Bill Simon, one of the most powerful men in America, formerly head of the Olympics and an enormously successful investment banker, on his knees in front of one cell after another, passing the bread and wine through the bars to a grateful, often weeping inmate kneeling on the other side. It was a reminder that the ground at the foot of the cross is level, and a glorious foretaste of the feast to come.

Traditions disagree whether the bread and wine is the actual presence of Jesus, as Catholics believe, or whether He is actually present at the altar, as Lutherans believe, or whether it is purely a memorial service, as most Baptists believe. The Reformed tradition teaches that Christ is really present, both in the elements and in His people, but only in a spiritual sense. Personally, as I hold that bread and look at that cup of wine, I am struck by the fact that the Holy Spirit, in His transforming work, is bringing about a real moment of communion with God. I hope I'm a good Baptist, but I feel that to the very core of my being.

I feel united not only to God but — however imperfectly — to my fellow believers as well, of whatever denomination. As it says in 1 Corinthians, "Because there is one loaf, we, who are many, are one body, for we all partake of the one loaf" (10:17).

The second sacrament, or ordinance, on which all but perhaps one Christian denomination would agree is baptism. Once again, there are many differences between Christian confessions on infant baptism, believers' baptism, sprinkling of water, or full immersion. I have my own strong feelings, which is why I am a Baptist. But the sacrament reveals for all that we have been buried with Christ and resurrected to walk in the newness of life. It is the sign that we are united with Him and now part of His body.

At Pentecost the people who heard the apostle Peter's message about Christ and His sacrifice were cut to the heart and asked, "What shall we do?" Peter's reply was, "Repent and be baptized, every one of you, in the name of Jesus Christ for the forgiveness of your sins" (Acts 2:38). People were told that they would receive the gift of the Holy Spirit. The new believer's baptism was the mark of life in Christ and Christ's Church. It is that same mark today.

As I've written elsewhere, I have a seventeen-year-old autistic grandson, Max, whose mother, Emily, has done an extraordinary job raising him to be a fine young man, able to function with help. Like most autistic kids, Max cannot handle crowds or confusion, so when Emily and Max are with Patty and me and we go to our church,

Max and Emily sit in the lobby watching the service on closed-circuit television.

One Sunday when Max was thirteen, he witnessed a baptism. He turned to his mother and said, "I want to be baptized by Grandpa in his pool."

We had two obstacles. Although this is not Baptist doctrine, I believe only the clergy should baptize, and knowing Max, he would never have gotten into the baptistery of the church, nor would he probably get into the pool at home with a stranger. I was able to solve that problem by asking the church to ordain me for one day, which it did. The second problem was more difficult. Believing as I do in believers' baptism, I could not baptize Max unless we were sure he understood what it meant.

Max learns by pictures. Happily, Emily is a gifted artist who draws little cartoon strips to help Max understand what is happening around him. So she did a cartoon strip entitled "Getting Baptized." The first box said when someone loves Jesus he can be baptized. The second box showed Max with his heart outlined, and it said: "Max loves Jesus, so Max can be baptized." The next frame showed Max in the pool with me. Max is saying, "I love Jesus," and in the next frame I am saying, "Because you love Jesus, I baptize you in the name of the Father, Son, and Holy Spirit." The fifth frame shows Max being immersed and coming out of the water, and the caption says, "Max is washed clean just like Jesus." The final frame shows Max with his arms raised to the sky. "Now Max is baptized, everyone knows Max loves Jesus."

Baptizing Max turned out to be a rich moment in my life — and Max's. He talks about it constantly. He recites the baptismal creed. Any time he comes to visit and gets in the pool he will announce that this is where he was baptized. I'm not sure that anybody has been baptized anyplace in the world that has had more significance than that pool did for this handicapped but beautiful young man.

Discipline

The third mark is the exercise of discipline. Because of the fall, none of us is capable of disciplining ourselves. Most of us, in fact, often do not recognize our own shortcomings; as I've written, we rationalize them away. But sin not dealt with diminishes the power of God in our lives, and habitual, serious sin can effectively quench the ministry of the Holy Spirit within us. The most miserable people are not free-wheeling pagans but Christians who know better and consistently sin anyway. So we need the Church's discipline in fighting the spiritual war that's always raging.[2]

After Watergate, and realizing what a mess I had made when I tried to be in charge of my life, I first submitted myself to a fellowship group that discipled me, and then to the board of directors of the ministry I founded. I would make no decision apart from them, and I've asked them to challenge me if at any time they see me straying in personal behavior or in orthodoxy. From time to time, they have done that. I've tried to have the same relationship with the pastors of my churches.

Sadly, discipline is not adequately practiced in most churches. Sometimes pastors and governing boards are unwilling to exercise discipline for fear of hurting church recruitment or — perish the thought — for fear of appearing intolerant in this golden age of toler-ance. But not to enforce church discipline, not to hold people ac-countable for holy and righteous living, is to make a mockery of the Church.

If you do not have an accountability group that will be honest with you, get one; if your pastor doesn't have a strong group around him, go to him or the church elders and urge that he get one. Church pastors have the toughest job imaginable, and they need trusted counselors. The close associate of a prominent pastor who fell once told me that this leader was "alone at the top." Too many are.

And discipline needs to be tough. I've never gotten over my Marine Corps training. Whenever I stepped out of line in officer's training, some wizened, old sergeant would kick me figuratively and literally until I did it right. Later, as an officer myself, there was always someone in command who would correct me, usually in colorful lan-guage. But the lessons were so engraved in my mind and heart that I came to obey them almost instinctively.

Why was that important in the Marine Corps? Because I was being trained to take other men and lead them into combat where their lives would be on the line.

Since we fight "not against flesh and blood," as the Scriptures tell us, but "against the spiritual forces of evil in the heavenly realms" (Ephesians 6:12), the Christian life is just as real a battle, except there's much more at stake — the spiritual destiny of both the believers and those yearning for God who look to us.

Community

Genuine community also characterizes the Church. The apostle Paul reminds the church in Rome, "In Christ we who are many form one body, and each member belongs to all the others" (Romans 12:5). How we belong to one another goes far beyond the "sweet fellowship" of potluck suppers and finding a comfortable social circle. True community involves a real *koinonia*, a deep communion — the kind the apostles described in Acts 4, which is the first real sign of the Kingdom on earth, where each person in need was helped (vv. 32–35). This is where people truly bear one another's burdens, pray for one another, and yes, even suffer for one another.

Instances of heroic virtue in this regard underline what Acts 4 *koinonia* can mean and even demand. Some years ago a *Dateline* television program told the story of a woman in Ohio, Diana Harrill, who sang in the choir and learned that another member of her church, Toni Whatley, was in line for a kidney transplant but might not live long enough to get it. Diana happened to be white; Toni black. They hardly knew each other. But Diana, finding herself impressed in prayer with Toni's need, offered her kidney. It was a match, and soon thereafter both were in the hospital. One church member giving a kidney to another. That's fellowship. That's bearing one another's burdens. That's commitment. That's the sign of the Kingdom.

Sharing of one another's burdens is something we do every Sunday, actually, in giving our tithes and offerings. Although we can view giving with the same jaundiced eye we reserve for taxes, what Christians do every Sunday by way of providing for their church and others is one of the Church's glories. This came home to me on Easter Sunday 2005 when then-Majority Leader and local Congressman Tom Delay and I and other Prison Fellowship visitors joined the inmates of the InnerChange Freedom Initiative (IFI) program in Sugarland, Texas, for worship. Prisoners receive a pittance for the work they do in prison and usually spend it in the commissary on toiletries and treats that make their lives a little better. But every Sunday in the IFI worship service this congregation of prisoners drops small items they have purchased from the commissary into the offering baskets for the benefit of the homeless. I watched in awe as one after another prisoners relinquished their last shreds of comfort to others.

Christian community demands commitment. When people ask me where I *go* to church, I correct them. I don't go; I'm a member. (John Calvin, like all the great Christian leaders, made clear that one could not be a Christian apart from the Church.) I've planted my flag—happily in a great church, First Baptist of Naples, Florida, with an unusually gifted pastor, Dr. Hayes Wicker—I'm proud to *belong*. We cannot treat the local church like a restaurant, picking and choosing from the menu, visiting another whenever we feel like it. Church membership involves making a covenant with fellow believers. It takes time to develop unity with others at any depth, and this never takes place, *ever*—not at any time or anywhere—without conflict.

The kind of community Christians achieve can have a powerful effect on culture. Harvard professor Robert Putnam, who wrote the landmark book *Bowling Alone*, is alarmed over the loss of community in American culture. Much of it he attributes to the emphasis on diversity, people "hunkering down" in their grievance groups and losing a sense of the common good. In his recent writings, Putnam (about whose spiritual life I know nothing) observes that the best example for assimilation in community today is being achieved by evangelical megachurches, where there is ethnic and cultural diversity in one community.[3] Once again, Christianity rises to the challenge of strengthening culture.

Where these marks are present—the preaching of the Word, the administration of the sacraments, the exercise of discipline, and the practice of community—the Church will inevitably transform the culture around it. The wholesale transformation of the culture of death in Colombia's prisons would be a case in point. So would South Africa's avoidance of civil war through its Christian heritage and the contribution Christianity made to the freeing of Eastern Europe from Soviet domination. When we *are* the Church as Christ commands us to be, we change and so does the world.

The Mission of the Church

The Church exists not only as a worshiping but also as a missionary community. Evangelism always has to be a primary call in the Church. It is with distress that I look back on the experience of my first forty-one years of life. I was taken to church at times; I even found myself in moments of great stress walking into a church and praying. I attended Sunday school sporadically, but I never *heard* the Gospel. Perhaps I hadn't been given ears to hear, and maybe I wasn't ready until the peculiar circumstances of my life when God used my conversion for a very dramatic witness.

But the truth is that the Gospel should be radiating out from our churches, the messages in the pulpit translated by those in the pew. We often think that evangelism belongs mainly to the clergy, but every church member has a particular ability and calling to extend the Church's witness into the world.

Not everyone is going to come into a church. As I have discovered, often the most effective way in which a church can evangelize is to seek out opportunities for its members to share the Gospel in the workplace, in homes, and in community halls, and draw people in however we can reach them.

I experienced a wonderful example of this through Prison Fellowship's Angel Tree program, in which volunteers buy gifts for prisoners' children.[4] One day the pastor of a small church in Oregon opened his study door to three small children: a five-year-old boy with his three-year-old brother and two-year-old sister. The eldest asked shyly, "Mister, can we see the church that brought us those Christmas presents?"

The pastor instantly realized the children had received Angel Tree presents. The three children belonged to a family where the father was behind bars and the mother was involved in drugs and prostitution. "Of course you can see the church," he said. "Come on in." He gave them the cook's tour of the building and then the children were on their way.

But fifteen minutes later they were back at the door. "What time does church start?"

"In an hour."

"We'll be back." The kids scampered away once more.

Fifteen minutes later, they were back again. "Is it okay for a person to come to church if his socks don't match?"

"Of course," said the pastor.

"What about if he doesn't have any socks? Mine don't match. My brother, he don't have any."

"You look more than fine to me," said the pastor. "Let me find you a seat."

A couple sitting nearby shepherded the children through the unfamiliar service. They puzzled over a brown paper bag the oldest boy was clutching. It turned out to contain one hot dog. The children were worried the service would last too long and had brought a lunch. They'd planned to split the one hot dog among them.

The kids were soon informally adopted and became a permanent part of the congregation. Christians had found them in their need, which brought them into a church they would never have thought of visiting otherwise. Their lives were soon filled with loving adults and hope for the future.

The Character of the Church

In our creeds we confess our belief in one holy, catholic, apostolic Church. What does that mean?

The Church is *one* because all true Christians, while we participate in different confessing congregations, are part of one body. That body is *holy* because its essential nature is found in Christ. The Church is *catholic* because it is universal, which is what *catholic* means — the

Church is open to everyone. Finally, the Church is *apostolic*, which means that its teachings are those of the apostles. We have not invented a religion. We are part of the faith God revealed.

———

As we've said, Jesus broke into society with a radical, transforming message. In His first sermon He announced that He had come to set the captives free, to preach the Gospel to the poor, to proclaim the favorable year of the Lord (Luke 4:18). It was more than just the good news of salvation. It was the announcement of a new Kingdom, that our God reigns, and He makes all things new, and all is under His authority—the world, the universe, the nation states, all people.

In between the announcement of the Kingdom and the fulfillment of the Kingdom comes the witness of the Kingdom. This is when God's people gather together to practice what the Kingdom promises even in the midst of this fallen world. It is the age of the Church in which we live. The Church makes the invisible Kingdom visible.

CHAPTER 11

BE HOLY —
TRANSFORM
THE WORLD

A major task of the Church is to make disciples, which means she guides us in the pursuit of holiness, the central call of every serious Christian. "Be holy, because I am holy," God says (Leviticus 11:45).[1] The words from Hebrews, "Without holiness no one will see the Lord" (12:14), convict us now as they did the British parliamentarian William Wilberforce in his twenty-year campaign to abolish the slave trade.

Of late, the Church has not done a good job of demonstrating holiness. The pedophilia scandals in the Catholic Church and accounts of evangelical ministers consorting with prostitutes, both male and female, have filled the newspapers. Often we wonder why the Church in America, which has such great resources at its disposal, has not done more to address racism, preventable diseases in the Global South, world hunger, the modern plague of AIDS, and human rights abuses.

The hard truth is that too many see Christianity in terms of self-improvement or as a guide to successful living; the command to holiness, the impetus for such change, is too often ignored.

What Holiness Is

What is holiness then? Most nonbelievers, and many Christians, confuse holiness with following a legalistic list of dos-and-don'ts or reduce it to piety and attentiveness to religious duties. In reality, holiness embraces piety, but it is much more; it is the heart of the Christian life and every Christian's destiny. As one devotional writer put it, God has one eternal purpose for us, that we should be "conformed to the likeness of his Son" (Romans 8:29).[2] We are to become holy as Christ is holy; we are to become true Christians, the root meaning of which is "little Christs." Indeed, through holy living, Christians are called to share in God's work of redeeming creation.

This holy life is the natural outgrowth of the exchange at the cross of our lives for Christ's life. Once reconciled to God, we enjoy, as Peter said, "a share in the divine nature" (see 2 Peter 1:3–4).[3] Jesus' relationship to the Father is one of perfect obedience in love. As we obey, God's grace enables us to live like Jesus.[4]

Jesus' Commands
and the Struggle for Holiness

How should we live in obedience to God? Jesus said that He came not to abolish God's law given in the Old Testament but to fulfill it. So He gave us His great commandment: "'Love the Lord your God with all your heart and with all your soul and with all your strength and with all your mind;' and, 'Love your neighbor as yourself'" (Luke 10:27).

The great commandment summarizes the Ten Commandments and focuses Christ's followers on obedience from the heart. The Sermon on the Mount and the Beatitudes show how God's law applies when God truly reigns. So we are not only forbidden from coveting our neighbor's wife, but we are commanded not to lust in our hearts. Christ's teachings take the Old Testament law and raise it to a new level.

But remember, the pursuit of holiness is a continuing struggle. Humanity still has the inclination to choose sin. The most saintly among us still want to do what's wrong and often do. This is why Paul, long after his conversion, writes, "For in my inner being I delight in God's law; but I see another law at work in the members of my body.... What a wretched man I am! Who will rescue me from this body of death?" (Romans 7:22–24).

True Christians who take this battle seriously will surely arouse the enemy and discover Satan as a roaring lion seeking to devour them, as the apostle Peter warned (1 Peter 5:8). To fight this spiritual battle, the first thing is to remember that we depend utterly on God; the Christian life is not about asserting our wills — our wills are corrupt even after we come to Christ. Our very love for God comes from God, and we only offer God's love back to Him. As Augustine writes, "Indeed we also work, but we are only collaborating with God who works, for his mercy has gone before us."[5] So the struggle for holiness is a joint effort.

The Key to the Holy Life

Paul gave an admonition to the Christians in Rome that is the key to the holy life: We are "to offer our bodies as living sacrifices, holy and pleasing to God" (Romans 12:1). This "spiritual act of worship" involves the "renewing of your mind" (12:2). There are at least four truths to remember about becoming living sacrifices.

Repentance

Christians everywhere recognize the need for continual repentance; we acknowledge our sin, resolve not to do it again, and take steps to avoid situations and circumstances that encourage it. The Scriptures both encourage us to confess our sins and assure us of God's pardon.[6]

We can always confess our sins directly to God, but it can also be helpful to discuss these matters with trustworthy fellow believers — another reason community is so important. Catholics, the Orthodox, and Anglicans direct their members to confess their sins to clergy, who then announce God's pardon. Similarly, Protestants have always availed themselves of the clergy's counseling. More and more evangelical churches today encourage accountability groups where participants follow the teaching in James to "confess your sins to each other and pray for each other" (5:16). The practice of accountability has been crucial to my own growth.

Genuine confession and repentance can be costly, as I have discovered in dealing with offenders. Take the case of the young man in the Washington area, deeply involved with his church and solidly converted to Christ, who came to visit one of our staff members several years ago. He had, he confessed, committed a murder in a drunken stupor many years earlier. He was never a suspect and had never been charged. But in his prayer time his sin greatly troubled him. He knew he was guilty in the eyes of the law. What should he do?

My associate counseled him that he had to follow his conscience; if he believed God was really telling him to turn himself in, he should do that. But he should also know God had forgiven him. In the weeks that followed, the man became increasingly convicted. He discussed it with his wife, also a believer, and both came to the conclusion, although it meant leaving the children, that he should turn himself in. He did, was charged, and sentenced to ten years in prison. Today this man is still serving his sentence in a Midwest prison, where he is one of the prison's Christian leaders. He is a living example of pursuing holiness at the kind of cost we talked about in chapter 8; but he is a freer man today than he ever was outside of prison.

Reforming Our Desires

Dealing with deadly sins like anger, envy, pride, sloth, avarice, gluttony, and lust is made all the more difficult in today's self-indulgent culture. We excuse anger as sticking up for ourselves. We choose luxurious options for our cars and houses and excuse the excess as resale value coverage. We brag about our achieving kids even to friends whose children aren't faring as well. And lust always poses a problem, especially for men. C. S. Lewis noted this, observing that while lust and gluttony are both temptations of appetite, they are grotesquely unequal in their allure. While many men are habitual patrons of strip clubs (and Internet pornography), no one pays a cover charge to see a platter of beef Wellington.

But the answer has always been found, as St. Benedict put it, in the replacement of one desire with another. It means wanting the things of God—the virtues—and God Himself more than what our pride or appetites demand.

I know how difficult it is to deal with habitual sins, some of which, like nicotine, are genuine addictions. When I became a Christian, I prayed hard to be delivered from cigarettes, but the appetite persisted. I used to go to great lengths when traveling to Christian meetings to conceal my habit. I would find a dark corner somewhere to catch a quick smoke. My young assistant at the time got used to carrying cigarettes for me, to his own disadvantage. One time after I'd finished speaking at a prison in Kentucky, I found a quiet area in the prison yard and lit a cigarette. At that moment my assistant spotted a *New York Times* photographer who had been traveling with us. I immediately handed the cigarette to my assistant, who cupped it down into his pocket. Less than a minute later, as the picture was being snapped, my assistant discovered that his jacket was on fire! For me, giving up cigarettes was a form of fasting—a way of ridding myself of a destructive habit in order to be a good steward of my body (and save my assistant's jackets).

All the traditional disciplines, like setting aside time for prayer and fasting, keeping periods of silence, or denying ourselves certain legitimate creature comforts—these disciplines all have the same character: they are not ends in themselves, but a means of replacing faulty desires with the desire for God.

Retraining ourselves to do what is right is just like physical exercise, and we have to work at it. Paul tells us that physical exercise is good, but spiritual exercise is far more important. Sin comes naturally; holiness doesn't. It requires the constant supervision of the Holy Spirit and constant prayer, study of the Word, and discipline of the individual Christian. But soon we find we can't live without it. We hunger more for virtue than for vice.

Renewing the Mind

Key to growing in Christ is not only subduing our natural appetite but beginning to think like Christ, to see the world as God sees it, by the renewing of our minds. A renewed mind in Christ allows us to direct our desires more in accordance with reason. This is a tremendous part of the freedom we gain in Christ from the slavery of sin. We no longer lie to ourselves as much; we stop being such phonies.

We also become discerning about the things we see in the culture around us, exploding the false myths that we are urged to live by. This means developing a view of the world formed by the Bible. Remember, as we have discussed, Christianity *is* a worldview.

Seeking the mind of Christ, seeing things in the world the way God sees them, is the only antidote to a culture that exalts the self above everything else. Watch the television screen long enough and you'll believe that the whole object of life is to gratify your desires as quickly and fully as possible. It is all focused on you.

I know how living a self-directed life distorts our views of others. I was heralded in the press as the most influential young political leader in Washington when I was President Nixon's assistant. Admirals and generals saluted. These things went to my head. And even in the early days of my Christian life I found that I enjoyed the plaudits that I received and the standing ovations I got when I spoke and gave my testimony. It can be frustrating how the old habits cling — as Paul knew well.

True holiness is thinking more of God and others than yourself. This leads to humility, which is the most elusive of the virtues. The reason is that once you think you have achieved it, you've lost it. Humility is clear evidence of holiness.

Acts of Charity

As we see the world through God's eyes, we actually do put others' needs ahead of ours. This is why, when the great novelist Flannery O'Connor was asked by one of her correspondents how he could experience God's love, her reply was, "Give alms." She meant do something for the poor, for those in need, which in fact is one of the most telling marks of Christian holiness, as the apostle James reminds us (1:27; 2:17).

When we care for God's favorites, the poor, who include the destitute, the widowed, the fatherless, the sick, prisoners, and anyone suffering injustice, we plunge immediately into the cosmic battle that's always raging between good and evil. We choose sides. Once on God's side, we come to understand God's point of view and position ourselves to experience God's love and friendship in a whole new way.

Holiness as a Way of Life

Reforming our desires, renewing our minds, and doing intentional actions in obedience to Christ on behalf of the poor result in the formation of new habits. In turn, a new way of living through obedience to God's will becomes second nature.[7] Dave Cauwels, a close friend and Prison Fellowship Board member, for example, has been spending one day a week in the notorious Santa Fe Prison, working with a group of long-term offenders. He recently told me that each Thursday, when he drives ninety minutes to the prison, is the day of the week he most looks forward to. Dave has brought dozens of released inmates into his own church. At seventy, he finds this holy habit — serving others — far more satisfying than his business.

One graduate of our worldview Centurions program, John Nunnikhoven, was busily teaching biblical worldview to a group of legislators in the Vermont capitol when a volunteer invited him to a prison. There he saw such needs, particularly of those being released, that he began bringing ex-offenders into his home. When I thanked John and his wife, Betty, they shrugged it off; it was a natural thing to do.

———

There are healthy signs that churches are getting serious about the spiritual disciplines that cultivate these holy habits. Some Catholic bishops are calling errant public officials, for example, to account for their pro-choice stands. (We need more of this in every confession.) In many churches, Alpha courses, an excellent study of the basics of the Christian faith, are springing up. Some local churches are now making discipleship mandatory. The Fellowship Bible Church in Little Rock, Arkansas, for one, requires each new member to sign a covenant, with the church's expectations for attending worship and participating in small "Discovery" study groups. Before people can become "active members" of Mariners Church in Irvine, California, they are required to sign a written agreement to abide by biblical commands about the Christian life, seek spiritual growth, and strive to fulfill one's life's mission or calling.

I have seen up close what happens when discipleship is intentionally cultivated in community. The prison units we run, known as the InnerChange Freedom Initiative, are around-the-clock, intense discipleship communities. The men and women agree to participate for eighteen months, and then another six months after their release. It is like a spiritual boot camp. They begin each morning with devotions; then they go to meals, classes, and work projects, and in late afternoon reassemble for Bible study, which in most cases goes until lights-out. There is no TV or other distractions. Some find the course so spiritually exhilarating that they have turned down parole in order to complete it. There is a strong bonding among believers in this program.

As noted, the results have been amazing: men and women coming through this program have had a recidivism rate of 8 percent after two years.[8] Every inmate, when released, is assigned a mentor, and the vast majority become members of local churches. This is a great model for the Church. It is holiness in action.

Social Holiness

Holiness doesn't stop with our own condition but carries over into actions that affect the world around us. John Wesley famously said there is no holiness apart from social holiness.[9] Many young evangelicals, including those in the emerging-church movement, are echoing this call, and they are right to do so. It's not enough to be comfortable in our gathering places of worship.

Look at the covenant with God we have entered into by virtue of our incorporation in Christ. In the Old Testament, the Lord says, "Be holy because I, the LORD your God, am holy" (Leviticus 19:2); and "I will dwell among the Israelites and be their God" (Exodus 29:45). The literal translation of "dwell" is that He "pitches His tent" among the people of Israel.

The covenant is repeated in the New Testament: John's Gospel tells us, "In the beginning was the Word ... and the Word became flesh and made his dwelling among us" (1:1, 14). Again, the literal translation is "pitched His tent among us." When God's Kingdom is established in the New Jerusalem, God promises, "Now the dwelling of God is with men, and he will live with them" (Revelation 21:3). For a third time the root meaning is "pitching a tent."

We clearly see why Peter, addressing the Church spread throughout the Mediterranean, reiterated God's first command, "Be holy because I am holy," reminding them that they were "a chosen people, a royal priesthood, a holy nation, a people belonging to God" (1 Peter 2:9). God living in our midst—how could we not be holy?

This is why the Church's mission is to make visible God's invisible Kingdom in the world. Since God lives in the midst of His people, we in turn are called to share in and reveal His loving character to our neighbors. We are to bring God's holiness to bear in every area of life. This understanding of holiness has moved Christians throughout history to some of the greatest advances in human dignity and freedom.

———

The great British parliamentarian who brought an end to the slave trade, William Wilberforce (1759–1833), was driven in that noble undertaking by his passion for holiness. He wrote about this in *Real Christianity*.* Throughout the book, Wilberforce argues for the holy, righteous life to be lived out in society. Along with other members of Wilberforce's intentional community, the "Clapham sect," Wilberforce modeled it, praying for three hours a day that justice would reign in Britain.

Early in his efforts, Wilberforce wrote in his diary that "God has laid before me two great objectives: the abolition of the slave trade, and the reformation of manners." By the latter he meant the morals of the British people. And throughout his career he pursued both

———

*The full title is A *Practical View of the Prevailing Religious System of Professed Christians in the Higher and Middle Classes in This Country Contrasted with Real Christianity*. That says it all.

goals simultaneously.[10] He realized that he needed not only to end the slave trade by law but to lead a spiritual renewal that would counter the sin motivating it.

Wilberforce's efforts at forming a new moral consensus in England accounted for the remarkable success of his movement. In 1807 the slave trade was abolished, but slavery as an institution continued. So Wilberforce kept battling to end slavery itself throughout the United Kingdom, a victory that was won in 1833, just days before his death.

———

This argument for renewal and holiness couldn't have come at a more critical time. Industrialization in the latter eighteenth and early nineteenth centuries had displaced millions from village life and left them vulnerable to exploitation. The newly wealthy factory and mine owners too often thought only of profit. The governing classes were blind to those in misery. This was Regency England, in which King George IV took legions of mistresses and the aristocracy followed his lead in dissipation and frivolity. Marital fidelity was regarded with scorn. The Anglican Church had been decimated by Enlightenment rationalism, her message reduced to a bland moralism unrelated to everyday concerns. Bishops took mistresses as perks of office.

God began to open the eyes of His people to the poor and the destitute, however, beginning in the generation before Wilberforce, with John Wesley (1703–1791) and George Whitefield (1714–1770). Both Wesley and Whitefield preached not only conversion—you must be born again—for which they are best remembered, but compassion for the disenfranchised and moral reform. Whitefield founded institutions to educate blacks and orphans in America. The Wesleyan movement aimed at a "reformation not of opinions ... but of men's tempers and lives."[11] Under their influence whole towns changed their dissolute ways.

One writer relates the story of a Durham miner who had been converted under the Wesleys. When ragged by friends as to how Jesus could turn water into wine, the miner reminded them of his family life before his conversion. "If Jesus could turn beer into provisions for his family, why should he not be able to turn water into wine?"[12]

Britain's nineteenth-century spiritual revolution may have been evangelical Christianity's finest hour, as God gathered his people into a reforming army. Following his success in abolishing the slave trade, Wilberforce took on sixty-five other causes, starting with prison reform and child labor in the coal mines. Waves of holiness swept across England as God's people, many of them ordinary Christians, unlike their unbelieving peers, put the needs of their neighbors before their own. God did nothing less than reveal the demands of social justice for an industrial age, in the process saving free market economics from its abusive tendencies and England from the violent revolutions of France and Russia. In his bestseller *God Is Not Great*, Christopher Hitchens argues religion is not good for society. Don't tell this to the freed slaves or the kids whose chains were loosened from machines.

The "reforming army" of nineteenth-century Britain culminated in William Booth's Salvation Army. Booth was an itinerant evangelist in 1865 when he came to the slums of East London. He had a frank and common way of speaking that was too fiery to be contained even within Methodist circles. When he arrived in East London, there were tens of thousands living on the streets, sleeping underneath bridges and in alley ways. Those in the ramshackle, firetrap tenements above were little better off. Everyone was in rags. Men and women and whole families survived on slices of bread and butter on the days they could find work and went without between times. There were 80,000 prostitutes in London—many of whom had been sold into the trade as young children by their families for as little as five pounds. The rich strolled through this scene of human misery as if the people were so much vermin—far less than trade animals.

After many years of working in the London slums, William Booth wrote *In Darkest England and the Way Out*, beginning with his analogy of "the cab horse ideal of existence." Every cab horse had shelter at night, food to eat, and work to do. Surely the poor deserved as much. So he came forward with his plan "to transform the living hell of the homeless into communities of self-helping, self-sustaining families."[13] The Salvation Army, drawing recruits with the clashing cymbals and beating drums of its colorful marching bands, did just that.

—

When you look at the history of these Christian awakenings and movements, you find one common denominator running through all of them. They did what they did not because it was some noble cause for society or because they believed in some social gospel or because they wanted political influence. They acted because they believed, as God's holy people, that they were called both to end systemic evil *and* reform cultural attitudes.

You'll find as well that the common denominator running through all of these efforts was a deep passion for the dignity and sanctity of every human life — the kids chained to the loading carts in the mines, the slaves crammed into the holds of ships so tight many died of suffocation, and the poor in East London who were dying wretched deaths on the streets. They were committed to the worth of every single living person, rich, poor, black, white, ill or in good health, at the beginning of life or its end.

CHAPTER 12

THE SANCTITY
OF LIFE

When Christians today see life through God's eyes, just as Wilberforce and his spiritual heirs did in the nineteenth century, we are compelled not only to care for the poor and vulnerable but to defend every human's God-given right. This is why Christians believe in the sanctity of life at every stage, from birth to death. In the Catholic view, the sanctity of human life is considered part of the Gospel itself;[1] among evangelicals it is considered integral to the Gospel.

Politicizing the Gospel—
or Believing in Life's Sanctity?

Some readers at this point are probably thinking, "Here they go again, the religious right, politicizing the Gospel." Strident voices in the culture as well as within the Church urge Christians to stay away from such divisive issues; to stop moralizing on sexual practices.[2] Conservative Christians are seen as concerned only with personal morality, issues related to the family and sexual practices, ignoring issues such as social justice, the welfare of the poor, and human rights. And daily we hear the hue and cry about conservatives wanting to "impose" their views on an unwilling society. Interestingly, that fearsome phrase originated not in response to Robertson and Falwell but goes back to the 1860 political campaign when Lincoln's opponents charged he was trying to "impose" his will upon slave holders. We can be grateful he did and freed the slave holders as well as the slaves from a morally corrupt and corrupting institution.

The simple fact is no one has the right in a free society to impose his will on anyone. All any citizen can do is contend for his point of view in the democratic process.

So Christians do not impose; they *propose* a vision of a culture of life, to educate and persuade, as a marvelous Evangelicals and Catholics Together document on life puts it, so that through "deliberation and decision: we might realize the promise of a more just and humane society, committed in life and law to honor the inestimable dignity of every human body created in the image and likeness of God."[3]

Why *should* we love our neighbor, sometimes sacrificially, if his life is not sacred? No secular philosophy has ever answered this question satisfactorily. The Christian commitment to the sanctity of life is the ground from which the Christian's love for his neighbor and community springs.

The Early Church and Its View of Life

Those who say the current abortion debate is the result of Christians plunging into politics after *Roe v. Wade* are simply ill informed about history. Sociologist Rodney Stark has traced Christian doctrine on life from the beginning of the Church, describing it as "absolutely prohibit[ing] abortion and infanticide, classifying both as murder."[4]

The Didache, a manual of Christian discipleship probably written in the first century, is unequivocal in its condemnation of pagan practices:

There are two ways [the document reads]: a way of life and a way of death. There is a great difference between them.... In accordance with the precept of the teaching, "you shall not kill," you shall not put a child to death by abortion or kill it once it is born. The way of death is this: they show no compassion for the poor, they do not suffer with the suffering, they do not acknowledge their Creator, they kill their children and by abortion cause God's creatures to perish; they drive away the needy, oppress the suffering. They are advocates of the rich and unjust judges of the poor; they are filled with every sin. May you be ever guiltless of all these sins.[5]

This Christian doctrine, "a vigorous defense of human life and care for the poor," has been consistent from the time of the Didache to today.

In his first apology, Justin Martyr, the great Church Father, put it bluntly. "We have been taught that it is wicked to expose even newly born children ... [for] we would then be murderers." To expose meant to leave a newborn child to die in the elements—a common form of infanticide.[6] The first recorded political appeal of the Church was in the second century when Athenagoras condemned abortion in a plea to the Roman Emperor Marcus Aurelius:

> We say that women who use drugs to bring on an abortion com-
> mit murder and will have to give an account to God for the abor-
> tion ... [for we] regard the very fetus in the womb as a created
> being and therefore an object of God's care ... and [we do not]
> expose an infant because those who expose them are chargeable
> with child murder.[7]

The Church's passionate engagement in politics in defense of life is not due to the emergence of the "big bad religious right," as Christianity's detractors might say (and many Christians mistakenly believe as well). It was the early Church that consistently challenged the state, describing abortion and infanticide in terms that would be politically incorrect today. The Church's defense of life unexpectedly turned out to be hugely popular in an ancient world where lions tearing people apart constituted entertainment. "Perhaps above all else," author Rodney Stark writes, "Christianity brought a new conception of humanity to a world saturated with capricious cruelty and the vicarious love of death."[8]

Christian Humanism Versus Secularism: Two Views of Humanity

But haven't medical advances changed the world utterly since the days of ancient Rome? Yes, but medical advances have only confirmed what the ancient Christians took as a matter of faith—that the essential identity of every human life remains the same from conception to death. Today, the moment when life begins is beyond reasonable dispute. At the moment of conception the genetic endowment of a human life is established. Life begins.

But people still dispute which human beings, whatever their developmental state, possess the right to life. This was certainly not a difficult question for our Founding Fathers, whose moral views were shaped by biblical revelation. They wrote, "We hold these truths to be self-evident, that all men are created equal and endowed by their Creator with certain unalienable rights, among these are *life*, liberty and the pursuit of happiness" (emphasis mine).

Whether we still believe this and are willing to accept responsibility for a child in the womb or someone whose quality of life has deteriorated dramatically depends today on our contrasting views of humanity.

The Christian View

Christians believe that men and women were created intentionally and purposefully in God's image.[9] God proves how dear men and women are to Him throughout the whole drama of human history. He acts consistently to bring the human person on whom He lavished such gifts back into relationship with Him—even sending His Son to give His life for *every* human being, even for those we ourselves hate—like mass murderers, child molesters, and terrorists. God puts no one beyond His mercy.

The Secular View

What is the alternative if the Christian view is not accepted? The secular view of humanity excludes the idea of an inherent purpose. Secularists emphasize the continuity of the evolutionary process, seeing humanity as just another example of evolution's chance handiwork, no different in kind than lice and lungfish. Since the universe came about for unknown reasons and life evolved by chance, humanity must invent its own reasons for being and the ethics by which we will govern ourselves. That means whose lives we value becomes a matter of choice.

But some argue that DNA sequencing has now discovered that the genetic makeup of humans and apes is 98.7 percent identical. So doesn't this prove evolution? Why should we consider ourselves different from the animals?[10] The DNA may be common, but the differences are vast. G. K. Chesterton once famously argued that if you look at a man and a brute you see similarities, but you also see that that which separates them is far greater than those similarities. An ape may have hands, but he does nothing with them; he can't create art or play the violin. Elephants, Chesterton observed, while their tusks are ivory, do not build colossal temples of ivory. And camels, who provide material for paintbrushes, do not paint.

And the same evidence that evolutionary scientists — some of whom are Christians — use to argue for common ancestry would point just as well to a common designer, which is entirely consistent with the biblical view and which preserves human dignity. The secular view of evolution cannot answer the question "What makes us human?"

I believe the Intelligent Design movement has provided good reasons for evolutionary theory to be reconsidered; what we have learned about DNA tells us that all of life is governed by intelligent information. But however we regard evolution, all serious Christians take issue with the secular view and affirm that God created humanity with a specific purpose in mind: that creation is intentional and cannot be random. The argument for design is clear in Scripture, which records that the "heavens declare the glory of God" (Psalm 19:1) — in other words, God has left his imprint on creation. Created by God and with His purpose for us clear, human life is sacred.

How Both Views See Body and Soul

Belief in the sanctity of life leads Christians to affirm not only the goodness of the human body but that the body and soul are one.[11] Genesis tells us that "God saw all that he had made" — including the human body — "and it was very good" (Genesis 1:31). "The glory of God is man fully alive," wrote Irenaeus, the second-century Church Father.[12] The goodness of the body is affirmed by Jesus Christ in that the Son of God came to earth in the *flesh* and was resurrected bodily from the grave.

Secularists tend to see the body, as one scholar puts it, as "the source of sinful corruption; nor is it a prison that the soul needs to escape."[13] This notion leads to the idea that the body can be separated from the true "self" and then used for the self's purposes. This common assumption, a form of dualism, is rampant in Western society. "I have the right to control my own body" is the chorus heard so often from postmodern secularists (and from some significant Supreme Court cases). But what if our bodies are one with our souls and do not belong ultimately to us but to God?

The secularist view reduces the body to a machine that's to be judged by its usefulness. The self becomes something we discover or invent. Jean-Paul Sartre, the existentialist philosopher popular on campuses in the 1960s, said, "Man is nothing else but that which he makes of himself."[14] Who we are in our bodies has nothing to do with it.

This dualism persists because it allows us to regard our bodies as instruments of pleasure. While young and vigorous, our bodies serve as our slaves, accumulating experiences of all sorts that we foolishly expect will leave our characters essentially unaffected. Once we grow old, find ourselves in constant pain, or suffer devastating bodily injury and our bodies cease to be a source of pleasure, we claim the right to discard them through "assisted suicide" or euthanasia. People say that what they do with their bodies is a private matter with no public consequences.

It's a short step from there, at least logically, for the powerful to say that people whose bodies are of no use to them or society should be discarded. These people's bodies are merely machines, after all, which are broken. The right to die becomes the duty to die.

In Pursuit of the Social Good

Secularist humanists, some decades ago, declared man to be the supreme being in the universe; "all thought begins with humans, not God; nature, not deity," so says Humanist Manifesto II. Having crossed this great divide, secularists found themselves obliged to produce an earthly utopia according to their own lights.

But if, as Sartre argued, there's no God and no objective basis for determining human nature, how can we know what's in people's best interests? What would utopia look like? The great thinkers of secularism, Rousseau, Freud, Marx, and others, all fashioned their own visions of manmade (and imposed) utopias. The twentieth century ended littered with the wreckage of every vain scheme that man could possibly conceive. Blood ran red from the Killing Fields of Cambodia to the gulags of the Soviet Union to the death chambers of the Nazis. Every promise of utopian salvation led to human catastrophe.

The secularist may genuinely believe that he loves his neighbor, but in the end he may love him so much that he decides to put him out of his misery. Without a biblically based set of ethics rooted in the sanctity of life, without the established natural order clearly expressed in law and practice, we are left to the tender mercies of those in authority. And we embrace that at our certain peril.

Contrast this with the Christian view in which love for neighbor begins with respect for the neighbor's right to life; that is, to exist. The ECT document reads:

> We propose a deeper and richer humanism that is firmly grounded in the bedrock of scriptural truth, that is elaborated in the history of Christian thought, that is in accord with clear reason, that honors the best in our civilization's tradition, and that holds the promise of a future more worthy of the dignity of the human person who is the object of God's infinite love and care.

This understanding of humanism is why Christians have historically been and are still today in the vanguard of human rights crusades.

Christian Humanism in Defense of All Human Rights

The popular atheist Christopher Hitchens says that the New Testament favors slavery and that the Church was totally supportive of slavery until it became unprofitable.[15] He completely ignores Wilberforce and his colleagues, engaging in bald-faced revisionism. From its beginning in the Roman Empire, Christianity has been countercultural in defending life. Although slavery was a generally accepted practice in the Greek and Roman cultures of the time, the apostle Paul, writing to the early Church, declared that "there is neither Jew nor Greek, slave nor free, male nor female, for you are all one in Christ Jesus" (Galatians 3:28). This planted a seed of sedition into Western culture.

It's true that some Christians have been hypocritical about slavery, condoning it for too long. The record of the Church is not without blemish. But the fact is that the writers of the New Testament, while acknowledging the reality of slavery, never embraced it. Paul included "slave traders" in identifying lawbreakers (1 Timothy 1:10). Indeed, one of Paul's most moving letters was to Philemon, in which he pleaded with him to take back a former slave, Onesimus. Having been a prisoner with Paul, Onesimus was now to be "no longer … a slave, but better than a slave, … a dear brother" (Philemon 1:16).

Stark has documented that as early as the third century, "a universalistic conception of humanity" was embraced by the Church. In the eleventh century, St. Wulfstan and Bishop Anselm sought to remove slavery from Christian culture entirely. "No man, no real Christian at any rate," writes scholar Marc Bloch, "could thereafter legitimately be held as the property of another."[16]

While the theological question was settled, it was centuries before abolition could be realized in practice. But the Church kept fighting the issue. When Spanish and Portuguese traders brought slavery to South America in the sixteenth century, Pope Paul III issued three papal bulls, or edicts, against the practice, demanding that the Indians native to South America "should not be deprived of their liberty or their possessions … and are not to be reduced to slavery."[17] To enforce his decree, a subsequent ruling was issued, decreeing excommunication for anyone engaging in slavery.[18] In the seventeenth century, Pope Urban VIII reaffirmed the earlier edicts, cracking down again on the practices of slavers. In the early nineteenth century, as the Spanish empire retreated and liberation came to South America, so did emancipation. And as we have seen, the story of Wilberforce and the ending of the slave trade in Britain is one of the great heroic chapters in Christian history. Lloyd Garrison, Lewis Tappan, and innumerable other Christians led the fight against slavery in America as well. One only needs to read Martin Luther King's "Letter from a Birmingham Jail" to see that his Christian faith was at the heart of his crusade.

The radical Christian commitment to equality revolutionized the status of women as well, who in prebiblical times were regarded, as they are in Islam today, as inferior to men. The early Church spread fastest among women because the Church offered them protection against abuse and exploitation that they could find nowhere else. The Church denounced divorce, incest, marital infidelity, and polygamy while these were practiced, much to women's detriment, in the surrounding cultures. The Church taught that "fidelity without divorce was expected of every Christian."[19]

And the Church also expanded most quickly among women because of the Christian teachings against abortion and infanticide. Christian families welcomed all the female children God gave them, while the Romans — as in China, India, and other parts of the world today — employed abortion and infanticide to produce more male workers and warriors than "burdensome" women.

In the light of this, it is not hard to understand why Christians were in the vanguard of movements for women's liberation, including the suffrage movement in the United States, led by such active Christians as Antoinette Blackwell, Lucretia Mott, and Anna Howard, all three ordained ministers; the former slave Sojourner Truth and, of course, Susan B. Anthony.

Today Christians are no less determined. Christian political activists led the successful efforts to free Christians taken as slaves by the Muslim government in Sudan. These same activists enlisted President Bush to lead the campaign against worldwide sexual trafficking. Legislation was passed in the United States and some European nations, and U.N. resolutions were finally adopted. Many Christians as well are working to combat AIDS in Africa and end religious persecution in North Korea and elsewhere.

A *New York Times* reporter visited my office when President Bush spoke on sexual trafficking to the UN, inquiring why Christians were involved with human rights. It was amusing to watch this reporter become flustered and almost annoyed as her stereotypical view that Christians are only concerned about abortion and "gay" rights was shattered. The resulting front-page story in the *New York Times* had an almost man-bites-dog character.

This is why I have spent the last thirty-four years taking the Gospel to the most forgotten people in our society, prisoners. Over that time I've discovered that every one of them—black, white, rich, or poor—is an image-bearer of the God I worship and thus is worthy of loving care. Only a humanism rooted in the Christian view of life causes men and women to care for, let alone sacrifice for, those who are a burden to society.

What about the Real World?

Belief in the sanctity of life may be fine as an ideal, many will say, but there are real-world problems that demand exceptions. It's hardly compassionate to bring millions of unwanted children into the impoverished nations of the world where they will experience hunger and be afflicted with disease from the moments of their births to their premature deaths. There are genetic "defects" that can now be detected in the womb that condemn children to lives of misery. Why should we be obliged to perpetuate their lives through modern medicine when nature has so clearly decided against them? And there are many less extreme but still difficult situations in which reasonable people believe the termination of a pregnancy or the practice of euthanasia offers the only way out. What about the promising, bright fifteen-year-old girl whose pimply-faced boyfriend as much as forces himself upon her in one overheated backseat encounter? Why should that young woman and her family's hopes and dreams be dashed unnecessarily?

Many Christians think this way; our secular neighbors generally all do. So many people, in fact, that even if the U.S. Supreme Court were to return the abortion issue to the states, half would vote to legalize it. Even many Christians have succumbed to a "lesser of two evils" mentality. After all, this world is hard—it truly is—and the prospect of avoiding what we fear may well be an overwhelming responsibility has a strong appeal.

———

I thought about this appeal when I visited my daughter, Emily, in Massachusetts. One Sunday afternoon we attended a special-needs basketball game in which Max, my autistic grandson, was participating. The game was in an elementary school on a tree-lined suburban road. The school itself was red brick, with white casement windows to each side of a main entrance, a small bell tower, and a steeply pitched roof—the epitome of New England architecture. But the gymnasium had been added on. It looked like a big sandy-beige concrete-block cube. I could see horizontal slit windows high up on the walls that would let in the only natural light. I thought it would be dreary inside.

But inside it was anything but dreary. There were about thirty children in attendance who suffered from autism, Down syndrome, cerebral palsy, or other conditions. Almost an equal number of parents and high-school-student volunteers had shown up as well so that each youth or child had his or her own caregiver. A coach, with a whistle around his neck, was backed by several strong assistants. Not one kid among the thirty could fully manage for himself or herself. One of the boys, who looked to be in his midtwenties, was helped onto the court by his middle-aged mother, who had a craggy, New England look but a warm smile. She held on to her son, keeping him drawn up with a tight grip on his jacket, in order for him to stand. He wasn't able to speak but evidently communicated well enough with his mother through his eyes. They both seemed equally glad to be there. The parents and volunteers were excited to see how eager the kids were to play.

After everyone had dribbled and thrown the balls about for a while, the group assembled for a prescribed warm-up. They formed a big circle around one of the baskets and every participant took a turn shooting baskets until he or she made one. A few scored on their first shot. Max was actually one of the more functional kids, although his first couple of shots missed wildly before he sank one. Most of the kids had to take five or six or as many as ten shots. Every time a participant scored, a look of pure joy appeared on his face and on the volunteers' faces and the family's. There was tremendous enthusiasm with whoops and hollers at every basket.

I worried when it was the turn of the young man whose mother had to help him stand. Another volunteer came over, got his hands on the ball, and then together they made a great sweeping gesture and let the ball fly. This young man got so excited when he saw the ball go into the air and swish through the hoop that he just beamed. And so did his mother.

Then they had a game. Half the kids composed one team and the other half their opponents. No one was allowed to interfere with anyone who had the ball. The coach, his assistants, and some of the volunteers now turned into helping-hand referees, supervising the kids as they dribbled, passed, and took the ball up and down the court the best they could. When they dribbled up to one of the baskets, the person with the ball shot, and then the others jumped for it. If a team member came up with the ball, he shot again, unimpeded, and if a member of the opposition came up with the ball, the journey down to the other end began. It was well organized and exciting for the kids.

After the game, the mother who had to help her son stand was about to leave a bag behind when Emily noticed it and brought it to her. It was filled with diapers. Imagine being the mother of a twenty-year-old whose diapers still need changing. I wondered whether I could ever summon the stamina and grace these kids demand of a parent. My daughter will tell you, however, that Max is the greatest blessing in her life. What occurred to me that day, though, was that all of these parents, as well as the coach and volunteers, displayed a love that was utterly missing in most of society today. Their reaction to the situation was, indeed, the exact opposite of what one might expect. They were the happiest group of people I had met in a long time.

Why were they so happy when so many others in Western society who live privileged lives, utterly free of such cares, are so miserable?

It's because, whether they know it or not, they are doing God's work. It's not that autism or Down syndrome or cerebral palsy are good things; they are consequences of the fall. It's not that raising such children or caring for the hungry in distant lands or becoming the unsuspecting grandparent of a fifteen-year-old daughter's child doesn't entail incredible sacrifice.

But when I reflect on the joy in that gym, I realize God gives a special anointing to those who care for others — even to those who don't believe in the God who is blessing their actions. The disabled and the poor end up being God's gifts to us, for they present opportunities to serve our common Creator, who has fashioned each of us in His image. As Mother Teresa said, "The poor, in whatever part of the world they are to be found, are the suffering Christ. In them, lives and dies, the Son of God. Through them, God shows us His face."[20]

I was left that day with two other thoughts. The greatest advocate in our day for utilitarian ethics, Professor Peter Singer, argues for infanticide and euthanasia as good things, since they free resources to maximize the happiness of the majority. And if life has no inherent worth, he's logically correct. So why don't we get rid of these burdensome kids? Because the truth about life is understood — the *imago Dei* is in us, even when we don't want to acknowledge it.

Also, how could anyone watch that game and still believe that Darwin's theory of natural selection is correct? According to his theory, natural processes would have selected out those characteristics which do not strengthen us in our struggle to live. In other words, the strong would eliminate the weak. But why hasn't that happened? It's because of what Darwin and his defenders could never understand — human kindness and altruism. Darwin's defenders would deny us the blessing of caring for people like Max and those who played basketball that day. It's not a burden, thank you. It's a joy.

The Modern Dilemma and the Abilities of Man

Many Catholics, Protestants, and Orthodox have argued that we are in a great struggle that pits a culture of life against a culture of death.

This is, in fact, the preeminent form the battle of good versus evil has taken in our day — as it did in the early days of the Church. This may sound inflammatory and extreme to some, but what could be more crucial than whether the worth of a life comes from being created in the image of God or from its usefulness to society?

Today the nature of the debate over human life is changing. Just consider the implications of the incredible technological advances we have made in genetic engineering in recent years. In the next decades we will likely master techniques of engineering human development. There is talk today of discovering the "crime gene" that causes a person to engage in antisocial behavior. Could we engineer such a gene out of the human makeup? Should we? Or a cancer gene? What will keep totalitarian governments, like the one in Aldous Huxley's *Brave New World*, from producing a class of slaves?

Today children can originate in petri dishes, sperm are implanted so that lesbian couples can raise children, and human embryos are being destroyed for research purposes. Huxley's world where humans are created on assembly lines of bubbling glass vials draws ever closer, enabling us to make children in our image. Fetal farms have been proposed where clones will be raised to produce replacement body parts. We are openly discussing creating life in test tubes and engineering human robots.[21]

C. S. Lewis said when we reach this point, as the designers of future generations, we will become the victims, the slaves, of our technological successes.[22] We will tell ourselves that we conquered the limitations of human nature while we will actually become the products of the worst in human nature — the desire to play God.[23] We will destroy humanity itself by ensuring that future generations will be ruled by our out-of-control appetites.

If humankind is not to bring about its own abolition, the destruction of its nature, Christians will have to persuade their neighbors that we should *not* employ various technologies simply because they exist. This type of debate has already begun with in vitro fertilization and stem cell research. And many other issues will arise, particularly in relation to "designer children."

We see other deeply troubling signs today. We no longer see children as gifts from God; we see them more often as commodities, something that we are "entitled to" simply because we exist. We decide to have children or not on the basis of whether they will enhance our lives. We evaluate pregnancies according to their potential to produce "good outcomes." When abortions are botched and "wrongful births" occur, people sue, the grounds being that "my life" has been adversely affected. What about the life of the child? Who thinks of that? As a result, the birth replacement rate in the most advanced nations is declining dangerously as people in affluent cultures want to live unencumbered (child-free) lives. We are endangering our own species.

———

This is why Evangelicals and Catholics Together, in perhaps its finest document, argues that "Christians who support the legal license to kill the innocent [must] consider whether they have not set themselves against the will of God and, to that extent, separated themselves from the company of Christian discipleship."[24] That is a tough statement, but this issue separates true Christians from those who are simply along for the ride.

Christians propose to society a biblical humanism "deeply grounded in the dignity of the human person at every stage of development, disadvantage, or decline." It would be difficult to find a more effective answer to the encroaching culture of death than the love and justice of God.

CHAPTER 13

LAST THINGS

Christians believe that Christ will come back. But this time He will return in glory and power, to judge the living and the dead and to make all things new. The Kingdom of God that we know now in Christ and His Church will then be finally established.

We cannot fully understand this—we see now only dimly—but Christ's postresurrection appearances and the Scriptures provide fascinating glimpses of what will happen when we are resurrected and reign with God forever. This is Christianity's ultimate hope and promise.

But is it only a hope, only a dream? What signs are there that God intends something more for us, as individuals and collectively, than mere death and extinction?

Justice:
A First Sign of Our Eternal Destiny

One of my visits to death row caused me to think about justice and its relationship to the afterlife. On Good Friday 1981, I was in Menard, Illinois, at a huge and dreary high-walled maximum security prison there. After addressing the prisoners as a group, I visited the segregation units.

On this occasion I was able to visit several Christians on death row. I had a worshipful time, particularly with a former Satanist who had brutally massacred innocent people and was deeply repentant. He knew he was going to die and was fully prepared for it, almost relieved.

Before I left death row, I was told that John Wayne Gacy, the man who had sexually abused and then murdered thirty-three young men, burying them around his home, was asking to see me. I agreed. After ten or fifteen minutes, two guards led Gacy into the room. His arms were shackled at the wrists to the chain around his waist, and his legs were in irons that barely allowed him to shuffle forward.

Gacy had been tried in February 1980. He pleaded not guilty by reason of insanity—a plea that was rejected. On March 13 he was convicted and sentenced to death.

Repulsed by the evil acts that Gacy had committed, I was not eager to meet him. As he was seated in a straight-backed chair opposite me, I found myself startled at his appearance. Unlike many of the murderers and violent criminals I've met, he was not tattooed, muscular, and brutish. He might well have been an accountant or vice president of a community bank; he was middle-aged, with a genial smile and well-brushed graying hair. He looked harmless and would easily have blended into a crowd of suburbanites—again, evil comes in ordinary packages.

In conversation he was intelligent and articulate, but also defiant. "I am a Christian," he told me, "and I have a right to see you on Good Friday!"

Gacy then professed his innocence, over and over. He did not deserve to be on death row, he insisted. I expected to be uncomfortable in Gacy's presence—what kind of terrible, sick, depraved person finds pleasure in sexually molesting boys, carving them up, and burying them in his basement? But as he talked, that wasn't what made me uncomfortable. Rather, it was that he looked so incredibly ordinary. I realized that there's something of John Wayne Gacy in all of us, as the Scriptures plainly teach.

Gacy's case raised a question that was personally uncomfortable because I was opposed to capital punishment. But how could there ever be justice, I asked myself, if a man like Gacy were to be sentenced only to life in prison? How could the parents of the young men he had abused then brutally killed ever feel that their sons' loss had been appropriately punished? Gacy was utterly unrepentant, still rationalizing his actions. But he knew what he had done; the insanity defenses failed. He was, in short, purely evil. So what did justice demand in his case?

Justice: Balancing the Scales

I couldn't get John Wayne Gacy out of my mind over the next several months. At the urging of one of my assistants, I started rereading the arguments for and against capital punishment. I'd always been against it, first because there's absolutely no evidence that it's a deterrent (except of course for the person executed). And second, having practiced law, I knew that the law is not infallible and could execute an innocent man. I agreed with Blackstone's ratio: better that ten guilty persons escape than that one innocent person suffer.

In the course of my study I reread C. S. Lewis's brilliant essay "The Humanitarian Theory of Punishment." Lewis rejects the rehabilitative model of justice on the grounds that crime is to be punished, not cured. Lewis feared the white-coated doctor who means to cure our abnormalities. Lewis argued that punishment was a matter of "just deserts," that the scales of justice must be balanced.

Carrying Lewis's argument to its logical conclusion, I began to see that there could be no punishment commensurate with the kind of crime that John Wayne Gacy committed, other than taking his life. Some believers argue, of course, that Christians should have a consistent ethic of life, protecting life not only in the womb but even in a serial killer. But there's a difference between taking an innocent life and a murderer's.

My study of the Bible eventually led me to conclude — albeit reluctantly — that capital punishment is warranted in limited cases *because of* the sanctity of life. How else might the true importance of the lives taken by someone like Gacy be acknowledged? How else could the scales be even remotely balanced? The Old Testament law, the *lex talionis*, "an eye for an eye," did not authorize revenge but decreed that the punishment should be commensurate with the offense (Genesis 9:6; Leviticus 24:20) — no more than the offense, but no less, if the standard of justice demands it.[1] Thanks to John Wayne Gacy, and to C. S. Lewis, I came to realize that if the scales of justice could not be balanced otherwise, then capital punishment must necessarily, if reluctantly, be carried out.

Whatever we believe about capital punishment—and good, faithful Bible-believing Christians come down on both sides—my experience with Gacy underscores what all of us share—a deeply ingrained sense that the scales must be balanced, that wrongs must somehow be righted. Christians believe this sense of justice arises from being made in God's image. As creatures of a just and loving Creator we long to see His character reflected in the world about us, if not always in our own actions. The moral law is written on our hearts (Romans 2:15).

We cry out for the demands of justice to be satisfied, and we even sense that they will be someday. Many consider this hunger for justice persuasive evidence of God's existence and His final balancing of accounts in the afterlife.[2] If the world were truly a random place, guided by no design or purpose, why would believers and nonbelievers alike have this sense of justice and look forward to its realization, in this life and eternity as well? This is why nearly every religion has embraced some form of judgment in the afterlife. Christianity confirms that our longing for the wicked to be punished and the good rewarded will on judgment day be fulfilled.

Justice: To Each His Due

Different aspects of justice testify to our need for God's redemption and its fulfillment in eternity. Besides a balancing of the scales, which is retributive justice, punishing wrongdoers, we also have a sense that life should have an essential fairness and equality of opportunity, a level playing field it often lacks. Ancient Greeks, when asked what they considered the most important question for any society, "What is justice?" arrived at a shorthand answer: "Justice is giving each person his or her due."

From the beginning, "giving each person his or her due" meant administering punishment to those who deserved it—*retributive* justice. But the Bible also instructed the Israelites to leave the gleanings of the field to the poor and to care for the needy. In fact, the prophets make caring for the poor a chief standard by which the nation will be judged. In modern times, following these principles, we have gained a greater sense that each person should be afforded similar opportunities and enough resources to make use of them. So under Christian influence, Western society evolved more and more in the direction of *distributive justice*—that is, seeing that needs receive equal treatment. Universal education, for instance, largely emerged out of Christianity's concern for the poor and the dignity of every person.

Most of the demands of distributive, or as it is often called, social justice are found in Scripture: demands for honest dealings in business, the use of just scales, and fair pay for workers. Scripture even calls for Jubilee years in which debts are forgiven.* Remember, too, the model in Acts 4 of the early Church, where each believer shared with the brothers and sisters in the community. Everyone's needs were met, but not because of a novel utopian economic theory like socialism; the Church was enacting, as far as it was capable, the distributive model of justice the Church foresaw would be realized in God's Kingdom. (Remember, this is the church doing it, not government—though both can play a role.)

Even with our best efforts, distributive justice applies unevenly. If I'd been born in another country, for example, I would probably not have had the education and advantages I've enjoyed throughout my life. Does the success I've had mean that I've been more virtuous or had more favor from God? Of course not. I've spent my life among the poorest of the poor in our society and have met few who've had the same chances in life I did.

And all of us could present examples of good people who die young while evil people live long and successful lives. How could we possibly live with the unfairness of this world if we did not have a belief that at some point the accounts will be reckoned? The nonbeliever has to chalk this up to the spin of the wheel and futile human remedies. But the believer, who trusts in a loving God, knows all believers have the same ultimate hope.

---

*By God's people, not the government. There can be no social justice without respect for human responsibility, which is why I am for safety nets but against the nanny welfare state.

Biblical Justice: "Shalom"

This world is out of kilter, with nations at war, violence rife even in stable societies, and nature herself the cause of catastrophe. We also see that our best models of justice fail when applied in a sinful world. The distributive model gave us the Great Society and the loss of individual responsibility. And the retributive model has filled our prisons without making our streets any safer. The best utopian solutions are doomed in a fallen world.

The biblical model gives us a clear sense of justice to come. While it embraces both the retributive and distributive models, it goes beyond both. It gives us a sign of the Kingdom to come by seeking to restore the order that pertained in the Garden of Eden. This is what we mean when we use the Old Testament word *shalom*. That word, so blithely used as a greeting, is translated in the Old Testament as "peace." But shalom means much more than the absence of hostility; it means concord and harmony in society. Shalom means creating a society in which there can be human flourishing, in which people can both do good and live well. Shalom addresses itself to the injustice of human society and nature's disorder and decay. Christ gives us His shalom to live with a measure of the blessedness or divine happiness that we will one day know fully when He returns to reign forever.

The biblical view of justice: help for the poor, punishment for the unjust, and shalom, signaling that the reign of sin will end and the Kingdom of God will come in its fullness. Our desire for justice is a sign of our eternal destiny. And the biblical model offers the only truly hopeful answers to the innate human desire for immortality.

Love:
A Second Sign of Our Eternal Destiny

Just as the desire for justice points to our eternal destiny, so too does the love we experience, as in the case of our families and friendships. Love always envisions a limitless future. Saying "I will love you *forever*" comes as naturally to lovers as breathing. Like most family men, I love my wife and children so deeply—sometimes with the most exquisite delight—that I care for them every moment and enjoy their company whenever possible. I pray fervently for them, as I did especially when my eldest son and my daughter were battling cancer at the same time.

But what happens if you lose a loved one? If death brought down the curtain forever, then our love for others would be a cruel joke, a passing feeling with no ultimate meaning. Death and its eternal separation from everything we've given, nurtured, endured, created, and enjoyed with those we love would cause horrific despair. When in love, even atheists act as if they believe in immortality.

Does anyone really believe that life is such a cruel hoax? The philosopher Albert Camus faced life's possible absurdity without God and determined that the first philosophical question anyone should ask is whether to commit suicide. Most do not face the question so starkly. Our common intuition that life and love must endure somehow serves as a working principle.

But is it possible that cold, impersonal nature created us and evolved such intimate feelings in us only to let us down in abject despair? Or is it more likely that God made us with an intense love for others that would help turn us, finally, toward our common Creator?

The Christian hope of immortality addresses—as no other religion does—what we cherish so much about human relationships. Christianity does not teach that at death our souls are reunited with an infinite, impersonal oneness, as in Buddhism, Taoism, and New Age beliefs. Neither does it allow, as in Hinduism, for reincarnation, when we will be punished in the next life for sins committed in this one, nor that our souls remain in a disembodied state, as in animism, paganism, and Platonism. Rather, Christians believe in bodily resurrection.[3]

The disciples could not contain the good news of the resurrection because it meant they had Jesus Christ back—for now and eternity. And Christ's resurrection meant that they—and we—will have believing wives and children back someday, as well as Christian friends and all those who long for this grand reunion.[4] It means we will experience the justice we long for. The resurrection is what Christianity is all about! Not life floating on a cloud, but the hard embrace of your living, breathing son or daughter as tears start to fill your eyes in gratitude. The resurrection caused the apostle Paul to say, "Where, O death, is your victory? Where, O death, is your sting?" (1 Corinthians 15:55).

Death:
A Look at Our Eternal Destiny

"Man is destined to die once," the Scriptures tell us, "and after that to face judgment" (Hebrews 9:27). Christians believe that immediately after death the person comes into God's presence and is judged as to whether he has accepted Christ's offer of salvation or rejected it. Jesus tells the good thief on the cross next to him, "Today you will be with me in paradise." This is usually called the "particular judgment" to distinguish it from the "general judgment" that will occur following Christ's second coming. The bodies of those who die in God's grace and friendship rest, awaiting Christ's return and our resurrection,[5] while we enjoy the continuous, active love relationship of Father, Son, and Holy Spirit. Those who do not die in God's grace are separated from God.

I imagine some readers have started bracing themselves: "Here comes the hellfire and brimstone stuff," they are thinking. "God wouldn't send anyone to hell. This is just scare talk on the part of Christians that reeks of fanaticism."

Well, people raising that objection are quite right. A loving God wouldn't send anyone to hell and He doesn't. He doesn't want "anyone to perish, but everyone to come to repentance" (2 Peter 3:9). He promises that every individual who comes to Him in genuine faith and repents of his sins will be saved and spend eternity with God.

But God gives each person a free will. Reluctantly, He respects the choice the person makes to remain alienated from Him while alive. He doesn't send the unrepentant person to hell; the unrepentant person chooses it.

What is hell like? It's a real place, and its chief punishment is eternal separation from God. The biblical images for hell, such as the lake of fire, are meant to wake us up to what an excruciatingly painful fate that will be.

Life's separations tell us something about what this will mean. When I was an eager young Marine officer, I contracted a strange form of hives that appeared to be an allergy to the underbrush at Camp Lejeune, North Carolina. I was treated repeatedly. On the final occasion the doctor said to me that if this persisted I'd have to be discharged from the Marines. It was a dreadful moment, as I faced the prospect of being "drummed out" of the Corps. To my great relief, the hives left and never returned. And I continued in my patriotic journey.

Many years later, I was indicted for my role in Watergate. Far more difficult than going to prison was to stand in the courtroom and hear the clerk read "The United States of America v. Charles W. Colson." The scars from that wound remain to this day. To be told that your country or your friends are casting you out creates unspeakable shame. How would it be to hear God say not, "Well done good and faithful servant," but, "Depart from me"?

Those Who Have Never Heard the Message

But what, you may ask, about those who have never heard the Gospel, who are ignorant of God and His commandments?

First, no one is entirely ignorant, that is, in the sense of *not knowing about* God: God reveals Himself by common grace through creation and conscience. As Paul writes, "For since the creation of the world God's invisible qualities—his eternal power and divine nature—have been clearly seen, being understood from what has been made, so that men are without excuse" (Romans 1:20). All people have some sense or awareness of God; there has never been a society of people in any setting without some form of religion, some means for seeking contact with God.

And yet, Paul talked about what he called the times of "ignorance" (Acts 17:30), that is, the times in which people pursued the knowledge of God wrongly or in vain and futile ways (Acts 17:23–29). Before the coming of Jesus Christ countless millions sought to know

God, following in good faith the dictates of tradition and culture, according to their inherited forms and rituals of religion. But there is good news about these times of ignorance.

First, it has pleased God to "overlook" the ignorance of those who have sought to know God in ways other than what He Himself reveals (Acts 17:30). That word, "overlook," is a most generous and mysterious word. We know God is good; God is just; God is merciful. He will do what is good, just, and merciful concerning all those who have never heard the Good News of Jesus Christ. (And, as we read in Romans 1:8, God's judgment is against those who, knowing the truth, still reject it.)

The second part of the Good News concerning those who dwell in the times of ignorance is that they don't have to be ignorant any longer! Now, Paul says, since the days of Jesus, God has been busy sending messengers to all the world to tell the Good News that He can be known, that He desires us to know Him, and that Jesus Christ is the One through whom we may enter into the knowledge of God which is eternal life (John 17:3).

Over the years, in many Christian communities, devoted teachers and theologians have taught that those who have not heard the message of Jesus Christ will be held accountable for the fullest extent of their knowledge and for the genuineness with which they seek to know God. At the same time, no one comes to the Father but through faith in Christ. Christ's redemption of creation and humankind opens the doors of God's Kingdom to those who have believed the Gospel.

So, while Scripture isn't entirely clear about how truth becomes known to people who have not heard the Gospel, and how God's perfect justice and mercy will apply to them, believers trust in the goodness and mercy of God and, obedient to His command, are calling all people everywhere to repent and believe the Good News of Jesus Christ (Acts 17:30). As the book of Job says, "It is unthinkable that God would do wrong, that the Almighty would pervert justice" (34:12).

The End of History

Science has confirmed what the Scriptures teach, that history will end. In 1929 the American astronomer Edwin Powell Hubble concluded the universe was expanding due to his observations of the "red shift," the increase in wavelengths of light returning to us from distant galaxies. This meant that the universe is not eternal; it has a beginning, in what we now call the Big Bang, and there are signs that the universe is experiencing entropy, a winding down just as it was once wound up. One day it will end.

History will not end when humanity reaches utopian goals, as some speculated in the 1990s,[6] but when Christ returns in glory at the second coming. As C. S. Lewis says, the author of history, like the producer of a play, will step onto the stage, bringing down the curtain.

There's probably no subject in history that has consumed more time, attention, and speculation than how this will happen. Christians disagree about events associated with the second coming, particularly the millennium—a thousand-year period of peace and prosperity. Evangelicals are especially fascinated with riddling out the figurative passages of Scripture that describe the end times, the Apocalypse, and the return of Christ.[7]

No one knows the hour or the season when Christ will return, but there are signs of the providential direction of history. Many scholars agree that the return of the Jews to their homeland is a crucial sign of the fulfillment of the eschatological promise; an even more particular sign would be recognition of Jesus as the Messiah by many among God's chosen people. So depending on one's perspective, the place of Israel and our support for it becomes critical. "I will bless those who bless you, and whoever curses you I will curse; and all the people on earth will be blessed through you" (Genesis 12:3). That verse applies to the Jews. This is why the Christian community should be unfailingly supportive of them, although that doesn't mean turning a blind eye to the state of Israel's political failings.

Still, because no one knows the time of Christ's return, prophecy must not be used as a wedge to divide Christians. The important thing to remember is what all true Christians confess—that Christ *will* return. I have my own convictions about how and when, which are mainstream evangelical, but I respect others who think differently. Different perspectives should never divide the body, which is why Luther, Calvin, and St. Augustine all disapproved of the kind of speculation that many engage in today.

Once, as a probably legendary story goes, St. Francis was weeding his garden when a visitor asked, "What would you do if you knew the world would end tomorrow?"

St. Francis replied, "I would finish weeding the garden."

This holy man knew that he was at his post, doing what God had called him to do at that moment. We too should live our lives in the same humble expectation. Everything we do should be done to God's glory so that we will be prepared at any moment for Christ's return, which will happen unexpectedly, He tells us, like a thief in the night.

Jesus Will Judge the Living and the Dead

All Christians believe that there will be a last judgment that will follow the second coming. When Christ comes again, the souls of those who have died in Christ will return from paradise to receive their incorruptible bodies, and living believers will be similarly transformed. The Athanasian Creed summarizes biblical teaching by saying that at the coming of Christ all men shall rise again "and shall give an account for their own works."

There would not be the justice we all long for if God, the Perfect Judge, did not reward *and* punish. We would expect John Wayne Gacy and Mother Teresa to each be judged differently.

Even for believers, there will be judgment. Remember that Christ warned the Pharisees that we will stand before the King and be judged by whether we fed Him when He was hungry, gave Him drink when He was thirsty, extended Him hospitality when a stranger, clothed Him when He was naked, cared for Him and visited Him in prison. When did we do these things for you, Lord, the people will ask. His reply, "Whatever you did for one of the least of these brothers of mine, you did for me" (Matthew 25:40). (Or as He later points out, what you did not do, you did not do for Him [25:45].) We are saved by our faith alone, but we will be judged by how we have extended God's graces to others. The universal call to holiness we wrote of earlier has eternal consequences (Romans 14:12).

When Jesus comes again, the world will be created anew. God's purposes must prevail in the end. Jesus Christ will come and reign supreme over everything. And then, as Scripture promises, all things will be brought into subjection to Him, and God will become all in all.

"In a flash, in the twinkling of an eye, at the last trumpet ... the dead will be raised imperishable, and we will be changed" (1 Corinthians 15:52).

CHAPTER 14

THE JOY
OF ORTHODOXY

True Christians understand that the faith was given once for all and is filled with life and excitement.

As you have seen in these chapters, true Christianity is a logical and coherent explanation of reality. It begins with the rational premise *God is*. And He's told us how His world works. He is the ultimate reality. Why then is there suffering? Because God gave humans free will. We chose not to obey, so evil came to the world. Satan's control didn't stand, however. God invaded earth in His Son. The battle raged, and the Son was arrested and executed, as the payment for evil. But the stone was rolled away, and God raised Him from the dead, and with His resurrection guaranteed our own new life. The Holy Spirit was sent to finish the invasion, establishing Christ's Kingdom through His body, the Church.

We can now exchange our lives for Christ's life. Reconciled with Him, we are reconciled with each other, living a holy life in community, defending life at every stage. One day Christ will come again and finally establish God's Kingdom. All those in Christ will enjoy God's fellowship eternally, as humankind was meant to from the beginning.

So how in the world do so many people these days talk about the Christian faith and its doctrines as being dry and brittle? You may say it's frightening, upsetting, life-changing, radical, extreme — but dull and boring, never. Yet that's what some are saying. How can this be?

One answer is found in the Church's failure to teach what the faith is. Shouldn't we hear Christianity described as a new Kingdom, an overarching way to see all of life, a worldview, the rule of God? Instead we hear shallow therapeutic messages or messianic political messages. People sit like dead weights in their pews, waiting to be entertained or told how to vote.

Second, we have become so self-absorbed, self-indulgent, and materialistic that we're blind to what makes life worth living. Americans are weighted down by credit-card debt or college tuition expenditures or the desire for a new car — or the new suit that already doesn't quite fit. According to one survey, we are the unhappiest nation on earth, with more mental disorders and depression per capita than any other country. Interestingly, by the same measure Nigeria is considered the happiest. If you were to contrast Lagos, Nigeria, with any major Western city, you'd wonder why.[1]

But if you go to worship services in Third World countries, you'll discover the tremendous joy of orthodoxy, which beats visiting the mall or chasing a golf ball any day. The most meaningful church experiences I've had have been either in prisons or in the Third World, sometimes under incredibly difficult conditions. Why? The people are excited because they have no false idols, no distractions, and they get the message of the new Kingdom.

Third, many Westerners today, I believe, are intimidated by cultural pressures. We certainly don't want to seem too extreme or talk with our secular neighbors about something as outrageous as the bodily resurrection or the parting of the Red Sea. Who wants to tell a sophisticated neighbor who got an advanced degree from Harvard that you really believe that God spoke the world into existence?

The Gospel can be upsetting. The first person who ever witnessed to me was Tom Phillips, a senior executive and, at the time, a client of mine. Tom is a shy, gentle man by nature. But I can remember to this day the words he spoke: "I have accepted Jesus Christ and committed my life to Him." He was so uncomfortable he didn't look me straight in the eye when he spoke; he was looking at the clock on the wall. He later told me that he had prayed the night before that he would have the courage to do it; God, he believed, told him, "Tell Chuck

Colson about me. He needs a friend." His words were upsetting—and exactly what I needed.

Yes, there is a risk, but don't let it stop you. People may call you an absolutist and accuse you of being judgmental. This fear of offending, I'm convinced, has caused many evangelicals to weaken their view of the Gospel. It's true many see it as politicized, which is sometimes legitimate, and absolutist, which is not true any more than any other truth-claim, such as the sun rises, is absolutist. Some younger evangelicals and the emerging-church movement, when they shy away from truth claims, are reacting to stereotypes, and so rather than preaching or taking strong positions, they basically want to start a conversation, hoping somebody discovers Jesus. But ever since the Gospel was first proclaimed, the Good News has had a specific content: Christ is risen! A bold truth-claim if there ever was one.

Fourth, our culture exalts progress—newer is better. True Christianity, however, finds its enlightenment in its historic orthodoxy, which is why I often use the term "radical Christianity"—a Christianity that draws its life from the faith's roots. The faith, again, has an ancestry, just as do families, in which its identity can be found.

Looking to Christianity's sources is countercultural today, because people in their pride, impressed by the latest trends, believe that we can invent utopian solutions for everything. This catches us up in fads—which fade as fast as they spring up. Technology may bring in a bountiful harvest, but that harvest still cannot provide relief to victims of famine if utopian dictators won't allow it to be delivered—their pride is an age-old problem. But the truth of the orthodox faith is what transforms people and cultures.

Finally, in this liberal, enlightened, tolerant age, all religions are seen as alike, and even some believers fall for this. After all, the people who worship sincerely in their communities are as entitled to be respected as we are. But the idea that all roads lead to heaven is the quickest way I can imagine to deaden any Christian's belief system. Why would you want to assert something that you don't believe is true? Truth is an exclusive claim, after all. Go to Africa today and ask Christian leaders whether they believe in such a thing as truth, and they will look at you as if you've lost your mind. Would someone stake his life on something they didn't deeply believe to be true?[2]

To the liberal mind, choice is more important than truth. That's fine when deciding what neighborhood you want to live in — but not when it comes to trusting your life to someone or something. As Chesterton so shrewdly observed, however, liberalism does not lead to liberalizing the world.[3] In fact, the opposite is true. The promise of liberation led to Marxist repression. Destructive higher criticism led to a church without beliefs and soon without followers, and then to the inevitable chaos of a society that believes nothing and lives for nothing. Liberalism, Chesterton argued, is actually illiberal, denying free thinking, denying miracles, and unable to countenance anything not within one's own sphere of knowledge and understanding.[4]

The Joy of Orthodoxy

The people who are drawn away from historic orthodoxy are missing the most exciting thing in life — a drama without equal in human history, the promise of incomparable joy. Is there anything more exciting than to know that you are part of God's great drama that has been played out through history? That you are taking your place alongside the saints who have gone before you? So you are with Luther at the Diet of Worms, with Augustine when Rome fell, with Aquinas as he wrote his magnificent opus, the *Summa Theologica*.

Remember, you and I today can believe exactly the same thing that the first-century apostles believed and for which they were willing to give up their very lives. Can anything compare to living in pursuit of virtues that God first expressed through Moses at Mount Sinai, which have proven over the years to be nothing less than enduring wisdom in virtually every culture? Don't you find joy in knowing that Jesus Christ is the same yesterday, today, and forever, the sustainer of all things, through whom and by whom and for whom all things were made?

People are always saying they want a more intimate relationship with Jesus Christ. That's good. If you do, start with the first-century apostles, their teaching, and their immediate successors. Go back to the early days of the Church and recover the orthodoxy of those who were with Jesus. What you will discover is the enduring, life-changing truth—and how we live in His presence. That's true intimacy.

The rewards of embracing orthodox truth are immense. First, anyone who goes through life fearful of offending his neighbors or being labeled an extremist will never have the joy of knowing that he has contributed to the transformation of another's life. He'll never experience the incredible excitement of knowing that the God who created him has His hand upon him and His Holy Spirit within him, that he's being empowered to carry to the world the most exciting story ever told.

Second, this robust, life-changing faith is the only thing that will sustain you in crisis. Everybody goes through periods of stress and doubt and pain and suffering. There are those moments when you question if God is real: "Am I deluding myself? Am I making all this up?" you ask. Everybody has those moments. Or maybe you're ill. If so, the feel-good gospel will be of no comfort. Therapy can only help you deal with a problem; transformation fixes the problem.

Most of the time life is tough. So in those times of stress and doubt and pain, you need to hear the words, "Be still, and know that I am God" (Psalm 46:10). If you listen to the still, small voice within you, you will have the quiet assurance that whatever you are wrestling with is nothing new.

Through two thousand years, millions upon millions have had this same experience. They have wrestled, have doubted, have raised questions for which there seem to be no answers. But believers in Christ have lived through the doubt and pain and suffering, and have resolved those questions, not by their own creative efforts or by some blinding new discovery, but by relying on the same enduring truth.

The Witness
of a Joyful Orthodoxy

Orthodoxy is not only important for enjoying life and understanding our relationship to God but also for our witness to the world. An essential factor in the success of Christianity in the early centuries was what Christians believed. Right doctrine led to right behavior, often with unforeseen but wonderful consequences.

Christianity, unlike the pagan religions of Rome, not only offered answers but moved people to act. While the Sophists prattled on about the exhaustion of virtue in a world grown old, Christians risked their lives on behalf of plague victims. In so doing they began constructing a new civilization in the midst of one doomed to decay. The same thing is happening today in the Third World and the Global South: sound doctrine and orthodox living are fueling incredibly dramatic growth and bringing a measure of justice to chaotic societies.

Scholar Phillip Jenkins, surveying the growth of religious movements, predicts for Christianity "a worldwide boom in the coming decades."[5] But the majority of believers will not be white, European, or American; they will be Asian, South American, and African. The growth will be explosive in the southern hemisphere.

The reason for this involves what the British sociologist Dr. David Martin reported in his study of the clash of liberal Catholicism and Pentecostalism in South America, *Tongues of Fire*. South Americans were not drawn to "liberation theology," the promise of social justice on the basis of political activism. This promise rang hollow to people who for generations had been oppressed by corrupt governments. Nor did they find much appeal in a liturgy celebrated by those who no longer believed in its supernatural basis. Liberal Christianity proved insipid.

The great appeal to the new converts in Chile and Brazil, whom David Martin interviewed, was the Pentecostal church's ability to "deliver the goods." The life-changing Gospel message attracted women in particular; when their husbands were converted, they no longer went out at night drinking in the bars and taverns but stayed home. They got their families back. That's what they cared about—the transforming power of the Gospel—and they in turn evangelized their neighbors.

The Bible itself singles out marginalized groups, the outcasts of society, the beaten-down and trampled upon, the forgotten. The Kingdom has come to deliver sight to the blind, set the prisoners free, feed the hungry, and give hope to the forgotten. It is radical, true liberation. What we are witnessing in the Global South today is the same thing that made the early Roman church succeed and through the centuries has advanced Christianity—a Gospel with the power to transform lives and cultures.

You can't help but be caught up in this if you put yourself in the place of those on whose shoulders we stand. I did this when I first visited Mars Hill, one of the most treacherous tourist attractions in the world, because one has to climb almost straight up tiny steps cut into a slippery rock to get to the top and the level surface where Paul confronted the Areopagus, the council of Athens's elders. From a distance, Mars Hill looks like a giant rock placed on the top of a mountain, just a few hundred yards down the hill from where the great Parthenon with its enduring columns stands.

But when I ascended that rock, I could see in my mind's eye the apostle Paul, the Jew, coming for the first time to the center of Greek culture and the great thinkers and philosophers of the day, proud Athens. And he came with the most radical message—that Jesus Christ died for our sins and rose again and reigns today. When I stood on that very spot, shivers went up and down my spine as I relived the drama of that confrontation. I looked over to the Parthenon where for centuries on Good Friday the flag has been lowered to half-staff, and raised full early Sunday morning. Only a few followed Paul the day he preached that remarkable sermon, but countless millions have followed since, and continue to today.

This faith, which once built the greatest civilization in human history, must now engage in the titanic struggle of our times.

CHAPTER 15

THE GREAT PROPOSAL

As we close these reflections, I would like to tell two stories: one that formed *us* and our civilization, and one that's shaping the future.

The Parable of Thorney Island

Parliamentary democracy in the West began humbly and with Christian roots. Elections of monastery officials like the story you're about to read really did happen. What's interesting in this account is how the election ran counter to worldly thinking and remade society in the process.

On Thorney Island by the Thames River in 1033, an election was held in the quadrangle of buildings that made up a Benedictine monastery. After the office of prime, forty-two monks in cinctured black habits gathered in the chapter house or central meeting hall to elect a successor to Father Romuald, the monastery's longtime abbot, their spiritual guide and leader.

The election of a Benedictine abbot in the eleventh century was a curious thing, although the order had been following the same procedure for five hundred years, ever since St. Benedict composed his *Rule* around AD 530.[1] The monks observed silence except during their afternoon recreation hour. This limited campaigning. More importantly, every monk, whether the son of the earl of Northumbria or an illiterate sheepherder from Wessex, received one vote — a practice that horrified the aristocracy.

Despite the absence of campaigning, three leading candidates for abbot had emerged. A subtle hand signal was used to indicate a monk's preference in the days before the election. The monks pressed their palms together for recollection as they walked along. A monk who wanted to indicate his choice would cup his right hand, making the sign of a *D*, and nod in the direction of his preferred candidate. The *D* stood for St. Dunstan, who, a century before, had rekindled Christianity throughout England after the devastation wrought by the Danes' invasions. St. Dunstan founded monasteries throughout England, including this Benedictine house on Thorney Island. The monks always hoped to elect an abbot who possessed a similar charisma.

The three leading candidates were Father Wilton, Father Aldhelm, and Father Cassian. Father Wilton deserved election as he had served the monastery in virtually every other capacity. He was also the finest philosopher and theologian and impeccable in his personal discipline. Fearless in the face of danger, he had once faced down a band of marauding Danes just outside the monastery's door.

But he had difficulty understanding the failings of his fellow monks. His indiscriminate application of discipline inspired long-held resentments. Father Wilton didn't have the voice to lead singing either.

Father Aldhelm was not an intellectual, but he loved everything associated with the daily life of the monastery. He loved keeping the books, devising or implementing new techniques to make their lands more productive, and making work assignments that fitted people's abilities. Father Aldhelm was certainly more diplomatic than Father Wilton and devised stratagems that avoided confrontations. This made him somewhat secretive, though, which inclined him to disguise his decisions. He would be a friend to the courtiers but hardly a match for any king. And in the opinion of some he would make the monastery little more than a farm, ruining its reputation as a center of thought.

Father Cassian, the youngest of the three, had already shown many of the evidences of being a saint, including a saint's tendency to cause trouble. Everyone believed he had the gift of contemplation;

he would often remain in private prayer from 2:00 a.m. till daybreak and still show no signs of fatigue. Cassian might have been resented were it not for his uncanny habit of performing kindnesses for his fellow monks. If a monk's shoes showed too much wear, the monk found a new pair by his bed courtesy of Cassian.

After Cassian was ordained and began hearing confessions, people began flocking to the monastery for his advice and counsel—often, too many for the other monks' comfort. But like St. Dunstan, he was a favorite of the monastery's school children.

Still, Cassian was young and in many ways untried. And yet, he was the only one among them likely to be remembered in future ages like St. Dunstan. Waves of enthusiasm for his election kept rising through the community.

In the chapterhouse hall, the monks sat in high-backed wooden choir stalls, which lined the back and side walls. The acting abbot, Father Theobald, sat before them in a central throne underneath the monastery's seal, a central cross on a blue background with a pelican, a lamb, a Bible, and a dragon in its four corners. They recited the "Our Father" together. Then, one by one, in order of seniority, each walked to the center of the hall, bowed before Theobald, and whispered a vote into his ear. Theobald kept the count in the ledger on his lap in his own private code.

After the first ballot, Theobald stood and announced that no one had received the 75 percent majority, or thirty-two votes, needed. Wilton had received nineteen votes; Cassian twelve; Aldhelm eight; with single votes going to Father Mark, Brother Levi, and Father Adeodatus.

At the mention of Cassian's vote total a commotion arose. Cassian had outpolled Aldhelm on the first ballot, and Aldhelm's support would likely go to Cassian on the second. Cassian would be elected. What this might mean for the monastery no one quite knew, but it was an exciting prospect.

Father Theobald commanded everyone to keep silence and led them in the Chaplet of Divine Mercy as a prelude to a second ballot.

When the vote was taken again, Cassian received twenty-one votes, Wilton fifteen, Aldhelm five, and Brother Levi one.

Everyone looked to Father Wilton to gauge his reaction. He seemed undisturbed. He glanced at Cassian, who looked far more troubled.

Cassian's vote total rose to thirty votes on the third ballot and on the fourth he was elected.

Father Theobald placed the ledger book to one side, walked to where Cassian was sitting, and the old man knelt before the young one and asked whether he would accept election as the community's abbot. Cassian took Theobald's hand and whispered something into his ear. The older monk stood up awkwardly and stepped back a few paces. He looked over to the abbot's throne as if considering whether to return to it.

Cassian pressed his palms together and closed his eyes. His face had turned as pale as skim milk. He was visibly shaking. For a long time he went deeply into prayer.

Finally, he opened his eyes and said, "Brothers, not yet." He said it with authority.

If Cassian had protested of his unworthiness, his demurrals would have been resisted. Instead, he confirmed that the responsibility must one day be his. But that day, his prayers told him, had not come.

On the following ballot Father Wilton was elected unanimously — except for Brother Levi's obstinate self-endorsement.

Thus was born the model for Western parliamentary democracy. The Greeks invented democracy as a means of choosing leaders, but voting rights in its ancient cities were strictly reserved to the wealthy. Benedictine monasteries were the first institutions in the world's history to enjoy universal suffrage.

The Benedictine monastery on Thorney Island by the river Thames really existed. In 1045, King Edward built his palace, St. Stephen's, a stone's throw away. King Edward also enlarged the monks' church, which became known as the "minster" (monks' church) to the West, or, as we know it today, Westminster Abbey. King Edward's palace was eventually transformed into the Houses of Parliament.

A Hymn to Christendom

This parable of Thorney Island speaks of how Christianity created Western civilization—the most dynamic culture the world has ever known. Like the very stones underlying Westminster Abbey, whose basement incorporates the ancient monks' dormitory, Christian principles are the foundation of the West.

The location of the Houses of Parliament speaks eloquently of the Church's role in generating the West's political institutions. But monasticism also played a role in the development of capitalism. The monks reinvested their wealth in the acquisition of new technology like mills run by overshot wheels, collars that allowed horses to replace oxen for plowing, and the heavy wheeled plow whose share (blade) dug the deep furrows needed in northern Europe.

The monks also learned to run their farms according to strict accounting practices, like the "rational firm" of modern day economics. They appointed managers on the basis of merit—as we saw with Father Aldhelm—not social position, which gave them another huge competitive advantage.

Benedictine monasticism embraced work as well, and specifically hard, physical labor, as a means of knowing God. This gave a dignity to work that the world had never known before, a dignity that was later expanded through the Reformation and the Protestant work ethic.

Originally the recipients of a noble's charity, a monastery often became that noble family's banker in later generations, and in so doing helped the Church distinguish lending at reasonable rates from usury.

Capitalism spread to the independently governed cities of Northern Italy, Venice, Genoa, Florence, and Milan, and from there to the Netherlands, Ghent, and Amsterdam, before finally revolutionizing the wool trade in England. A host of technical innovations assisted in the process, particularly windmills and the kind of inventions we now take for granted, like accurate clocks and eyeglasses that prolonged the careers of artisans. The cities of Northern Italy were particularly responsible for the spread of international banking. They invented financial instruments that allowed capital to follow opportunity and early forms of insurance that limited risk.

Capitalism also came into being in the West because the Church recognized civil society must enjoy a rightful independence from its control. Theocracies like those Islam produces or unified political-ethical theories like Confucianism in China always produce command economies by their nature. Both Eastern fatalism and Islamic theocracy under a central spiritual leader kept the East and the Islamic Middle East from creating truly dynamic economic systems.

The belief of Christians in reason — the very meaning of *Logos* — also drove the scientific revolution. In fact, science itself might never have been invented if not for Christianity's belief that all the world could be explored for God's glory, thus initiating the inductive methods essential to scientific advance. It did not develop earlier where it might have, in the civilizations of China and Islam, which possessed sufficient wealth and technical expertise. These civilizations lacked the necessary faith; that human reason could discover the Reason in all things. The great figures of the scientific revolution, Mendel, Copernicus, Kepler, Galileo, Newton, and Boyle, were all profound Christians. Newton wrote far more on theology than any other subject, and Boyle sponsored Christian missions and translations of the Bible into far-flung languages. As one sociologist wrote, alchemy developed in China but chemistry in the West.[2] The historical record belies the reckless statements of Hitchens, Dawkins, and other anti-theists that faith opposes reason and is antiscience. The truth is, the scientific method owes its existence to Christianity.

Christian influence led to the establishment of the first universities, not just trade schools as had been the case in China, but communities of scholars where knowledge could be pursued because it was good for human beings to learn. The first two universities were in Paris and Bologna in the middle of the twelfth century. Oxford and Cambridge followed shortly thereafter. And then the universities spread through Europe. Christians also developed public education, fueled by the faith's embrace of equality, as all were created in God's image.

While the West embraced reason during its Christian centuries, our civilization also depended upon the authority of Christian revelation. The common moral standards that Christianity engendered in Western culture were crucial. People must be able to govern themselves, to practice self-restraint, before they can rule themselves via elected government.

The sanctity of life made Christians defenders of each individual's dignity; we see men and women as sovereign creatures who ought to enjoy as much liberty as possible. That's why the Church has always defended the right of private property, another hallmark of the West, because it belongs to each person's sovereign nature to rule a piece of ground or field of endeavor.

At the same time Christians do not exalt the individual at the expense of community. Our Trinitarian God *exists* in community. Christians insist that we are "made for each other," and we defend the rights of the family, businesses, and voluntary associations to nurture community as only they can, free from governmental control, a principle underscored in the Reformation's concept of "sphere sovereignty."

"It is for freedom that Christ has set us free," Paul writes (Galatians 5:1). Through reflecting on the implications of the Gospel, Christians became the great advocates and protectors of human freedom, which resulted in this freedom's institutionalization in the West.

In Beijing, an American journalist recently encountered one of China's foremost scholars, a man who had spent long years studying the West. His colleagues and he had investigated the reasons for the West's success and preeminence, examining our history, politics, economics, and culture. Their first conclusion was the West's success was due to its more advanced military; later they believed it might have been the political system; or perhaps the economic system. But "in the past twenty years," one investigator said, "we have realized that the heart of your culture is your religion: Christianity. That is why the West has been so powerful. The Christian moral foundation of social and cultural life was what made possible the emergence of capitalism and then the successful transition to democratic politics. We don't have any doubt about this."[3]

In the Land of Rembrandt

In the land of Rembrandt, in the city of Amsterdam on a cloudy, damp morning in the early winter of 2004, a middle-aged man was riding his bicycle on a downtown street. His name was Theo van Gogh, a distant relative of the famous painter. TV personality, columnist, and film-maker, he was known throughout Holland for his social criticism.

He was about to be murdered. The first gunshot targeted his sagging stomach and sent him staggering to the other side of the street. His assailant shot him several more times in the stomach until he lay on his back with his arms over his head.

At this point, Van Gogh was still conscious, and once he saw his assailant looming above him in his gray raincoat and Muslim prayer hat, he asked, "Can't we talk about this?"[4]

His assailant, a twenty-six-year-old Dutch citizen of Moroccan descent named Mohammed Bouyeri, was carrying a machete and promptly slashed the filmmaker's throat. To free his hands he then planted the machete in the victim's chest. Several eyewitnesses noted his unhurried and matter-of-fact manner. He took out pen and paper from a small bag and calmly wrote out a note before carefully folding it. He took a smaller knife he was carrying and stabbed it through the letter into the victim's chest.

Then Bouyeri, after giving the corpse a few last kicks, walked away, not hurrying, making no real attempt to escape. While he paused to reload his gun, a woman who had seen what had happened screamed at him, "You can't do that!"

"Yes, I can," Bouyeri replied, "and now you know what you can expect in the future."[5]

Bouyeri ambled off into a nearby park, where the police who had rushed to the scene caught up with him. Standing his ground, Bouyeri shot at the police, hitting one in his bulletproof vest and wounding a passerby with an errant shot. Bouyeri expected to die in this confrontation, in his mind as a Muslim martyr, but he was only wounded and arrested.

The note that Bouyeri had left so cruelly at the scene explained his action. It was not addressed to Van Gogh but to Ayaan Hirsi Ali, a Somali-born member of parliament who had become radical Islam's chief critic in the Netherlands. As someone brought up in Islam and educated in its traditions, she said forthrightly that violence and oppression belonged to the heart of Islam. Islam was not a religion of peace that had been co-opted for destructive purposes by radicals. What the radicals were doing came straight out of the Quran. She called on the Dutch to wake up to this reality and protect their traditional freedoms.

Bouyeri's death epistle called Hirsi Ali a "soldier of evil" and accused her of "turning her back on the Truth." He prophesied she would be destroyed, along with the United States, Europe, and Holland.[6]

Bouyeri had delivered this message via the murder of Theo van Gogh because Ayaan Hirsi Ali and Van Gogh had collaborated on a film, *Submission* (which is what "Islam" means), a graphic protest against Islam's oppression of women. In the film, passages from the Quran are projected onto the skin of half-naked women as their frustrated prayers rise to Allah recounting episodes of rape and abuse sanctioned by the passages.

The lives of Ayaan Hirsi Ali, Theo van Gogh, and Mohammed Bouyeri provide important perspectives on today's clash of civilizations. Their drama represents the challenges of our times as Thorney Island epitomizes how Christianity built the West.

Ayaan Hirsi Ali, the daughter of a Somalian political activist, grew up primarily in Kenya under the guidance of her traditional Muslim mother and even more conservative grandmother. Her grandmother saw to it that she underwent a horrific female circumcision — what Hirsi Ali prefers to call an "excision," and rightly so — at the age of five. After going through a period of religious enthusiasm in her early teens, Hirsi Ali began to have religious doubts as Islamic practice began taking away her independence.

In 1992 she was being shipped off to Canada and an arranged marriage when, on a layover in Germany, she decided to bolt. She made her way to the Netherlands, lied about being a political refugee from Somalia, and was given residence. Within ten years she learned to speak perfect Dutch, studied political science at Leiden University, became a favorite of café society, and finally was made a member of the Dutch parliament.

As she became part of Dutch society, Ayaan Hirsi Ali pursued one all-important question: Why was it that Americans and Europeans were able to enjoy free societies under the rule of law? What had produced such liberty?

She was told this was the result of the Enlightenment—of reason unfettered from religious influence. She read Herman Philipse's *The Atheist Manifesto* and chose unbelief. "I saw that God was a fiction and that submission to his will is surrendering to the will of the strongest."[7] She saw a role for herself as Islam's Voltaire, believing reason alone could bring progress.

———

If Voltaire's Enlightenment was a rebellion against tradition and traditional religion, then Theo van Gogh was certainly its true son. By his own admission, he played the "village idiot." On TV talk shows, in newspaper columns, and through his films he criticized radical Islam, Jews who "made too much of the Holocaust," those in the Netherlands who had collaborated with the Nazis, those who overstated the Netherlands resistance to the Nazis, and the Netherlands Catholic and Calvinist past. In other words, anyone and everyone.

But why did Theo van Gogh make these criticisms? Criticizing one and all afforded Van Gogh the license, he felt, to live life as one ongoing party.

After his death, his Website continued to run selections from his work that his friends felt were a fitting tribute.[8] Included were pictures of Theo van Gogh with a crest that featured a limp phallic symbol and the words, "I Shall Struggle and Stand Up," scenes from Van Gogh's nightclub life, and erotic clips from his movies.

After they made *Submission*, Van Gogh told Ayaan Hirsi Ali that as an apostate from Islam she was the one whose life was in danger. No one could possibly take him seriously. Tragically, his murderer, Mohammed Bouyeri, credited Van Gogh with believing in something —a decadence Islamists detest.

At his trial, Bouyeri told Van Gogh's mother that he honored her son for not being a hypocrite, for speaking his own mind. "I acted out of faith," Bouyeri said. "If it had been my own father, or my little brother, I would have done the same thing."[9] He went on to say that his religion demanded he "cut off the heads of all those who insult Allah and his prophet." He found Dutch society as a whole intolerable, for the divine law of Islam, *Shari'a*, forbade the practice of free speech.

The Dutch could not understand why one of their citizens, who had been given every benefit of Dutch society, including an education, welfare benefits, and lenient treatment when he fell into trouble as a youth, would want to destroy the Netherlands. The Dutch knew their problem went far beyond this isolated case, as Bouyeri had been part of a terrorist cell and radical Islam was spreading among the Netherlands Muslim population, which constituted 5.5 percent of the country.

The Dutch would not have been surprised if they had known Bouyeri's past. After three halfhearted attempts at earning a university degree, Mohammed Bouyeri had become the disciple of a radical imam from Syria, Abou Khaled.[10] Over the course of a year he became an Islamist radical. Intoxicated with the ideal of worldwide salvation through Islam, he was convinced that any sacrifice to this end was justified. Murder and suicide became his sacrament and path to God.

Today's radical Islam, represented by Bouyeri, was partially generated by Western thinkers and Western universities and, ironically, shares habits of mind with postmodern secularism.

Sayyid Qutb is an example. In 1954 this Egyptian radical was imprisoned by then-President Nasser. Sayyid Qutb had received a traditional Muslim education and committed the Quran to memory by the age of ten. He was well educated at a Cairo university before coming to the United States in the late 1940s, where he received a master's degree at Colorado State College of Education. The decadence he experienced in America radicalized him. Christians, he believed, had had an opportunity to build God's society in the West, but they had squandered it. And so the only hope was to destroy Western civilization and replace it with Islam.

Sayyid Qutb was tortured brutally in Nasser's prisons but somehow managed, between 1954 and 1962, to write an amazing Islamic manifesto. It was entitled *In the Shade of the Quran*. Copies smuggled out of prison and published after his death are now widely circulated along with his book *Milestones*, an extensive study of the Quran that has been translated and published in fifteen volumes. These are the handbooks of the Muslim brotherhood and of radical Islamists everywhere.

Sayyid Qutb accepted the idea of a superior culture formed by the will of God, or Allah. He called on the Muslim world to bring about universal salvation through imposing God's law, the *Shari'a*, everywhere. They were to sacrifice themselves to this end. Qutb's Allah is a god of pure will, who is known through obedience that results in compulsion and even violence, not a God of love who suffered so that we may know Him.

Nasser finally had Qutb hanged in 1966. But four years later, *In the Shade of the Quran* was published. Qutb's brother Muhammad fled Egypt and settled in Saudi Arabia, where he became a professor at the university. One of his prize students, who absorbed Qutb's philosophy, was Osama bin Laden.[11]

In the murder of Theo van Gogh we see how post-Christian the West has become and with what devastating consequences. Immigrants such as Ayaan Hirsi Ali and the Moroccan-Dutchman Mohammed Bouyeri are taught that the Enlightenment's atheism produced the West's glories. Rarely, if ever, does anyone mention Christianity's formative role. (Ayaan Hirsi Ali accepted that salvation came from the Enlightenment; many, like Bouyeri, find a purely secular society — or what they see as a corrupt Christian one — intolerable.) Immigrant students like Bouyeri attend Western universities that advocate eliminating the last vestiges of Christianity from culture. These foreign students also learn that truth does not exist, or it's completely relative to one's own culture — except when Western secularists identify Western imperialism as the scourge. Then, comic pornographers like Van Gogh are held up as the best we have to offer. Could this situation be more suicidal?

We should not be surprised when young men like Bouyeri seek a better answer to life's questions than Van Gogh's self-absorbed hedonism.

———

The orthodox faith is the one source that can renew Western culture. Why? Because the faith teaches how God can change humanity, and faithful Christians have demonstrated time and again this truth. If I didn't believe Jesus changed my life or could change the lives of others, I'd have gone back to the law long ago.

The critic who calls himself an anti-theist, Christopher Hitchens, is a clever and engaging writer, but his claim that all religions, including Christianity, have made nothing but a negative contribution to human history is belied by the evidence, only small samples of which we have sketched here. We saw how Christianity met the needs of the late Roman Empire when paganism proved insufficient to maintain the Roman colossus. We have seen how Christian monasteries served as the leaven of their cultures, fostering progressive developments that then spread to the larger society. We saw how the great evangelicals of eighteenth- and nineteenth-century Britain helped the United Kingdom and the rest of the West cope with injustices spawned by the Industrial Revolution. That the same could happen again is our hope.

Common Roots of Today's Threats

In this parable of our times from Holland we see the essential elements of today's clash of civilization and their respective sources, the Enlightenment, Islamo-fascism, and Christianity.

While many have backed away from the term "Islamo-fascism," we have already seen part of the reason for it in Sayyid Qutb's writings and Bouyeri's murderous nihilism. The enemy of the West today is not a peace-loving movement seeking to evangelize. It is a deeply radicalized, extreme fascist movement, correctly called Islamo-fascism. That term, incidentally, came not from modern-day Christians or

Westerners but from a French Marxist writer, Maxine Rodinson, who used the label to describe the Iranian revolution of 1978.[12]

Qutb's maniacal hatred of the West was influenced by the works of Nietzsche, Heidegger, DeMan, and other European intellectuals whose writings helped inspire the rise of Adolph Hitler's Nazi party. He feasted as well on anti-Semitic literature like *The Protocols of the Elders of Zion*, which fed his belief that Jews and Christians must be destroyed.

The supreme irony is that these German intellectuals who paved the way for Hitler's fascist regime and who helped Qutb shape Islam in a fascist mold have also shaped postmodern literary criticism and thought in the West. The dominant idea of these intellectuals is one we have already discussed: that all philosophies are expressions of their cultures. This can be taken in two directions: (1) either truth does not exist, or (2) the only way to know truth is through the world's foremost culture. The first direction leads to existentialism; the second to fascism—or radical Islam. So the Twin Towers came both from a common and an alien view of life.

The Nazis of the 1930s wanted to merge their own identities into the greater reality of the Aryan race. They wanted to purify their society of anything alien to Aryan culture. And they fell in love with death as a means of doing so—just like Van Gogh's murderer, Mohammed Bouyeri.

Most Westerners have ignored the fact that the Nazi roots go deep into the Middle East, not only filtered through dangerous Islamic radicals like Sayyid Qutb, but directly into the politics of Syria and Iraq. When the French government fell in World War II, the Vichy regime turned over control of both of those countries to the Nazis. The Bath party that emerged in these nations after World War II was heavily influenced by fascist thought.

Europe has lost its ability to employ reason against reason's enemies because it has lost the authority for reason, that is, its faith. It is left with nothing but the tattered remains of a belief in the rationality of humans. But reason alone, without faith, cannot deal with today's clash of civilizations. This was Pope Benedict's point in his magnificent speech at Regensburg, which the press totally misunderstood.

While he rightly condemned Islamic violence, the central point of Benedict's speech was to challenge the secular West's separation of faith and reason. "A reason which is deaf to the divine," he said, "and which relegates religion into the realm of subcultures is incapable of entering into the dialogue of cultures."[13]

The problem in Islam is that it is a blind faith that neither supports reason nor is informed by it. The Allah of Islam is strictly a god of pure will whose dictates, as known through Islamic law, cannot be questioned.

So we have a dilemma: in the West, reason alone without faith leads to chaos; in Islam, faith alone without reason leads to tyranny.

And the tragedy is that the two sides can never find common ground. Theo van Gogh's last words were "Can we talk?" Obviously not.

Does the West Have the Will to Continue?

Many have questioned whether the West even has the will to continue, for secularism has produced a society without sufficient hope to reproduce itself. Today, the fertility rate in Europe is 1.4 — far below the 2.1 necessary to maintain its population.[14] So Western culture is doing today exactly what Rome did when Christianity began, importing immigrants to take the place of workers not being produced by families. It's simple to project statistically when Europe will have a totally immigrant population. If the West doesn't fall, it will simply be absorbed by an expanding Islamic population, and very likely ruled by radicalism.

This is why orthodoxy matters, for a renewal and strengthening of the orthodox Christian faith can provide not only joy and meaning for Christians but a bulwark of sanity and reason against barbarism. Do we want Westminster Abby and the Houses of Parliament facing one another? Or do we want to leave it to the merry pranksters of café society to confront an evil they cannot understand, appreciate, nor defend against? This is the great battle of good versus evil of our time.

Pope Benedict has made the principal mission of his papacy the development of Christian communities in Europe, who, like the monks of old, will keep alive the virtues of the West. It's time for all Christians to contribute to the "oases of civilization" that the world so desperately needs. Christianity is growing dramatically around the world; no doubt the Global South, as well as China and Korea and other Eastern countries, may supply providential help in the present struggle. But it is also our mission as Westerners to reevangelize the West.

The Great Proposal

We are always hoping to be rescued by moderate Muslim leaders, and while we thank God for them and for the millions of Muslims who desire to live in peace, we have to recognize Ayaan Hirsi Ali's conviction that violence and oppression are inherent in the faith of Islam. The radicals, alas, have developed a stronger theology, at least as it is being lived out. *New York Times* columnist Thomas Friedman has wondered aloud, "Where is the Islamic Martin Luther King?" Where are the responsible Muslim leaders who would take charge of their own communities? Who would come up, he asked, with a "Muslim counter-nihilism strategy that would delegitimize the mass murder of Muslims by Muslims"?[15] A Syrian poet, Ali Ahmad Said, lamented, "We Arabs are in a phase of extinction, in the sense that we have no creative presence in the world."

The orthodox Christian faith is the one source that can renew culture because it relies on a wisdom far beyond humankind's own that can yet be known by reason. It constantly calls people to the practice of virtue and charity guided by this greater wisdom. Theologian Michael Novak argues that this is why Christianity is so vital to culture. All societies experience what Lincoln in his Lyceum Address called "the silent artillery of time"; that is, there is a built-in inertia as a culture matures. People get comfortable in their ways and become less creative and inventive — and certainly less adventuresome. In later generations people lose their drive and become self-indulgent. Entropy and decadence set in.

Orthodox Christianity alone among worldviews, however, provides a stop to this inertia through the renewal of the soul and the regeneration of people that transforms cultures. We have seen this revolutionary influence of orthodox Christianity being exerted repeatedly from the early centuries to the monastic movement to the great Protestant Reformation to the Great Awakenings in England and America and today in the Global South.

Chesterton explains why Christians are change agents. There are, he says, optimists and pessimists in the world. The optimists are always trying to do good things, and the pessimists are always wringing their hands in despair. But the Christian, he argues, is the only one with a balanced view—a pessimist because he knows that this is a fallen world and things do need fixing, but an optimist because he knows that God is all powerful and in charge and that all things therefore can be fixed. "We have said," Chesterton writes, "we must be fond of this world, even in order to change it. We now add that we must be fond of another world (real or imaginary) in order to have something to change it to."[16]

If there's ever been a time in which renewal was essential, it is today when Christianity is pitted against not only hostile influences within Western secularism but a massive, monolithic force, Islamo-fascism, that is pledged to destroy us.

And Christianity is, decidedly, an other-directed religion, as the Danish philosopher Søren Kierkegaard often wrote. By the very character of what we believe in our orthodox faith, we don't want to force beliefs down a person's throat; rather, we're perfectly willing to lay our lives down for others as Chinese Christians did amid the Cultural Revolution's madness, as Christ did for us.

Christianity does not seek to impose, it proposes. The Gospel is the great proposal: Come to the wedding feast, one and all—black, white, rich, poor, East, West, Muslim, Jew, Christian—all are welcome, and it's never too late. God turns no man or woman away, not one. Through His Son, Jesus Christ, the Father brings us into His Kingdom. This is the promise He holds out to individuals and nations alike, a Kingdom not of eating and drinking or of marching armies and clashing swords, but a Kingdom of righteousness, peace, and joy forever in the Holy Spirit.

NOTES

Prologue

1. Rodney Stark, *The Rise of Christianity* (San Francisco: HarperOne, 1997), 160.

2. Stark, *Rise of Christianity*, 89.

Chapter 1: Everywhere, Always, by All

1. When Christopher Wren rebuilt the church, he discovered Roman urns and ancient Christian graves on the site.

2. For instance, Oxford professor Richard Dawkins, in his editorial review of Kimberly Baker, ed., *Fundamentals of Extremism: The Christian Right in America* (Boston: New Boston Books, 2003) at the Barnes and Noble website (*www.bn.com*), states, "The Christian Right is America's Taliban."

3. Peter Berkowitz, "The New Atheism," *Wall Street Journal* (July 16, 2007), A13.

4. Michael Novak has commented on the new anti-theists: "And yet, there's an odd defensiveness about all these books—as though they were a sign not of victory but of desperation. Everywhere on earth except Western Europe, religion is surging. Each of the authors admits that most people, especially in America, do not agree with him. Each pictures himself as a man who spits against the wind. Each rehearses his arguments for atheism, mostly, it seems, to convince himself." *First Things* (June/July 2007).

5. Brian Burrell, "So Help Me God: Words of Obedience: Loyalty Oaths and Pledges of Allegiance," *The Words We Live By* (New York: Free Press, 1997). President Eisenhower's quote was from an address given on Flag Day, June 14, 1954.

6. *BreakPoint WorldView* (June 27, 2007).

7. Michael Weisskopf, "Energized by Pulpit on Passion, the Public Is Calling: 'Gospel Grapevine' Displays Strength in Controversy over Military Gay Ban," *Washington Post* (February 1, 1993).

8. To consider some more examples of biblical illiteracy, read Steven Prothero's new book, *Religious Literacy: What Every American Needs to Know and Doesn't* (San Francisco: HarperOne, 2007).

9. Gene Edward Veith, "Stray Pastors: Only Half of America's Ministers Hold to a Biblical Worldview, but Even Many Who Do Aren't Imparting It to Their Congregations," *World Magazine*, vol. 19, no. 5 (February 7, 2004), accessed at *www.worldmag.com*.

10. "Our Churches, with common consent, do teach that the decree of the Council of Nicaea concerning the Unity of the Divine Essence and concerning the Three Persons, is true and to be believed without any doubting."

Chapter 2: God Is

1. Sam Harris, *Letter to a Christian Nation* (New York: Knopf, 2006), 52.

2. As quoted in Joseph Cardinal Ratzinger, *Introduction to Christianity*, rev. ed. (Fort Collins, Colo.: Ignatius, 2004), 153.

3. This illustration is drawn from Ratzinger, *Introduction to Christianity*, 154.

4. Ratzinger, *Introduction to Christianity*, 150–56.

5. Freeman Dyson, as quoted in Martin Gardner, "Intelligent Design and Phillip Johnson," *Skeptical Inquirer* (November 21, 1997), 197.

6. Stark, *Rise of Christianity*, 209–15.

7. A study done by two eminent British social scientists in the early 1990s, on the spread of evangelical Christianity in largely Catholic South American countries and the tensions it created, came to precisely the same conclusion. David Martin, *Tongues of Fire: The Explosion of Protestantism in Latin America* (Oxford, UK: Blackwell, 1990).

8. See Stark, *Rise of Christianity*, 167ff.

9. *Hardwired to Connect: The New Scientific Case for Authoritative Communities*, sponsored by the YMCA of the USA, Dartmouth Medical School, the Institute for American Values (2003). See also the following references: 1. Ian Sample, "'God Spot': Researchers See the Light in MRI Study," *The Guardian* (August 30, 2006); 2. Daniel Goleman, *Social Intelligence: The New Science of Human Relationships* (New York: Bantam, 2006); 3. James Randerson, "Humans 'Hardwired for Religion,'" *Guardian Unlimited* (September 4, 2006); 4. Marc Hauser, *Moral Minds: How Nature Designed Our Universal Sense of Right and Wrong* (New York: Ecco, 2006).

10. Jim Holt, "Beyond Belief," *New York Times Sunday Book Review* (October 22, 2006).

11. Charles Colson, *God and Government* (Grand Rapids, Mich.: Zondervan, 2007), 79.

Chapter 3: He Has Spoken

1. Facts related to the incident and Speratus's words are taken from J. A. Robinson, trans., in *Acts of the Scillitan Martyrs*, in original supplement to the American edition in *Ante Nicene Fathers*, ed. Alexander Roberts and James Donaldson, (repr. Grand Rapids, Mich.: Eerdmans, 1955), x, 290–91. I have retranslated, paraphrased, and edited the historical record of the trial to fit this rendering's form.

2. David Aikman, *Jesus in Beijing* (Washington, D.C.: Regnery, 2003), 56.

3. For the sake of brevity we have attenuated the following history: The Three-Self Patriotic Movement (TSPM), the state's Protestant agency, and the Catholic Patriotic Association (CPA) were themselves subjected to persecution during the Cultural Revolution. These agencies were founded early in the communist takeover and then brought back after the Cultural Revolution as a means of exercising control over Christian churches.

4. Johnny Li of Open Doors USA, personal interview (June 29, 2007).

5. Both texts were known and rejected by the Church Fathers. Ireneas declared the Gospel of Judas heretical in approximately AD 180.

6. James the brother of John was the first apostle to die a martyr's death, during the first persecutions in Jerusalem. Peter and Paul died later at about the same time, AD 66–67, in Rome during Nero's persecution of the Christians. The apostle and evangelist John led a very long life and may have died as late as AD 100.

7. The differences in the four Gospels were duly noted. The early Church Fathers could see that the evangelists present the life of Christ in different chronological orders. They also represent Jesus' teachings from different angles with a particular audience in mind. Rather than being disturbed by this, scholars in the early Church understood that the different accounts broaden and enrich our understanding of Christ's life. They also served as proof against the one-sided interpretations that characterized false teachings in that day—and ours as well.

8. Contrary to what many suppose today, any book that falsely claimed apostolic authorship was rejected immediately.

9. Luke's authority derived in part, for example, from being a companion of Paul and his acquaintance with other apostles.

10. Also, the *sensus fidelium*, the "sense of the faithful," that is, the judgment of Christians within all the local churches of the faithfulness of the text to the apostles' teaching, provided another test of a text's authoritative status. The wider the acceptance, the greater likelihood it was inspired.

11. Before the close of the first century, the rule of faith was also summarized in early versions of the Apostles' Creed. In fact, the Church Father Tertullian (155–230) insists that part of the rule of faith—the apostolic tradition—can be found in early versions of the Apostles' Creed.

12. During Paul's ministry as well, the faith had to defend itself against false teaching, particularly the influence of the "Judaizers"—those who thought potential converts must become Jews before becoming Christians. There were also *docetists* who taught that Christ did not truly come in the flesh but only appeared to be a man. Both Paul and John implicitly condemn this heresy. (See Colossians 1:19, 2:9 and 1 John 1:1–3, 4:1–3; and 2 John 7).

13. Protestants and Catholics differ, of course, about what books should be included in the Old Testament. Catholics accept a list based on the Septuagint, a Greek translation of the Hebrew Scriptures that originated in Alexandria, a city in ancient Egypt. The Alexandrian Septuagint included seven books, Tobit, Judith, Wisdom, Ecclesiasticus, Baruch, and 1 and 2 Maccabeus, not included in the Hebrew Scriptures as they were known in Jerusalem. This difference in Jewish traditions was then picked up by the Christian community and became a long, running conversation. Protestants accept only the narrow Hebrew canon of Jerusalem.

14. Paul Johnson, "A Historian Looks at Jesus," speech given at Dallas Theological Seminary, 1986, reprinted as a Wilberforce Forum Booklet.

15. Ibid.

16. Carl F. H. Henry, "The Uneasy Conscience Revisited: 1947–1987," a speech delivered at the seventy-fifth anniversary of Northern Baptist Theological Seminary (November 2, 1987).

17. See *www.johnankerberg.org/Articles/_PDFArchives/apologetics/AP2W0604.pdf* referencing Norman Geisler, *Christ: The Theme of the Bible* (Chicago: Moody, 1969), 29n, citing D. J. Wiseman, "Archeological Confirmations of the Old Testament," in Carl F. Henry, ed., *Revelation and the Bible* (Grand Rapids, Mich.: Baker, 1958), 301–302.

18. Walter C. Kaiser and Duane Garrett (of Gordon-Conwell), *The Archaeological Study Bible: An Illustrated Walk through Biblical History and Culture, New International Version* (Grand Rapids, Mich.: Zondervan, 2006).

19. The earliest manuscript is a papyrus called P52, which most scholars have dated to the first half of the second century.

20. Christopher Hitchens, "An Atheist Responds," *Washington Post* (July 14, 2007).

21. Pastor Greg Sempsrott of the First Church of God in Vero Beach, Florida.

Chapter 4: Truth

1. As quoted by Gabriel Josipovici, *The Book of God: A Response to the Bible* (New Haven: Yale University Press, 1990), 29.

2. Dr. Mark Hauser, professor of psychology, organismic and evolutionary biology, and biological anthropology at Harvard.

3. David Van Biema, "God vs. Science," *Time* (November 5, 2006).

4. Barna, cited in Dale Buss, "Christian Teens? Not Very," *Wall Street Journal* (July 9, 2004).

5. See Scott McKnight, "The Future or Fad? A Look at the Emerging Church Movement," *The Covenant Companion* (February 2006). *www.covchurch.org/uploads/3F/7L/3F7LxAd37g_jWSGgttqDVw/0602-Future-or-Fad.pdf.*

6. Dorothy Sayers, *Creed or Chaos?* (Manchester, N.H.: Sophia Institute, 1974), 25.

7. Deane William Ferm, "Protestant Liberalism Reaffirmed." Found at *www.religion-online.org/showarticle.asp?title=1829.* The article originally appeared in the *Christian Century* (April 28, 1976), 411–16. At the time of writing this article, Dr. Ferm was the dean of the chapel at Mount Holyoke College, South Hadley, Massachusetts.

8. Interview with Katherine Jefferts Schori, *Time* (July 17, 2006).

9. George Barna and Mark Hatch, *Boiling Point: It Only Takes One Degree* (Ventura, Calif.: Regal, 2001), 185, 202.

10. Just as reason without revelation had produced the French Revolution's Reign of Terror.

11. See Joseph LeConte, "Christianity without Salvation," *Wall Street Journal* (May 5, 2007).

12. Subsequently, Federal Judge Robert Pratt declared IFI unconstitutional, ordering that the Iowa IFI program shut and that Prison Fellowship pay the $1.5 million Iowa had paid for the secular services correc-

tions officials said were ably provided by our
fellowship.

Chapter 5: What Went Right, What Went Wrong

1. The Bible frequently alludes to this larger story within which the human story fits. Paul reminds us, "For our struggle is … against the spiritual forces of evil in the heavenly realms" (Ephesians 6:12). When the seventy-two that Jesus commissions to spread the Good News return from their mission, the Lord connects their activities with this cosmic warfare: "I saw Satan fall like lightning from heaven" (Luke 10:18). The Revelation of John helps us integrate these passages and others from the Old Testament into a comprehensive picture.

2. "Flight 5191 didn't get updates," Associated Press (July 23, 2007).

3. Theodore Dalrymple, *Life at the Bottom* (Chicago: Ivan R. Dee, 2001), 7–8.

4. Samuel Yockelson and Stanton E. Samenow, *The Criminal Personality: A Profile for Change*, vol. 1 (New York: Jason Aronson, 1982), 19–20, 36.

Chapter 6: The Invasion

1. For statistics see "Normandy Invasion." *Encyclopædia Britannica* (2007). *Encyclopædia Britannica Online* (September 29, 2007): *www.britannica.com/eb/article-9056146>* and *en.wikipedia.org/wiki/Normandy_Invasion*.

2. "English Bishop Calls Christ's Resurrection Conjuring Trick," Associated Press, *St. Louis Post Dispatch* (October 28, 1984).

3. See Jon D. Levenson, *Resurrection and the Restoration of Israel: The Ultimate Victory of the God of Life* (New Haven, Conn.: Yale University Press, 2006).

4. Charles Colson, *Loving God* (Grand Rapids, Mich: Zondervan, 1996), 61–70.

Chapter 7: God Above, God Beside, God Within

1. St. Caesarius of Arles, *Sermo 9, Exp. Symb…*: CCL 103, 47 as found in *Catechism of the Catholic Church* (Liguori, Mo.: Liguori Publications, 1994), 62.

2. Account of Estes' speech and facts about his background drawn from Rebekah Allen, "Speaker Shares Views on Islam,

Christianity" (November 14, 2005), *www. lsureveille.com/media/storage/paper868/ news/2005/11/14/CampusLife/Speaker.Shares. Views.On.Islam.Christianity–2054087.shtml*.

3. Ibid.

4. As quoted in Stephanie Hill, "Middle Tennessee State U. Student Says Move to Islam Act of Honesty," *Sidelines* (copyright 2004 Sidelines via U-Wire) (March 15, 2004).

5. As quoted in Susan Hogan-Albach, "Drawn to Islam: Clear Message, Strict Morals Attracting Americans," *The Dallas Morning News*, Lifestyle section (November 8, 2001).

6. Muslim Student Association of University of North Texas website.

7. The story of Idris and Nafia Abdur-Rahim is found in "Keeping Faith—Under Scrutiny; Laurel Muslims More Cautious as Authorities Probe Hijackers' Pasts," *The Washington Post*, Metro section (January 6, 2002), C01.

8. The following discussion relies, in part, on John Stott, *Christian Basics: An Invitation to Discipleship* (Grand Rapids, Mich.: Baker, 2003).

9. Gregory of Nyssa, on "Not Three Gods" NPNF 2 V, 331–36, cited in Thomas Oden, *Systematic Theology* (Peabody, Mass.: Hendrickson, 2006), 182.

10. See Stott, *Christian Basics*, 49.

11. As Peter preached, "By his wounds you have been healed" (1 Peter 2:24).

12. Stott says, "First, in the Greek of John's Gospel Jesus is recorded as referring to the Holy Spirit five times by the emphatic pronoun *ekeinos*, 'he' (John 14:26; 15:26; 16:8, 13–14). This is the more striking because the masculine 'he' is in apposition to the neuter noun *pneuma*, 'Spirit'. Thus theology triumphs over grammar! The Holy Spirit is not a vague, indefinable influence, but a living person, not an 'it' but a 'he'" (*Christian Basics*, 61).

13. See Stott, *Christian Basics*, 61.

14. The Spirit also has "spoken by the prophets" being the source of inspiration for both the Old and New Testament writers. Like the Son who is "begotten not made," the Spirit "proceeds from the Father" and

exists in eternal relationship with the Father and the Son.

15. We note the long-standing disagreement between Roman Catholics and the Orthodox over whether the Creed should stipulate that the Holy Spirit "proceeds from the Father and the Son," or as the Orthodox would prefer, proceeds only from the Father. The addition of "and the son," in Latin *filioque*, came into use in the West as an extra protection against Arianism in the Spanish church following the Goths' conversion in the late seventh century. The Orthodox protested against this growing Western usage based on the decrees of the Council of Ephesus (431), and the Fourth Council of Chalcedon (451) that no further additions to the Creed were to be admitted. The Latin Church considered "and the son" biblical and a logical extension rather than a substantive change to the Creed. The Orthodox Church disagreed.

16. For those who want to explore the Trinity in more depth, I recommend *God the Holy Trinity*, ed. Timothy George (Grand Rapids, Mich.: Baker, 2006), an excellent collection of articles by fine scholars. Gregory of Nyssa's rainbow analogy is referenced on pages 32–33 in an essay by Alistair McGrath.

17. Stott, *Christian Basics*, 47.

18. James D. Bratt, ed., *Abraham Kuyper: A Centennial Reader* (Grand Rapids, Mich.: Eerdmans, 1998), 488. Italics in original.

19. Charles Colson and Nancy Pearcey, *How Now Shall We Live?* (Wheaton, Ill.: Tyndale, 1999), 295–98.

20. Timothy George, "What Time Is It?" Prison Fellowship Board Retreat (October 22–23, 2005). We are deeply indebted to theologian Timothy George for his reflections on this subject.

21. The poet T. S. Eliot gave classic expression to time being both tedious and fleeting in "The Love Song of J. Alfred Prufrock": "In a minute there is time / For decisions and revisions which a minute will reverse / For I have known them all already, known them all:—/ Have known the evenings, mornings, afternoons, / I have measured out my life with coffee spoons."

22. George, "What Time Is It?" 3.

23. St. Augustine, *Confessions* (cited in page 5 in Timothy George talk).

24. George, "What Time Is It?" 5.

Chapter 8: Exchanging Identities

1. Charles Haddon Spurgeon, *Morning and Evening* (Wheaton, Ill.: Crossway, 2003).

2. Elizabeth Raum, *Dietrich Bonhoeffer: Called by God* (New York: Continuum, 2003), 59.

3. Ibid., 67–68.

4. Ibid., 104–109.

5. Eberhard Bethge, *Dietrich Bonhoeffer: A Biography* (Minneapolis: Fortress, 2000), 656.

6. Ibid., *Bonhoeffer*, 204–205.

7. Ibid., *Bonhoeffer*, 204.

8. Ibid., *Bonhoeffer*, 655.

9. Raum, *Bonhoeffer*, 100.

10. Bethge, *Bonhoeffer*, 275.

11. Raum, *Bonhoeffer*, 135.

12. "Above all he delighted in the early church fathers, whom he tracked down in the Tegel library. They seemed more 'contemporary' to him than the reformers, since they had done their thinking during a non-privileged period for the church. Their ethical conflicts in a non-Christian environment seemed incomparably more exciting that the problems of the Augsburg national synod of 1530." Bethge, *Bonhoeffer*, 843.

13. From Payne Best, as in Bethge, *Bonhoeffer*, 920.

14. According to Bethge, *Bonhoeffer*, 926–27.

15. Raum, *Bonhoeffer*, 150. Earlier he wrote, "We may pray that death from without does not come to us till we have been made ready for it through this inner death [to ourselves for the sake of Christ]; for our death is really only the gateway to the perfect love of God." Bethge, *Bonhoeffer*, 661.

16. Bethge, *Bonhoeffer*, 928.

17. The life of Dietrich Bonhoeffer exemplifies Paul's thought "Now if we [have] died with Christ, we believe that we will also live with him" (Romans 6:8).

18. L. B. Cowman, *Streams in the Desert*, ed. James Reimann (Grand Rapids, Mich: Zondervan, 1997), 277.

19. But any form of suffering, not just persecution, can be offered to Christ for His

purposes. He calls us to unite everything we are as mortal creatures to him.

20. Cowman, *Streams in the Desert*, 48.

21. Ibid., 271.

Chapter 9: Reconciliation

1. As quoted in *Stories of Mercy*, an Exposure International Production (Newmarket, New Zealand) for Prison Fellowship International.

2. *The Mahabharata of Krishna-Dwaipayana Vyasa*, trans. Kisaria Mohan Ganguli, *Baharatadesam*; at *www.sacred-texts.com/hin/m05/m05/m05033.htm*, see Book 5, chapter XXXIII of "Udyoga Parva."

3. In the Lord's Prayer we ask God: "Forgive us our debts, as we also have forgiven our debtors" (Matthew 6:12).

4. Letter from John Calvin to William Fare (May 11, 1541). See *Letters of John Calvin*, ed. Jules Bonnet, vol. 1 (Philadelphia: Presbyterian Board of Publication, 1859), 260.

5. Article by Professor Henry Drummond, "Some Impressions and Facts," *McClures's Magazine*, vol. 4, no. 1 (December 1894).

6. Abraham Kuyper, *Christianity: A Total World and Life System* (Marlborough, N.H.: Plymouth Rock Foundation, 1996), 110

7. J. Gresham Machen, *Christianity and Liberalism* (New York: Macmillan, 1923), 52.

8. This paper was embraced at the Vatican and taught to synods coming in for the millennium.

9. Francis Schaeffer, *The Mark of the Christian* (Downers Grove, Ill.: InterVarsity, 1976).

10. Charles Colson, *God and Government*, 415–16. This quote has been slightly modified for economy.

Chapter 10: The Church

1. T. M. Moore, "The Joy of the Whole Earth?" *BreakPoint WorldView* (January–February 2007), 4–5.

2. The apostle Peter counsels: "Be self-controlled and alert. Your enemy the devil prowls around like a roaring lion looking for someone to devour" (1 Peter 5:8). Paul in his letters set up procedures for resolving factional disputes among church members and for expelling those who will not be dis-

ciplined. The writer James admonishes us: "Therefore confess your sins to each other and pray for each other so that you may be healed. The prayer of a righteous man is powerful and effective" (James 5:16).

3. Robert Putnam writes, "In many large evangelical congregations, the participants constituted the largest thoroughly integrated gatherings we have ever witnessed." See Daniel Henninger, "Death of Diversity," *Wall Street Journal* (August 16, 2007).

4. Prison Fellowship delivers gifts on behalf of their incarcerated parents to over half a million children a year.

Chapter 11: Be Holy — Transform the World

1. In the Sermon on the Mount, Jesus makes explicit the demands of this universal call to holiness: "Be perfect, therefore, as your heavenly Father is perfect" (Matthew 5:48).

2. Cowman, *Streams in the Desert*, 62.

3. In 2 Peter we read: "His divine power has given us everything we need for life and godliness ... so that through them you may participate in the divine nature and escape the corruption in the world caused by evil desires" (1:3–4).

4. As Jesus said, "If you obey my commands, you will remain in my love, just as I have obeyed my Father's commands and remain in his love" (John 15:10).

5. On God's love: "It has gone before us so that we may be healed, and follows us so that once healed, we may be given life; it goes before us so that we may be called, and follows us so that we may be glorified; it goes before us so that we may live devoutly, and follows us so that we may always live with God: for without him we can do nothing." As in *Catechism*, 484. St. Augustine, *De natura et gratia*, 31:PL 44, 264.

6. "If we confess our sins, he is faithful and just and will forgive us our sins and purify us from all unrighteousness" (1 John 1:9).

7. This is how God completes the work He began in us (Philippians 1:6).

8. "The InnerChange Freedom Initiative: A Preliminary Evaluation of a Faith-Based Prison Program," study by the University of Pennsylvania, Byron R. Johnson with David

B. Larson. Eight percent refers to the reincarceration rate of IFI grads within two years of release. A texas comparison group had a reincarceration rate of 20 percent. The reoffense rate after two years for IFI grads was 17 percent. The Texas comparison group had a reoffense rate of 35 percent after two years. Nationally that goes up to 59 percent after two years and 68 percent after *three* years. The source for IFI and the Texas comparison group is the U. of Penn. study. The source for national figures is the Bureau of Criminal Justice Statistics.

9. As quoted in Garth Lean, *Strangely Warmed* (Wheaton: Tyndale, 1979), 62.

10. Wilberforce recognized that culture is a far more powerful force than politics. It shapes people's "manners," how they treat others; culture determines whose life is valued and to what degree. And the movement he led recognized this.

11. Herbert Schlossberg, "Religious Revival and the Transformation of English Sensibilities in the Early Nineteenth Century," at *www.victorianweb.org/religion/herb3.html*. This story is based on his citing of Hugh McLeod, *Religion and the People of Western Europe, 1789–1989* (London: Oxford University Press, 1997), 40.

12. See *www.victorianweb.org/religion/herb3.html*.

13. Trevor Yaxley with Carolyn Vanderwal, *William and Catherine: The Legacy of the Booths, Founders of the Salvation Army* (Bloomington, Minn.: Bethany, 2003), 221.

Chapter 12: The Sanctity of Life

1. John Paul II, *Evangelium Vitae* (March 25, 1995). See *www.vatican.va/edocs/ENG0141/_INDEX.HTM*.

2. One prominent pastor just before the 2004 presidential election preached six sermons urging Christians to steer clear of politics and stop moralizing on sexual issues. See Laurie Goodstein, "Disowning Conservative Politics, Evangelical Pastor Rattles Flock," *New York Times* (July 30, 2006).

3. Evangelicals and Catholics Together, "That They May Have Life," *First Things* (October 2006).

4. Stark, *Rise of Christianity*, 124.

5. Evangelicals and Catholics Together, "That They May Have Life," 9.

6. Stark, *Rise of Christianity*, 124.

7. Ibid., 125.

8. Ibid., 214.

9. In fact, three times in Genesis, God refers to making humans in His (or "Our"—an implicit reference to the Trinity) image. God wanted us to understand that our likeness to God distinguished us from all other living things.

10. Michael D. Lemonick and Andrea Dorfman, "What Makes Us Different?" *Time* (October 1, 2006). See *www.time.com/time/magazine/article/0,9171,154128,00.html*.

11. Philip Graham Ryken, *What Is a Christian Worldview? Basics of the Reformed Faith* (Phillipsburg, N.J.: P&R, 2006).

12. Irenaeus as quoted in Evangelicals and Catholics Together, "That They May Have Life."

13. Ryken, *What Is a Christian Worldview?* 21.

14. Jean-Paul Sartre, *Existentialism Is a Humanism*. Trans. Philip Mairet. Public lecture, 1946.

15. Christopher Hitchens, *God Is Not Great* (New York: Twelve Books, Hachette Book Group, 2007).

16. Marc Bloch, *Slavery and Serfdom in the Middle Ages* (Berkeley: University of California Press, 1975), 30, as found in Rodney Stark, *Victory of Reason* (New York: Random House, 2005), 30.

17. Stark, *Victory of Reason*, 201.

18. Ibid.

19. Robin Lane Fox as quoted in Stark, *Rise of Christianity*, 104.

20. As found at *www.mariancatechist.com/html/formation/aboutthemariancatechistapostolate/motherteresaservicetosouls.htm*.

21. "Research Cloning and 'Fetus Farming'; The Slippery Slope in Action," United States Conference of Catholic Bishops (August 31, 2005). You can view it on the Center for Bioethics and Culture Network website, *www.thecbc.org/redesigned/research_display.php?id=249*; Matt Slagle, "Robot Maker Builds Artifical Boy," *Associated Press* (September 13, 2007), *ap.google.com/article/ALeqM5jkS53pEFigyo4pMaf_GefNTFuY5w*. See also Greg Bluestein, "Study

Finds Human-Robot Attachment," *Washington Post* (October 2, 2007), www.washingtonpost.com/wp-dyn/content/article/2007/10/01/AR2007100101040.html.

22. C. S. Lewis, *The Abolition of Man*, (San Francisco: HarperOne, 2001), 44.

23. Ibid., 41. "At the moment, then, of Man's victory over Nature, we find the whole human race subjected to some individual men, and those individuals subjected to that in themselves which is purely 'natural'—to their irrational impulses. Nature, untrammeled by values, rules the Conditioners, and through them, all humanity. Man's conquest of Nature turns out, in the moment of its consummation, to be Nature's conquest of Man."

24. "That They May Have Life," *First Things* (October 2006), www.firstthings.com/article.php3?id_article=5358. For a more substantial treatment of these principles and ideas, see Charles Colson and Richard John Neuhaus, eds., *Evangelicals and Catholics Together: Toward a Common Mission* (Dallas: Word, 1995).

Chapter 13: Last Things

1. For those interested in the subject of capital punishment, resources are available; see Daniel W. Van Ness, *Crime and Its Victims* (Downers Grove, Ill.: InterVarsity, 1986). We note that many Christians disagree about capital punishment, major communions and denominations arguing that it should never be used except where the innocent cannot be protected otherwise.

2. See N. T. Wright, *Simply Christian: Why Christianity Makes Sense* (San Francisco: HarperOne, 2006), 3–15; and Charles Colson with Harold Fickett, *The Good Life* (Wheaton, Ill.: Tyndale, 2005), 247–54.

3. "Do not be amazed at this, for a time is coming when all who are in their graves will hear his voice and come out—those who have done good will rise to live, and those who have done evil will rise to be condemned" (John 5:28–29).

4. When Jesus counters the Pharisees' attempt to stump him by saying that in heaven people do not marry, He is not implying that we will not know each other's particular identities and remember our relationships and their personal histories (Matthew 22:23–31).

5. Our word *cemetery* derives from the Latin word for "dormitory," that is, the place where we sleep.

6. See Francis Fukiyama, *The End of History and the Last Man* (New York: Free Press, 1992).

7. Some believe the millennium is a description of the age we live in now, the age of the Church; others think that the Church will largely accomplish her goals bringing about a much-improved world before Christ returns; while still others, particularly evangelicals, see the millennium as a period of peace that follows the second coming and leads to a final battle, Armageddon, after which God will create the world anew. Many evangelicals believe that the Church will be taken out of the world—"raptured"—before the world undergoes tribulation at Satan and the Antichrist's hands.

Chapter 14: The Joy of Orthodoxy

1. "Nigeria Tops Happiness Survery," *BBC News* (October 2, 2003). news.bbc.co.uk/2/hi/Africa/3157570.stm.

2. David Wells, *Mars Hill Audio Journal* (September–October 2006).

3. G. K. Chesterton, *Orthodoxy* (New York: Dodd Mead, 1955), 125–27.

4. Ibid., 120.

5. Phillip Jenkins, "Believing in the Global South," *First Things* (December 2006), 12.

Chapter 15: The Great Proposal

1. St. Benedict's *Rule* is a spiritual and practical guide to living the monastic life.

2. Stark, *Victory of Reason*, 14.

3. Aikman, *Jesus in Beijing*, 5.

4. Ayaan Hirsi Ali, *Infidel* (New York: Free Press, 2007), xi.

5. This account of Van Gogh's murder is based on Ali, *Infidel*; Ian Buruma, *Murder in Amsterdam* (New York: Penguin, 2006), 2–8; and newspaper sources.

6. Buruma, *Murder in Amsterdam*, 5.

7. As quoted in Buruma, *Murder in Amsterdam*, 165.

8. As of May 21, 2007, www.theovangogh.nl/indexc.html.

9. Buruma, *Murder in Amsterdam*, 189.

10. Also known as Mohammed Radwan Alissa.

11. See Paul Berman, "The Philosopher of Islamic Terror," *New York Times* (March 23, 2003). Also see Paul Berman, *Terror and Liberalism* (New York: Norton, 2004); and also Berman's interview at *Mars Hill Audio Journal*, vol. 54 (Sept./Oct. 2003).

12. Roger Scruton, "Islamo-fascism" op-ed, *Wall Street Journal* (August 17, 2006).

13. Pope Benedict XVI, "Faith, Reason, and the University: Memories and Reflections" (September 12, 2006). The full text of Pope Benedict's lecture is available at *www.vatican.va/holy_father/benedict _xvi/speeches/2006/september/documents/hf_ ben-xvi_spe_20060912_university-regensburg _en.html.*

14. See "A Tale of Two Bellies: The Remarkable Demographic Difference Between America and Europe," *The Economist* (UK) (August 14, 2002). *www.mindfully.org/ Reform/2002/Demographic-Difference — US-EU24aug02.htm* (May 25, 2007).

15. Thomas Friedman, "Martin Luther Al-King?" *New York Times* (January 24, 2007).

16. G. K. Chesterton, *The Collected Works of G. K. Chesterton I: Heretics, Orthodoxy, The Blatchford Controversies* (San Francisco: Ignatius: 1986), 310. The quoted passage is a summary of Chesterton's general argument throughout the chapters "The Paradoxes of Christianity" and "The Eternal Revolution" of *Orthodoxy.*

WITH GRATITUDE

Editors are as important as writers when it comes to producing a significant book. We have been incredibly blessed to be assisted by Zondervan's Stan Gundry, Senior Vice President and Editor-in-Chief, and Executive Editor John Sloan. Stan Gundry is not only a solid editor but an impressive theologian. He helped us pursue an ecumenism grounded in the truth. John Sloan did an especially helpful job in keeping the focus of the book clear, maintaining its pace, and ensuring the book's readability. John might well be the best editor in the industry. Not that the process was without pain and suffering: watching your most inspired sentences fall on the editorial floor is a pain that only authors know; but the book wouldn't have made it without it. Finally, Senior Editor-at-Large Bob Hudson did the copyediting and gave the book an excellent final polish. For me, Judith Markham, who edited *Loving God* and *Kingdoms in Conflict* while at Zondervan in the 1980s, has always set the gold standard for editors. I didn't think anyone could equal her, but these editors turned out to be tops (perhaps in part because both John Sloan and Bob Hudson were trained by Judith).

In writing this book we were guided for theological purity by T. M. Moore, the estimable theologian and writer who has worked with me for more than twenty years. T. M. is now Dean of the Wilberforce Forum and the Centurion Program through our ministry, which teaches biblical worldview to leading laymen across the country. I also drew heavily upon the writings of Timothy George; his guidance and counsel to me over the years—recognized in the dedication of this book—have been formative. He has been to me, in the last ten years, what Carl Henry and R. C. Sproul were in the years before that, a loving and incredibly gifted mentor. I am especially grateful as well for the counsel and support of my very able pastor, Dr. Hayes Wicker.

We also consulted with many experts on various parts of the book—apologies in advance for any whose names we have omitted. We acknowledge with gratitude for their tremendous expertise David Aikman, Dale Allison, Jeannine Brabon, Paul and Carol Bramsen, David Carlson, Bruce Gordon, Dr. John Edmund Haggai, Jochen Katz, Johnny Li, Tom Oden, Joel Pilcher, and Ron Tappy. We also especially want to acknowledge the team at *www.answering-Islam.org* and the real-life person whose story is told under the pseudonym "Farid."

Profound thanks are due to Sherrie Irvin who has mastered the art of reading my otherwise totally unintelligible notes. She takes my often erratic dictation and somehow turns it into smooth copy. Sherrie not only has a great capacity for work but, good student that she is, picks up many of the errors I would have otherwise made. A very helpful sounding board and constructive critic, she is indispensable.

Finally but by no means last, our thanks to our families. Only authors know what a particular burden an author's spouse must carry. I think of all the nights when I came out of my office, steaming with frustration over that elusive paragraph or idea that I couldn't quite capture. Patty has been an incredibly calming influence in my life (often a humbling influence as well, whenever I have pretensions of being a great author). Somehow we've managed to get through twenty or more books with our marriage intact, indeed stronger.

Harold wishes to thank his beautiful and loving wife, Karen, and his three children, Hal, Will, and Eve. As Harold has written full-time these past ten years, they have allowed him to keep faith with a challenging vocation. Harold also wants to thank his mother, Mary Frances Fickett. The story goes that Harold and his family are taking care of her, but she does just as much taking care of them.

My special thanks to Kim Moreland, longtime research associate; and Catherine Claire, one of our very able young editors at Prison Fellowship. Summer intern Sy Hoestra wrote a particularly helpful background memo on the new anti-theists. Arlene Aiello, Nancy McDonough, and Carol Halperson also helped type various parts of the manuscript. I'm grateful as well to Linda McGraw who organizes me and my schedule so ably that I have time to write.

I want to give special thanks also to those to whom we sent prepublication copies for their critiques, evaluations, and in some cases, important corrections.

As has been the case in the last four or five books that I have written, Harold Fickett and I have enjoyed a wonderful fellowship and a great collegial relationship.

THE FAITH GIVEN
ONCE FOR ALL

Since this book was written as a straightforward narrative—interlaced with stories and relevant to contemporary concerns—it may be difficult for some readers to identify clearly the essential doctrines that constitute the Christian faith. We have therefore listed those doctrines below, indicating the chapter in which they are discussed:

- God Is—Chapter 2
- He Has Spoken—Chapter 3
- The Fall/Original Sin—Chapter 5
- The Incarnation—Chapter 6
- The Cross and the Atoning Death of Christ—Chapter 6
- The Bodily Resurrection—Chapter 6
- The Nature of God/His Sovereignty—Chapter 7
- The Trinity—Chapter 7
- Justification by Faith/Conversion—Chapter 8
- Forgiveness and Reconciliation—Chapter 9
- The Church—Chapter 10
- Sanctification/Holiness—Chapter 11
- Dignity of Human Life—Chapter 12
- The Return of Jesus and the End of History—Chapter 13

All of these doctrines can be found in the historic creeds of the Church and, obviously, in Scripture. Here, for example, is the Nicene Creed, the historic late–fourth-century statement of faith endorsed in some form by all major Christian communions. In parentheses we indicate which chapters of this book address the doctrinal concerns outlined here:

We believe (1) in one God, the Father Almighty,
    Maker of heaven and earth,
    of all things visible and invisible (2, 3, 7, 12).

And in one Lord Jesus Christ, the only begotten Son of God,
    begotten of his Father before all worlds,
    God of God, Light of Light,
    very God of very God,
    begotten, not made, being of one substance with the Father (7);
    by whom all things were made;
    who for us and for our salvation
    came down from heaven,
    and was incarnate by the Holy Spirit (6, 7) of the virgin Mary (6),
    and was made man (6);
    and was crucified also for us under Pontius Pilate (6, 8);
    he suffered and was buried;
    and the third day he rose again according to the Scriptures (6),
    and ascended into heaven, and is seated at the right hand
        of the Father (6, 7);
    and he shall come again, with glory, to judge both the living and
        the dead (13);
    whose kingdom shall have no end.

And we believe in the Holy Spirit, the Lord and giver of life,
    who proceeds from the Father and the Son (7);
    who with the Father and the Son together is worshiped and
        glorified (11);
    who spoke by the prophets (3);
    and we believe in the one holy catholic and apostolic church (10, 11);
    we acknowledge one baptism for the forgiveness of sins (5, 8, 9, 10);
    and we look for the resurrection of the dead,
    and the life of the world to come (12, 13).

The faith once for all handed down to the saints has been faithfully preserved by them from age to age, so that any reliable assertion of Christianity today, or in any age, must be able to demonstrate its continuity with the ancient past and ongoing tradition of the faith. At the same time, in every age it is the task of theologians and thinkers to restate the ancient faith in contemporary terms, as theologian E. L. Mascall observed:

Because both the thought forms and needs of the concrete situation of Christians in one age differ from those in another, the theologian has a continual duty to relate the unchanging Gospel to the contemporary situation in order that Christians themselves shall understand their faith as adequately as is possible and feel at home in it as contemporary men and women.*

This is what we have endeavored to accomplish in *The Faith*. It is the duty of serious disciples to examine all such statements as this in the light of Scripture (Acts 17:11) and the doctrinal guides and aids of their own traditions. For additional study of *The Faith* in the light of Scripture and the historic creeds of the Church, see the study guide for this book, which is available through the publisher's website *www.zondervan.com* and at Prison Fellowship *www.pfm.org*, *www.prisonfellowship.org*, and *www.breakpoint.org*.

If you would like more information about *The Faith*, or information about the study guide that has been prepared to go with it, visit *www.zondervan.com*, *www.breakpoint.org*, or *www.prisonfellowship.org*. You can also call Prison Fellowship toll-free at 1-877-478-0100 or write us at:

PFM
P. O. Box 1550
Merrifield, VA 22116-1550

---

*E. L. Mascall, *The Secularization of Christianity* (New York: Holt Rinehart Winston, 1965), 3–4.